Edward Dana Durand

The Finances of New York City

Edward Dana Durand

The Finances of New York City

ISBN/EAN: 9783744791151

Printed in Europe, USA, Canada, Australia, Japan

Cover: Foto ©Suzi / pixelio.de

More available books at **www.hansebooks.com**

THE FINANCES
OF NEW YORK CITY

BY

EDWARD DANA DURAND, Ph.D.

Late Legislative Librarian in the New York State Library,
Assistant Professor of Economics and Administration,
Leland Stanford, Jr., University

New York
THE MACMILLAN COMPANY
LONDON: MACMILLAN & CO., Ltd.
1898

All rights reserved

PREFACE

ERRATUM.

On page 336, line 18, instead of "two or three" read "twelve or thirteen."

differ so greatly among themselves that a comparative study cannot be made off-hand. Moreover, if mere magnitude of sums involved makes a subject important, New York's finances are entitled to careful consideration on this score. The yearly expenditures of all classes in the consolidated metropolis will be more than five times greater than those of the state of New York, nearly two-thirds as great as those of all the states in the Union

PREFACE

AT first glance the subject of the finances of New York city may appear a narrow one, scarcely deserving extensive treatment. As a matter of fact, however, very little work has yet been done in this country in the study of municipal finance — indeed only recently has there awakened interest in the general subject of city government — and some detailed investigation of the finances of individual cities is necessary as a basis for more comprehensive discussion. The accounts kept by our American municipalities are so complicated and differ so greatly among themselves that a comparative study cannot be made off-hand. Moreover, if mere magnitude of sums involved makes a subject important, New York's finances are entitled to careful consideration on this score. The yearly expenditures of all classes in the consolidated metropolis will be more than five times greater than those of the state of New York, nearly two-thirds as great as those of all the states in the Union combined, and more than a seventh as great as those of the Federal government, while the gross debt of Greater New York will exceed that of all the American states. And finally it is evident that the management of the finances touches intimately every other phase of the municipal administration, and that, if we consider the subject broadly in its relations to the general city government and in its actual working, we shall come very close to the core of some of those practical problems which are to-day arousing such widespread interest. It is certainly true that a more thorough understanding of the financial system on the part of New York's citizens and officials is highly desirable. Such an understanding might well lead to a change in some of the present complicated and anomalous features of the finances, as well as to greater economy and responsibility in the general administration.

The official records on which, in almost every case, the chief financial statements of fact in the following pages are based, are often so unsatisfactory, and the system of accounting has been so different at different periods, that I can hardly hope to have escaped errors altogether. For the year 1896 the comptroller's report had not yet appeared at the time of going to press, and nearly all figures for that year are taken from manuscript records in the office of the finance department. For the convenience of those not having access to full sets of documents who may care to verify facts or figures, it may be said that the same statements are often found in several different sources. The city Manuals from 1850 to 1870 copy some of the more important tables of the comptrollers' reports; since 1873 the proceedings of the aldermen, of the board of estimate and apportionment, and many other documents have been printed separately as well as in the *City Record*, to which latter publication reference is usually made. Recent comptrollers' reports, moreover, contain comparative tables on many subjects, running back either ten or twenty-five years.

Notwithstanding the great financial importance of the consolidation of Greater New York, which is being effected as this book leaves the press, I have not deemed it necessary to enter into detailed study of the financial history or conditions of Brooklyn and the smaller united municipalities. Their experience has had little influence in the framing of the new charter, which follows mostly the previous laws regarding New York itself, while an attempt to combine their financial statistics with those of New York would only produce confusion, owing to the different conditions and different methods employed. The present tense is usually used in speaking of the charter provisions existing in 1897, the future of those of the charter going into effect January 1, 1898.

Thanks are due to Dr. Albert Shaw for suggestions, and to Prof. J. W. Jenks and Prof. C. H. Hull for careful criticism of the text throughout. I am also under obligation to the officials in the city hall and comptroller's office, who have given free access to the records as well as direct information and suggestion. Mr. Isaac S. Barrett, general book-keeper, has rendered specially useful assistance.

E. D. D.

DECEMBER, 1897.

CONTENTS

PART I

HISTORY OF THE FINANCES TO 1871

CHAPTER I

	PAGE
INTRODUCTION	1
§ 1. General survey of history	1

CHAPTER II

THE EARLY CITY, 1652–1830	7
§ 2. The Dutch city	7
§ 3. The English charters	13
§ 4. The finances, 1665–1783	17
§ 5. The tax laws and finances, 1784–1830	25
§ 6. The city debt	32
§ 7. General character of the government	37

CHAPTER III

COUNCIL GOVERNMENT UNDER THE CHARTER OF 1830	41
§ 8. The charter of 1830	41
§ 9. The budget	46
§ 10. The city debt	51
§ 11. Special assessments	58
§ 12. General character of the period. Conclusion	59

CHAPTER IV

	PAGE
THE PERIOD OF LEGISLATIVE INTERFERENCE, 1850–1869	66
§ 13. The charter of 1849	67
§ 14. The charter amendments of 1853	70
§ 15. Charter changes of 1857, etc.	76
§ 16. The budget and the independent departments	80
§ 17. Legislative interference in the budget	88
§ 18. The city debt	97
§ 19. Special assessments, taxes, and accounts	107
§ 20. General progress of expenditures	112
§ 21. General character of government. Conclusion	114

CHAPTER V

THE TWEED RING	119
§ 22. Origin and growth of the Ring to 1870	120
§ 23. The charter and other laws of 1870	125
§ 24. Events of 1871. The 'two per cent law'	129
§ 25. Fall of the Ring	134
§ 26. General character of Ring financial management	137
§ 27. Special assessments	142
§ 28. The city debt	145
§ 29. Finances during the period of reconstruction	150

PART II

PRESENT WORKING OF THE FINANCIAL SYSTEM

CHAPTER VI

INTRODUCTION	154
§ 30. Adoption and character of charter of 1873	154
§ 31. Charter changes since 1873	163
§ 32. The Greater New York charter	166
§ 33. Outline of financial system and plan of study	172
§ 34. Preliminary view of receipts and expenditures	177

CHAPTER VII

	PAGE
ASSESSMENT AND TAXATION	187
§ 35. Outline of the tax system	187
§ 36. Practical character of tax assessments	190
§ 37. Collection of taxes	198

CHAPTER VIII

SPECIAL ASSESSMENTS	201
§ 38. Changes in the system since 1871	201
§ 39. Assessment procedure	213

CHAPTER IX

CITY PROPERTY AND FRANCHISES	221
§ 40. General character and importance	221
§ 41. City property — its management and revenues	224
§ 42. Municipal franchises	230

CHAPTER X

THE BUDGET AND CITY EXPENDITURES	253
§ 43. Outline of the budget system	253
§ 44. Powerlessness of the city council. Fixed appropriations	258
§ 45. Procedure of the board of estimate and apportionment	264
§ 46. Character and motives of the board	269
§ 47. The budget system of Greater New York	277
§ 48. The Tilden Commission plan	281
§ 49. Analysis of city expenditures	285
§ 50. Growth of expenditures since 1871	289

CHAPTER XI

THE CITY DEBT	295
§ 51. Constitutional limitation of debt	296
§ 52. Legislative and local authorization of debt	300

	PAGE
§ 53. Debt redemption — act of 1878	306
§ 54. Debt redemption under present laws	315
§ 55. General progress of the debt since 1871	319
§ 56. Chief bond issues since 1871	325
§ 57. Present state of debt; effect of consolidation	333
§ 58. The sinking fund and future debt issues	336

CHAPTER XII

AUDIT, ACCOUNT, AND FINANCIAL RESPONSIBILITY	345
§ 59. Auditing and accounting system	345
§ 60. Financial records and reports	349
§ 61. Inspection of accounts and official responsibility	352
§ 62. CONCLUSION	359
TABLE OF WORKS CITED	365

TABLES

I. Appropriations and Taxation, 1830–1896	372
II. The City Debt, 1830–1896	374
III. Expenditures by Decennial Periods, 1830–1890	376
IV. Modifications in the Budget Estimates, 1874–1897	378
V. Summary of Debt Issues, 1812–1896	379

DIAGRAMS

A. Appropriations, Taxation, and Special Assessments	380
B. The City Debt	381
C. Fixed and Contingent Appropriations, 1874–1896	382
D. Chief Heads of Appropriations, 1874–1896	383
E. Index Numbers of Appropriations, 1876, '86, '96	384
INDEX	385

PART I

HISTORY OF THE FINANCES TO 1871

CHAPTER I

INTRODUCTION

§ 1. *General Survey of History.*

In studying the history of the finances of New York city, it is necessary to pay considerable attention to the development of the general municipal organization, which constantly reacts upon the financial management. In fact, the four main periods in the history of the city government will furnish us the best lines of division for considering the finances. These periods may be roughly described by the following titles:—

1. The early city — 1652-1830;
2. Council government under the charter of 1830 — 1830-1849;
3. The period of independent executive departments and of legislative interference — 1849-1869;
4. The Tweed Ring — 1869-1871;
5. The modern period — 1871-1897.

1. It was in 1652 that the city of New Amsterdam received its charter from the Dutch West India Company. During the succeeding thirteen years of Dutch rule, the city burgomasters and schepens were involved in a constant struggle with the company's director, Stuyvesant, for independent authority, and especially for municipal revenues. They disliked to levy direct taxes and sought to secure various duties, fees, and property rights from the company. Citizens were called upon to perform many public services directly, while special assessments were also laid for the cost of local improvements.

Under the English rule which followed, the government was reorganized into something approaching its present form. More liberal grants of indirect revenues were made to the city, especially by the Dongan charter of 1686, and these long sufficed to cover the meagre ordinary outlay, although occasionally for reducing the floating debt or for extraordinary purposes a property tax was levied, under special authority from the provincial legislature. About the middle of the eighteenth century, however, it became necessary to levy taxes almost yearly, but by force of custom special sanction of law was still required, and when the state government was established after the Revolution, this requirement was continued. During the early period, however, the legislature did not abuse its control; in fact, its action was almost purely formal, and the council was really the sole power in financial management. The system of finance was still crude and irregular. In particular there was considerable carelessness in creating floating debt, and it was chiefly to fund this that permanent debt was first incurred, in 1812.

2. In 1830 the first considerable modifications in the city charter were made, as the result of the work of a municipal convention. Influenced by the precedent of national and state governments, the convention proposed to draw a sharp line between executive and legislative functions, transferring the former from committees of the council to independent departments appointed by the council. In connection with this change the system of annual appropriations was introduced. The city council, however, failed to carry out the spirit of the rather indefinite charter, and its committees continued to dictate executive business, while the management of the appropriations was so loose that they served to place practically very little restriction on expenditure. The city council was growing decidedly corrupt, and partisan motives influenced it largely. Perhaps the most important financial event in this period was the construction of the Croton aqueduct, which swelled the city debt to a high figure.

3. Growing dissatisfaction with the council government led at last to the passage of the charter of 1849, which actually accomplished the removal

of executive power from the council, and its transfer to independent departments. Considerable charter amendments were also made in 1853 and 1857. About the latter year the legislature began extensively the policy which prevailed throughout the remainder of this period, of actively interfering in the management of city affairs. Not only were several very important departments placed under commissions appointed by the state government, but the city and county organizations were separated, and the latter so constituted as to be largely in sympathy with the dominant party in the state. Above all, this interference was exercised by means of the annual tax laws, which had persisted from the early days. The details of city expenditure came now to be prescribed in these acts, and local wishes were almost absolutely disregarded in fixing the sums allowed. The motive of this general policy was to give the Republicans and Unionists in the outside state control of the city, instead of leaving it to the disloyal and largely corrupt majority in the metropolis. The city council and other officers actually chosen by the local voters grew constantly worse and worse. After the war, moreover, the independent departments and the state legislature gradually became corrupt, and the way soon lay open for the entry of the Tweed Ring upon the field.

4. As soon as this immensely powerful circle of conspirators had gained the complete ascendant,

they sought to perpetuate their power by securing a new city charter. This law, which introduced many features that still persist in the government of New York, did away with state commissions and with legislative interference in the appropriations. It did not, however, increase the power of the degenerate common council, but parcelled out authority among well-nigh autocratic departments headed by commissions. The control of expenditures was placed in the hands of a 'board of estimate and apportionment' composed of four executive officers, who were at this time precisely the four chiefs of the Ring. To this body was also given power to 'audit' many classes of claims and to issue bonds, and it was by virtue of its action that a large proportion of the enormous additions to the city debt during the few years of Ring rule were made. Such gigantic corruption as that which prevailed in 1870 and 1871 is unparalleled in the history of any city.

5. The Tweed Ring was finally overthrown by a general popular uprising in September, 1871. An attempt was now made to secure a new charter practically reëstablishing that domination of the city council which had prevailed before 1850, but the proposed bill was defeated, and as public feeling subsided a law was finally adopted which did not depart radically from the Tweed charter. Under this law, which, with some amendments, is still in force, the council has become less and less

a significant factor in the government. The mayor has gradually centred large power in himself, while the board of estimate and apportionment, somewhat changed in composition, by its control of expenditures and by the power in debt management and in other directions that has been conferred upon it, has likewise gained largely in authority. The state government has still retained a considerable degree of control. The Greater New York charter, which goes into effect January 1, 1898, seeks to make some important changes in the frame of government, and especially to give greater autonomy to the city, but it is questionable whether it will accomplish all that its authors have anticipated.

The first four periods above outlined will each be made the subject of a separate chapter. The character and working of the financial system in the period since 1871 will, however, require more minute study, and Part II is devoted to this subject. The financial tables and diagrams at the end of the book will be found useful in connection with the text.

CHAPTER II

THE EARLY CITY — 1652–1830

§ 2. *The Dutch City.*

The beginnings of New York city government carry us back to a time when the conception of a municipality was considerably different from the one now most common. An old-world town of those days came very much closer to the every-day life and business of its citizens than does a modern city. Its charter, granted — often not over graciously — by the sovereign or feudal lord, freed it from many of the burdens imposed on other parts of the community; and conferred upon it, along with political and judicial powers, special business privileges and a marked degree of authority over the industry and commerce of its inhabitants and of the neighborhood. The bestowal of lands and other property rights, and of power to levy all sorts of indirect taxes, tolls, and dues, assured the municipality an income. The city was a close corporation, and the conditions of entrance to its full citizenship were frequently severe; while to the 'freemen' were restricted many of what are now often considered natural rights. Practically only they could engage in any craft or business.

They were exempt from many charges that were exacted from their less fortunate fellow-townsmen and from outsiders; and they alone enjoyed the privileges of the common property. The influence of this system of city government[1] has left traces upon the administration and finances of New York which are not found in American cities of more recent origin.

The fact that New Amsterdam was originally the colony of a private corporation, bent upon its own pecuniary gain, for a time modified the application of European municipal precedents materially.[2] Despite frequent demands, no form of local self-government was granted by the West India Company to the town till 1652, and then the imperious Director-General Stuyvesant insisted upon retaining the appointment of the two burgomasters and the five schepens in his own hand, although a year or two later the city fathers succeeded in obtaining the right to nominate to him a double number of citizens for appointment as their successors. Not a stiver of revenue, moreover, could be raised in any way without the director's consent, and con-

---

[1] What is said here of European cities generally was not equally true of all of them. Conditions differed widely in different countries, and even within the same country. The best picture of early English town life is in Mrs. Green's *Town Life in the Fifteenth Century*.

[2] For fuller account of the early relations between the city and the West India company, see the writer's paper, *The City Chest of New Amsterdam*, in the Half-Moon Series.

stant conflicts between him and the city magistrates comprise most of the financial history of the Dutch municipality. Stuyvesant, on his part, hesitated to violate the traditions of free Holland by levying direct taxes on behalf of the company without consent of the people's representatives; and the latter used this fact as a lever to extort from him the first of those forms of indirect revenue which the good burgomasters and schepens so much preferred to unpopular property taxes. Almost immediately after the establishment of the new government, a considerable loan had been made by the director and the municipal authorities jointly for the construction of a wall and palisade about the city. The magistrates thereupon refused to raise subsidies to redeem the debt unless the revenue from the tavern-keepers' excise should be turned from the company's treasury into the city chest. With much grumbling this was finally conceded in November, 1653, and New Amsterdam received its first regular income. On the failure of the burgomasters and schepens, however, not only to pay the debt, but even to support the ministers whose salaries had been made a charge upon them, Stuyvesant, in the following year, took away again this important revenue. Meantime, however, the 'burghers' excise' on liquors, of nearly equal value, had been granted the city, and this was to the close of Dutch rule the chief regular means of supporting the government. As was the general custom regarding indirect charges in those days, this excise was farmed out to the highest bidder. It brought 4200 florins in 1657.

The old fortification debt of 1653 continued to be a bone of contention to the end of the Dutch period, and to the end the city fathers managed, by one shift or another, to avoid paying it. To be sure, they did levy one tax, in 1655–6, specially for repairing the fortifications. This was the nearest approach to a modern property tax which we meet until the British conquest, and even here an attempt was made to give it the appearance of a voluntary contribution, although citizens who refused to give freely, or who offered less than seemed proper, were compulsorily taxed. No formal assessment of property was made, but the magistrates assigned roughly to each burgher what they deemed his fair share — ranging from 4 to 150 florins. The total amount as listed was 6305 florins. The unpopularity of the tax is shown by the extreme difficulty in collecting it.

Other minor revenues were obtained from time to time, with more or less difficulty, but in spite of these the chest remained so chronically empty that the city magistrates were even driven to beg the payment of their own salaries by the company. Dues for slaughtering cattle and for marking measures and barrels, fees for admission to the burgher-right, wharfage charges, and special taxes, of uniform amount on each household, for the rudimentary fire protection and night-watch, were the only recurrent sources of income aside from the excise. The vast importance of the present system of municipal docks makes the establishment of the first city wharf of special interest. This was in 1658; the new dock appears to have adjoined the great bridge across the *Heere Gracht* or Grand Canal. The city was allowed to collect eight stivers per *last* (about two tons) for loading or unloading from this wharf. The burgomasters and schepens petitioned also repeatedly for the revenue from the ferry to Brooklyn, then farmed by the West India Company, but it was not till the English period that this was conceded to the city.

The most significant feature perhaps of the financial administration of New Amsterdam was the reliance upon individuals especially benefited by public works. This took two forms — the simple one of requiring each citizen to perform the work from which he was to receive special advantage, and the vastly preferable one of local assessment of the cost of work performed by the municipality itself. The first method was employed in 1654, when residents along the water-front were required to build a *Schoeyinge* or sheet-piling to protect their lots; in default the city was to build it and collect the cost from the owners. This same system was employed for the paving of the street along the *Prince Gracht* in 1660, and appears to have been used several times during the years immediately following the British capture in 1664. The method of special assessment was introduced in 1657 for the pavement of *Brouwer Straate* (now Stone Street), the first street to be paved in New Amsterdam. On petition of the owners, who agreed to pay the cost, the work was done by two overseers appointed by the city, who were authorized "to assess proportionably for the expense incurred each house standing in the aforesaid street."[1] This system was also used in the reconstruction of the *Schoeyinge* along the *Heere Gracht* in 1660, when the abutting lots were assessed at the rate of 40 florins per rod. The full list of assessments is recorded. In this case there was no petition of the property-owners offering to bear the expense; indeed, they were apparently not even warned that it would be laid upon them. Accordingly there was a great outcry when an attempt was made to collect the assessment. Poor Hendrick Willemsen, the baker, whose tax was the highest of all, declared that he had not only received no benefit from the work, but had actually lost a lot of valuable stone which had been undermined. He vowed he would not pay, and only after he had been conveyed to the prison chamber for an hour or two was he frightened into agreeing to contribute the amount due in four instalments. The privilege of defraying their assessments in

---

[1] Records of the Burgomasters and Schepens (translation), vol. 3, pp. 5, 34.

instalments was later given to all who chose to ask it.

Perhaps the difficulty encountered in this enterprise accounts for the apparent cessation of the use of local assessments hereafter.

§ 3. *The English Charters.*

In the year after his capture of New Amsterdam, Colonel Nicolls, the British governor, reorganized the city government somewhat on the English model,[1] although retaining quite closely Dutch customs. Instead of two burgomasters, a mayor was constituted, and the five schepens became aldermen. The appointment of these officers, following Stuyvesant's precedent, was kept by the governor, but was still apparently from a double nomination by the city council. A greater degree of autonomy than had yet been enjoyed was, however, allowed the municipality, and especially were greater financial privileges given. Nevertheless, the city fathers felt not only that their previous rights and traditions had insufficient protection from encroachment under the exceedingly brief charter which Colonel Nicolls had granted, but that additional powers and privileges, of both political and financial character, were needed to give dignity and strength to the growing municipality. Accordingly, upon the arrival of the new governor, Thomas Dongan, in 1683, the citizens

[1] Order quoted in Hoffman, *Estate and Rights of New York*, Appendix, p. iii.

made a movement for a more extended and formal charter;[1] and at last, by aid of a skilful present of £300 to that worthy, who felt it no unseemly thing to receive some recompense for his trouble and his benevolence, they succeeded in obtaining the famous charter of 1686. Additional property rights were granted or existing ones confirmed by Governor Cornbury in the 'charter of Queen Anne' in 1708; while Governor Montgomerie in 1730, on the petition of the citizens, gave the city yet another general charter, confirming all the rights of the previous ones, adding a few others, and making some slight changes in the frame of government. Thereafter few important modifications were made in the organization of the city down to 1830; indeed the general outlines of government, and not a few details prescribed by these early laws, still persist. The property rights and privileges then secured especially constitute a factor of great consequence in the present finances.

The Dongan and Montgomerie charters[2] declared New York a 'Free City,' a phrase borrowed from European municipalities; yet the independence which had been, in fact, so firmly possessed by many of the older cities of Europe was considerably curtailed. Indeed the charter of 1686 was granted at a time when in England

---

[1] Petition in Hoffman, Appendix, p. v.

[2] Both these charters are quoted in almost every edition of the laws relating to the city, in the Manuals, etc.

itself the Stuart kings were making marked encroachments on the liberties of the municipalities; when not only were the newly incorporated cities denied many privileges enjoyed by the older ones, but attempts were even made to wrest from the latter their ancient charters. Perhaps, too, because New York was in a dependent colony, more control over its affairs was retained by the general government, while the influence of the traditions of New Amsterdam tended in the same direction. The mayor and recorder were appointed by the governor, taxes could not be levied save by special authority of the provincial assembly, and the city ordinances were binding for only a year[1] unless approved by the governor. However, the colonial authorities were by no means inclined to abuse this power as the autocratic Stuyvesant had done. The city was at least allowed to elect its own councilmen, and these were empowered to regulate by ordinance many matters, such as the number and functions of the various subordinate officers, over which in the present century the legislature has arrogated very minute control.

 The city council was composed of seven aldermen, and seven assistant aldermen, elected annually. These did not constitute separate bodies, but met together, the mayor and recorder also having seats in the board. A 'chamberlain or treasurer,'

[1] Under the later charter; under the Dongan law only three months, § 8.

elected by the council, completed the number of important officers.

The city long continued to be a close corporation, whose members only could carry on business in the city or upon the Hudson River, and enjoy the other municipal privileges. These restrictions became by custom and by the growth of the democratic spirit gradually less stringent; but the provision for the admission of freemen, which required as a condition either birth from a freeman, a long apprenticeship, or a money payment, remained till after 1812.[1] From the beginning, however, the municipal suffrage, contrary to the practice in many English cities, was not confined to freemen, although in accordance with general custom a property qualification was required. This qualification was not specifically fixed for the city, as distinguished from the province as a whole, and that fact caused uncertainty and dissension. Finally, in 1771,[2] by act of the assembly the freehold requirement for voting was set at £40 in lands and tenants within the ward, a citizen being allowed to cast a ballot in each ward where he possessed the required property. The limit was reduced in 1787[3] to £20 and again in 1800[4] to

---

[1] Laws and Ordinances of New York, 1812, Chap. 40. The fee at this time was $12.50 for a trader, $2.50 for a mechanic.

[2] Laws of New York, 1691-1773, Van Schaack's ed., p. 620.

[3] Laws, 1787, Chap. 42; 1 Greenleaf, p. 376.

[4] *Ibid.*, 1800, Chap. 35.

$50; while a law of 1804[1] permitted in addition that any person might vote who rented a tenement of the yearly value of $25 and paid taxes. The constitution of 1821[2] made the payment of taxes a sufficient qualification for any election in the state, and even this requirement was removed by the amendment of 1826. Special elections on financial matters, however, may still be restricted to taxpayers, and in many villages and smaller cities this custom prevails; but no such limitation has ever been made in the few elections of this sort held in New York city. Although the metropolis is thus not without early experience of the system of property qualification for municipal suffrage, now so often advocated, the conditions then were so different from our own that we can gain practically no light as to its present advisability.

§ 4. *The Finances* — 1665-1783.

From the beginning of British rule a more liberal policy regarding the city finances was adopted by the central authorities, which were no longer, as in the Dutch period, those of a grasping private corporation. No longer was there a constant struggle for the wherewithal to fill the city chest. This change, together with a somewhat greater readiness to resort to direct taxation, chiefly distinguished the early days of New York under Nicolls and Andros from the times of Stuyvesant.

[1] Laws, 1804, Chap. 62.   [2] Art. 22.

The tavern-keepers' excise was restored forthwith to the city by Colonel Nicolls; a few years thereafter a municipal ordinance abolished it, but a little later it was reëstablished, in quite different form.[1] Moreover, the right to farm the Brooklyn ferry, so long coveted, appears to have been secured soon after the English capture; at any rate, we find a municipal ordinance regulating its management, and in 1682 an offer was made to the city council of £20 a year for twenty years for the privilege of maintaining it.[2] The title to this and to all other ferries from the city thereafter established was confirmed by Governor Dongan, and still more specifically by the charters of 1708 and 1730. The ferry became soon the chief source of municipal revenue. The Dongan charter was specially prized by the city fathers and the people, because of its confirmation and extension of those property rights which contributed so much to the municipal revenue. It gave the city the ownership of the market houses, extended its rights so as to cover all docks and wharves, and finally it granted to the municipality all unappropriated lands on the island to low-water mark — a grant which, had these lands been retained as other municipal properties then bestowed were retained, would ultimately have been vastly the most important of all. The Montgomerie charter gave

[1] Records of the Common Council, MS., vol. I, pp. 24, 31, 153.
[2] *Ibid.*, p. 215.

the city all land under water for four hundred feet about the island, a grant of very great value in connection with the dock system.

The rights and properties thus acquired by New York over two hundred years ago have been down to the present day of immense financial importance, but, in view of the limited expenditures of the early town, they possessed far greater relative consequence then. Indeed, till the middle of the eighteenth century, the revenues from these sources were usually sufficient without taxation to meet the recurrent outlay for city purposes proper; while occasionally when extraordinary needs arose, such as for fortifications or for the new city hall which was completed in 1704, some of the corporation lands would be sold.[1]

Great as was this reliance on indirect sources of revenue, the general English policy, both in state and municipal finance, did not shun direct levies with such thorough aversion as the Dutch had shown. The traditions of the mother country were more in favor of property taxes than had been those of Holland. For a year or two after taking possession, Governor Nicolls had required special taxes for quartering his troops, but the first tax for municipal purposes, based upon a formal assessment of the value of the property of the individual, was levied in 1676. The dock es-

---

[1] Black, *Municipal Ownership of Land on Manhattan Island*, pp. 22–24.

tablished in 1658 had just been rebuilt and much enlarged, and this expenditure, added to other older obligations, left the city with a debt which was reckoned up at the high figure of £24,505.[1] The assessment list for the 'taxacion' laid for reducing this debt is preserved complete; most of the amounts are round sums of £50 or multiples thereof, showing that the work of the assessors was rather superficial. The entire assessment was £99,695; on this a tax of one and one-half pence in the pound was levied. In the following year another tax for this same purpose was raised, and at three or four other occasions during the next decade direct taxation was resorted to, chiefly for reducing the debt.[2]

After the establishment of the provincial assembly in 1691, taxes for strictly civil purposes of the municipality were levied only by special acts of that body, and up to about 1750 such acts were called for but rarely, to meet some unusual expenditure or to pay off accumulated debts.[3] To be sure, under an act of 1693[4] recurrent taxes were raised, after the British custom, for supporting

---

[1] The figure is given in the original record, but seems scarcely possible from its magnitude. A tax of 1½d. per pound would make almost no impression in reducing this debt. Records of the Common Council, vol. 1, pp. 41, 61, 82 ff.

[2] *Ibid.*, pp. 93, 152, 265, 287, 334.

[3] The chief acts were in 1699, 1702, 1717, 1737, 1741. Van Schaack's Laws, pp. 35, 50, 105, 199, 209.

[4] *Ibid.*, p. 18.

the established church, and, in connection therewith, for poor relief; but these were collected by the vestrymen and did not come to the city treasury.

It is worthy of notice that from the first these various taxes were levied in proportion to the assessed value of property,[1] according to the fashion then prevalent in the mother land. Americans are so unaccustomed to any other form of general taxation (aside from the indirect taxes of the national government) that this fact may not appear in its full significance; but, in fact, many other modes of taxation then existed and still exist in Europe, while even in England municipal taxes are now levied on an entirely different basis — occupiers of buildings being assessed upon their annual rental. Had the Dutch retained control of the city longer, various forms of indirect taxation, or levies based on other criteria than property, might have become permanent features of the city finances; even such unjust taxes might long have continued as those laid in Stuyvesant's time for watching the city and protecting it from fire, which were collected in uniform sums from each household.

Up to the close of the war between England and France which ended in 1697, the chief city expenditure was for the watch, this item amounting to about £150 per year, but this was there-

[1] For general discussion, see Schwab, *History of New York Property Tax.*

after reduced greatly. The mayor and city council no longer received pay as in the Dutch days; indeed, they were subject to a considerable fine for failure to serve. Valentine, in the city Manual of 1859, gives the following summary for 1710, which shows well the general nature of the finances at this period:[1]—

Income

	£	s.	d.
Rent of the ferry	180		
Rent of the dock	30		
Received from 68 (tavern) licenses	51	19	6
Received from 15 freedoms, 8 to merchants and 7 to handicraftsmen	10	2	
Miscellaneous items	22	6	
	294	7	6

Expenditure

	£	s.	d.
Town clerk, salary	20		
Marshal, salary	10		
Treasurer's commission	20		
Bellmen's (watchmen's) salaries	36		
Lanterns and hour-glasses for watch	3		
Fire and candle for the constable's watch	3		
Bonfires on four occasions	20		
Repairs on city hall and jails	50		
Repairs at the ferry house	40		
Repairs on bridge and stairs at the dock	10		
Incidents on sundry occasions	42		
Making and repairing cage, pillory, and stocks	10		
Repairing the common sewer	10		
Miscellaneous	3	4	
	277	4	

[1] Page 505. The figures are apparently given only roughly, in round numbers.

Several public tasks which are now performed at general expense, such as lighting and cleaning the streets, were required to be done by the citizens individually; and for a time after 1742 they were even called upon to serve in rotation on the watch.

The system of special assessments for street improvements, which had been used in such perfect form by the Dutch, apparently gave way during the early English period to the other practice inaugurated in New Amsterdam of requiring such tasks to be performed directly by the adjoining owners.[1] Without further proof of the historic continuity of the assessment system in the colony, it would be perhaps hardly safe to assert that the early custom had special influence in securing the passage of the act which in 1691 firmly established the 'betterment' principle in New York finances. The phraseology of this law, at any rate, was borrowed directly from England. The first recorded application of the principle in the mother country was in 1662, for improving certain streets in London; while from another statute of 1667, for the improvement of that city after the great fire,[2] the New York law[3] was copied almost word for word. The latter act authorized the city to pave, grade,

---

[1] *E.g.* paving of street along *Heere Gracht*, 1676, Hoffman, Appendix, p. iv, and other cases in Records of the Common Council.

[2] Seligman, *Essays in Taxation*, p. 341. Dr. Rosewater, in 1891, first called attention to the act of 1667. See his *Special Assessments*, p. 16.

[3] Van Schaack's Laws, p. 8.

sewer, and otherwise improve streets, and "to impose any reasonable Tax upon all Houses within the said City, in proportion to the Benefit they shall receive thereby, for and towards the making, cutting, altering, enlarging, amending, cleansing, and scouring all and singular the said Vaults, Drains, Sewers, Pavements, and Pitching aforesaid."

The English betterment laws cited had been temporary and special, and the system there soon fell into complete disuse. The New York act was the first to establish this vastly important financial method of special assessments as a general and permanent thing, and the act of 1787,[1] which lies at the basis of the more recent legislation, was merely an extension of the statute of 1691.

The extent of the financial operations increased but slowly during the first half of the eighteenth century, as compared with the growth of population. The gross revenue in 1740 was only £747.[2] Soon after this, on the occasion of several extraordinary expenditures for docks and other improvements, it became the custom to incur temporary loans, and thenceforth the city had usually considerable floating debt.[3] To reduce this from time to time public lotteries, against which no scruples then existed, were resorted to, the first being

---

[1] Laws, 1787, Chap. 88; 1 Greenleaf, p. 441.
[2] This and following figures from Valentine, Manual, 1859.
[3] In 1784 it was £12,827, on which £5444 back interest was due.

authorized in 1756.[1] We find this device still employed in the early years of the present century. At this period, too, the ordinary expenses of the corporation took a rapid upward movement. In 1741 [2] a small annual tax for maintaining wells and pumps was authorized, and in 1761 [3] began the yearly levy of a rather larger amount for street lamps and watchmen. These taxes were added to the poor rate and collected by the vestrymen. Laws permitting the levy of other taxes for general or special purposes now became more common. In consequence of all these additions, the city income grew to no less than £10,395 in 1769, about £3000 of which went to the minister and the poor.

§ 5. *The Tax Laws and Finances* — 1784–1830.

The Revolution made no important changes in the city government or in the finances. Immediately after the war, however, the general movement toward greater personal freedom caused the abolition of the rates which had so long been levied for the support of the Episcopal ministry,[4] and therewith the collection of the poor taxes, and other taxes which had been embodied with them, passed from the vestrymen to civil officers.[5]

---

[1] Van Schaack's Laws, p. 363.
[2] Livingston and Smith's Laws, vol. 1, pp. 297, 343; 2, p. 233.
[3] *Ibid.*, vol. 2, p. 233.
[4] Laws, 1784, Chap. 38; 1 Greenleaf, p. 98.
[5] *Ibid.*, 1787, Chap. 62; *ibid.*, p. 419.

Down to the present day continual difficulty has been caused in the financial administration of New York city by the custom of collecting the taxes to cover the expenditure of the calendar year in its very last quarter, which makes necessary the borrowing of money during a large part of the time. This unfortunate system existed, as regards state taxes, at least as early as 1703;[1] but the rate for the minister and the poor, which had been so long practically the only city tax, was collected in January until 1775. At that time, because it was "inconvenient to the Assessors from the Coldness of the Weather," and also to the inhabitants since "there is but little Circulation of Money and their Family Expences higher than at any other Season of the Year," this local tax was made payable on August 1.[2] It was natural that mere convenience should lead ultimately, in 1788,[3] to the collection of city and state taxes at the same time, in the latter part of the year.

The same act which made this change laid down the first definite regulations as to the duties of the chamberlain. He was directed to keep "just, true, and distinct Accounts," and annually, between September 29 and December 14, to exhibit them, with the vouchers, to the mayor and council, as

---

[1] Van Schaack's Laws, p. 54.
[2] Laws, 1775, Chap. 57.
[3] Laws, 1788, Chap. 67; 2 Greenleaf, p. 181. The change was, perhaps, made in practice earlier.

well as to publish a summary, on the first Monday in November, in one or more newspapers.

The state legislature was quite as jealous of taxation by the city as had been the provincial assembly. The natural growth of expenditure for other purposes, as well as the change which placed the burden of poor relief on the municipality itself, now rendered it necessary to raise regular annual property taxes. The excuse for state control, which had perhaps existed when direct taxes were needed only on extraordinary occasions, no longer existed, but the legislature nevertheless insisted that annual tax acts be secured; and for no less than ninety years, beginning in 1784, the city remained subject to this central control. Similar annual tax laws were for a time passed for other cities in the state, but they soon gave way to general authorizations. The greater magnitude of the metropolitan finances doubtless led to the long continuance of the practice in this instance. The control thus exercised was, to be sure, for a long time almost purely formal, and was not the source of abuse such as became so flagrant in later days. Little if any change was ever made in the tax laws sent up for approval, nor did they prescribe the details of the city budget, as came to be the case about the middle of the present century. They fixed usually only two gross sums, one assessed on the whole county for the poor, roads, and miscellaneous expenses; the other, assessed on the more limited district especially benefited, for watching and lighting.[1] Occasionally additional sums for some specific improvement were inserted.

In conformity, doubtless, with the theory at the basis of this system, that taxation is a peculiarly sovereign prerogative, the power to levy city taxes was conferred upon the supervisors of the county of New York, as being more directly an organ of the state government, instead of upon the council itself. Down to 1857 this awkward distinction was a merely formal one, as the mayor, recorder, and aldermen served also as supervisors.[2] The assistant aldermen did not share this empty honor, but that fact was of no practical importance, since the levying of taxes in the city is little more than a mechanical function, while in voting the expenditure on which taxes were based, the assistants had equal power.

In the details of the financial system little progress was made up to 1830. By far the most important step was the creation of the office of comptroller in 1801. This was an act not of the legislature but of the common council, which, indeed, dictated the entire constitution of the executive departments. The comptroller, who was destined later to possess most powerful influence in municipal affairs, had at first but little authority,

---

[1] These two main divisions persisted till 1837, when the lighting and watching districts were separated. Laws, 1837, Chap. 80.

[2] Laws, 1787, Chap. 62; 1 Greenleaf, p. 419.

the council itself retaining control even of financial details. It was his duty, declared the ordinance,[1] "to examine and to liquidate all claims, to audit all accounts against this corporation in all cases whatever, and to report the same to the Board at each subsequent meeting, for its order in the premises; and also to countersign all warrants to be drawn on the Chamberlain or Treasurer of the city, for the payment of all monies directed by the Board; and in case where the Comptroller can not adjust the same without the interference of the Board, he shall examine such claim, and report the facts concerning it, with his opinion thereon. . . ." He was to exhibit a balance sheet every six months to the council.

There was at this period no system of appropriations in advance of expenditure, either annual or special. The council often ordered public works, and counted the cost only after it had been incurred. Some estimate, however, had to be made in order to apply to the legislature for the proper tax law. So long, moreover, as the council itself directed the details of the administration and even audited the smallest bills, there was somewhat less need of limiting expenditures by previous appropriations. Nevertheless, the absence of such a system tended toward careless management and extravagance, and often resulted in considerable deficiencies.

[1] As reënacted in 1812, Laws and Ordinances of New York, 1812, Chap. 9.

Especially after the War of 1812, when times were unusually hard, deficiencies kept accumulating till finally, in 1820, it became necessary to fund about $200,000 of floating debt.[1]

The expenditures during these early years appear very low from the present-day standpoint, and even after certain of the miscellaneous revenues had been set aside for the sinking fund (1813), these continued to cover a considerable part of the annual outlay. The first tax law (1784) had authorized the collection of £6000 ($30,000) for the poor, roads, etc., and £4000 ($20,000) for the watch and lighting.[2] The following figures show the relative importance of the various objects of outlay in 1798:[3] —

Schools	$ 2,000
Poorhouse and bridewell	40,000
Contingencies	30,000
Watch	23,000
Lamps	13,000
	$ 108,000

The receipts from the ordinary revenues — ferries, rents, etc. — were in that year about $20,000. This expenditure represents less than two dollars for each inhabitant of the city at that day,[4] a marked contrast with the present time, when the annual outlay, excluding state taxes, has reached

---

[1] Laws, 1820, Chap. 101; Valentine, p. 518.
[2] Laws, 1784, Chap. 43.
[3] These and other figures herein are from Valentine, pp. 514 ff.
[4] Population in 1800 about 60,000.

over twenty dollars *per capita*. The small expenditure indicates, however, not necessarily economy, but rather the limited character of the services which the city did for its people. Nothing was spent for fire protection, water supply (save a small sum for wells and pumps), or street cleaning, and the city was 'watched' only at night. In comparison with population and wealth, city expenditure increased less rapidly from 1800 to 1830 than at any succeeding period. Although the annual outlay multiplied about fivefold, the regular budget reaching $676,618 [1] in 1830, the population had meantime more than tripled while the assessed valuation had grown sixfold,[2] the tax rate being thus reduced from 50 cents on $100 to 42 cents. By 1830, however, some new municipal activities had been introduced; considerable sums were now spent for street cleaning, for the volunteer fire department, for public reservoirs and pipes (largely for fire purposes), and for courts,[3] while the cost of schools had risen to over $25,000. The support of the almshouse and the asylums and correctional institutions connected with it, and that of the watch, continued to be the most important city expenses. The revenues from sources outside taxation had increased even more rapidly than the taxes.

[1] Figures all from Comptroller's Report, 1830.
[2] From $20,703,000 in 1801 to $125,288,518 in 1830.
[3] $25,976, $23,462, $32,275, and $38,417, respectively.

During this period special assessments assumed great importance. In 1830 the expenditure to be recovered by this method reached $202,301, equal to nearly one-half of the amount raised by tax in that year.[1] Besides all sorts of street improvements, the law authorized the building of wharves and piers along the water front by assessment on the adjoining property[2] — a method long since abandoned. By an act of 1807 the system was extended to payment for the cost of land taken for opening new streets, where it has ever since been largely employed.[3] This change was introduced in connection with a comprehensive plan for laying out streets by state commissioners. The city was authorized at discretion to collect the entire cost of street openings from property benefited, but later acts have often required a part to be paid from the city treasury.

§ 6. *The City Debt.*[4]

The first decade of this century witnessed great activity in the making of permanent municipal

---

[1] Comp. Rep., 1830, p. 30.

[2] Laws, 1787, Chap. 88, 1 Greenleaf, p. 441; Laws, 1801, Chap. 129.

[3] *Ibid.*, 1807, Chap. 115. The distinction between assessments for opening streets and those for paving and improving them must always be borne in mind, as the provisions relating to the two often differ widely.

[4] Many details in this section based on Black, *Municipal Ownership of Land on Manhattan Island*, pp. 41-52, and Valentine's article, pp. 513-519.

improvements. The present city hall was built, an almshouse was erected, and large outlay was caused by filling in the lake or swamp called the Kolck, north of what is now Central Park. Not a little of this extraordinary expenditure was defrayed by the sale of lots belonging to the city, whose value had risen greatly with the rapid prosperity of the time; but the larger part of it went to swell the floating debt which had so long hung over the city treasury. The short-time loans were continually falling due, to the considerable embarrassment of the city fathers, who at last resolved to petition the legislature for permission to issue $900,000 of funding bonds. The petition, which set forth the extraordinary outlays which had been made, and which would still be required for opening streets, was granted in 1812,[1] and the history of the funded debt of New York city was begun. Seven hundred thousand dollars of the stock was immediately issued, the remainder a few years later. The term of the bonds was fourteen years, and the rate of interest 6 per cent.

The establishment of the sinking fund, which has had such far-reaching consequences, dates from 1813. It is noteworthy that this step was taken by the local authorities without legislative action. The law of 1812 had pledged "all and singular the revenues" of the city to the payment of the debt, and had promised that in default a

[1] Laws, 1812, Chap. 99.

special tax would be levied upon the citizens, but no definite provision was made for setting aside funds. It was the city comptroller, Thomas R. Mercein, who first proposed the plan of devoting certain kinds of revenue to a sinking fund.[1] He estimated that with accumulated interest these would amount by 1826 to $400,000, and suggested that the remainder of the debt could then be either postponed or met by the sale of lands. On August 9, 1813, the council passed an ordinance following closely these suggestions.[2]

This measure, which made no provision for interest, appropriated to the redemption of the city debt the income from: (1) commutation of water lot rents on grants prior to 1804 and quit-rents not commuted on such grants, (2) pawnbrokers' and second-hand dealers' licenses, (3) coach and (4) street vault licenses, (5) market rents and fees, and (6) 25 per cent — a few years later extended to all — of sales of city real estate. The control of these revenues and of the investments of the sinking fund was placed in the hands of an *ex officio* commission, consisting of the mayor, recorder, comptroller, chamberlain, and chairman of the finance committee of the board of aldermen — a time-honored body whose membership is un-

[1] Report of the Comptroller on the Establishment of a Sinking Fund, printed separately.
[2] Manuscript ordinances, Mayoralty of DeWitt Clinton, p. 105, copied closely in printed Ordinances, 1821, Chap. 32.

changed to this day. They were directed to purchase preferably city stock, but were not to pay more than par, and, if need be, might buy temporarily United States bonds or stock of New York banks. As a matter of fact, resort to this alternative proved necessary only to a very limited extent, and that for but a few years after the creation of the fund.[1]

The policy adopted by this ordinance was crude as compared with the stringent regulations, now common in many states, for the redemption of municipal debts by setting aside annually sums precisely sufficient to pay them at maturity; and by too long continuance it has needlessly complicated the city finances. Nevertheless, the measure was a fairly advanced one for that day. It was not many years before 1812 that the United States government had pursued the policy of appropriating specific revenues for debt reduction; while in England the fallacious idea that debt could be extinguished practically without effort by accumulating compound interest was still in vogue, and had led even to the absurdity of borrowing money to keep up the regular payments to the sinking fund. The entire absence of this famous 'sinking fund fallacy' in the discussion by the city comptroller is noteworthy. The accumulation of interest on securities purchased does not necessarily imply the holding of that theory. Almost the only

[1] Comp. Rep., 1858, pp. 46–49.

argument given by Mr. Mercein for the proposed sinking fund, aside from "a well-grounded belief that its utility must be obvious to all," was that it would aid in maintaining the high credit of the city, which was important "because emergencies may happen, which will require new loans." So, too, the preamble of the ordinance simply refers to the advantage that "the said stock will be prevented from depreciating, and the redemption of the same will be regularly progressing."

The revenues devoted to the fund constituted at first considerably less than half of the income of the corporation from other sources than taxation. Rents from docks, ferries, and real estate, and other miscellaneous revenues, were still paid into the general treasury. The receipts of the sinking fund in 1816 represent about the average between 1813 and 1820, if we disregard special sales of real estate in 1818 and 1819.[1]

SINKING FUND RECEIPTS, 1816

Commutation quit-rent	$ 1,667
Sinking fund — water lot rent	1,969
Market fees	8,038
Street vaults	1,638
Pawnbroker's licenses	650
Hack licenses	465
Commutation wheat quit-rent	1,999
	$16,427
Interest on accumulations	2,824
Total	$19,251

[1] Comp. Rep., 1858, p. 46.

Had it not been for a very rapid increase in market rents, due to the erection of Fulton Market in 1820–21, the comptroller's estimate of the accumulations of the fund in 1826 would have proved too low. As it was, however, the fund then amounted to nearly half a million.[1] To meet the remainder of the debt temporary loans were made, and finally, in 1829, $300,000 of 20-year refunding bonds were issued.[2]

In 1820 another loan of $400,000 was made, half of which was for funding floating debt, and the rest for constructing Fulton Market. A portion of the amount was redeemable at an early date; in 1830 the remainder outstanding was $270,300. The total funded debt in that year was accordingly $570,300, while the assets of the sinking fund were $227,744.[3]

§ 7. *General Character of the Government.*

The question, how well the city was governed in these early days, or in what respects, if any, the system was superior to the present one, is very difficult to answer. The common council centred in itself practically all power, the government being indeed very similar to that which is so successful in England to-day. They organized all the executive departments and chose the officers to fill them, even the appointment of the mayor, who had

---

[1] Comp. Rep., 1858, pp. 46–48, by computation.
[2] Under authority of a law of 1826, Chap. 93; Black, p. 57.
[3] Comp. Rep., 1830, p. 4.

long continued to be named by the governor, being given over to the council by the constitution of 1821. Though the old provision that ordinances should remain in force only a limited time unless approved by the legislature still persisted,[1] this was not made a means of active central interference. This method of council government remained almost unmodified up to 1849, and in the later period at least did not escape considerable abuses; but it is probably true that before 1830 the system worked considerably better, although the halo of distance has materially brightened the reputation of these 'good old days.' Certain it is that the citizens of that time itself were not entirely satisfied, for in 1829 a city convention, whose action was endorsed by popular vote, urged strenuously the removal of all executive functions from the council.[2] However, the charges brought by the convention were hardly severe and specific ones, and theoretical considerations had special weight in its discussions. It is beyond question that during the first decade of this century a much higher class of citizens composed the city government than is now the case. One would hardly expect to-day to see a man, who had already been governor, resign from the United States Senate to become mayor of New York, as did DeWitt Clinton.

One erroneous impression exists regarding the

---

[1] Extended from one to three years in 1806, Laws, Chap. 126.
[2] See § 8.

government of this period. It was not free from party politics. Just what peculiarity of our American character or what unique external conditions caused the development here of an evil which European municipalities have to considerable degree escaped, it would be hard to say. The first conflicts of national politics were mirrored in New York city, and though in the federal government the spoils system did not at first find undisputed sway, it was very soon almost universal in the city. In the harmonious Federalist days Richard Varick had held the mayoralty for twelve years.[1] But from the very outset of party strifes at the opening of this century, the appointment of the mayor was considered at Albany a legitimate spoil; and as often as the political complexion of the council of appointment changed, New York had a new chief executive. From 1801 to 1823 the mayor was changed nine times. In the city itself, despite the fact that municipal elections were held in April, the parties fought bitterly over the choice of aldermen. In 1801 a number of young men in two wards, shut out by the freehold requirement, bought jointly a house and lot, "upon the principle of a tontine," and were allowed to vote, though the election was afterward contested on this ground. The Democrats first secured a majority of the council in

[1] Most of what follows is based on an article by D. T. Valentine, "Political History of New York City," in the Manual of 1854, which gives official figures and documents.

1804, and the minutes of a caucus which they held record, one after another, motions to remove all but one of the city officers, each vote being 'unanimous.' The influence of the city's precedent was considered specially important in national elections. Party feeling was unusually strong during and after the War of 1812. One of the many flaming campaign circulars used in the purely local elections has these words: —

"REPUBLICANS! Do you wish again to see this city in the hands of tories — to be governed by traitors and cowards? *Awake!* . . . *To the polls*, then, every man of you — devote the whole of this last day to the preservation of your rights — to the salvation of your COUNTRY!"

Surely party politics were not absent here. The frequent almost total change of membership in the council shows how far short the city fell of the standard now held up to us by English municipalities where councillors and aldermen frequently retain their positions for half a life-time.

CHAPTER III

COUNCIL GOVERNMENT UNDER THE CHARTER OF 1830

§ 8. *The Charter of* 1830.

The so-called charter of 1830 was a comparatively brief act, in the nature of constitutional legislation, the details of government being left to the council to work out. The purpose of the zealous reformers who framed it, however, was to institute far more radical changes than were in fact accomplished. They proposed nothing short of an entire remodelling of the city government after the pattern of the federal and state constitutions, but the spirit of their too general enactments was little carried out in practice.

The agitation for some such changes had been long brewing among the people. One of the chief amendments which was sought — the separation of the aldermen and assistant aldermen into two independent boards — had been twice, in 1824 and 1828, submitted to popular vote,[1] but had been rejected, perhaps because the proposed change was coupled with an extension of the term of the upper board.

---

[1] Laws, 1824, Chap. 155; 1828, Chap. 249.

But the movement did not subside. At last, in 1828, in accordance with the traditions of home rule then prevalent, a city convention was held, composed of five delegates from each ward.[1] The charter it recommended was ratified by the people, while on the question as to the term of the council, submitted to separate vote, the decision was for a single year's term for both aldermen and assistants. The charter as adopted was passed by the state legislature unmodified.[2]

The principles expressed by the convention of 1829 are of great interest. Most stress was perhaps laid upon the separation of the council into two boards, "for the same reason which has dictated a similar division of power into two branches, each checking and controlling the other, in our general government."[3] Most of the delegates favored also a longer term for the upper house, aiming to make it approximate in nature to the United States Senate. A provision excluding the mayor henceforth from the council and giving him the veto power was designed to furnish an additional check. The convention proposed also that the mayor should thereafter be elected by the people instead of by the council, but as this required a con-

---

[1] Journal of the Convention, printed in Kent's edition of the Charter of New York, 1836.

[2] Laws, 1830, Chap. 122.

[3] This and following quotations from "Address of the Convention," New York Commercial Advertiser, October 24, 1829.

stitutional amendment, the change was not effected till 1834.[1] These changes were intended also to aid in the second great reform that was advocated, — the division of executive from legislative power. With a view to completing this separation, it was enacted that

"The executive business of the Corporation of New York shall hereafter be performed by distinct departments, which it shall be the duty of the common council to organize and appoint for that purpose."

As we shall see, the council neglected to carry out this too indefinite command, but the intent of the convention is clear from the address to the people with which the charter was submitted : —

"At present most of the revenues of the city are expended, and its most important executive business in relation to public works, buildings, repairs, &c., are performed, by committees of the same board which orders the work or the expenditure. By separating these duties, by expressly confining the Corporation to the legislation of the city, the appropriation of monies, the appointment of officers and the supervision of their accounts, and by entrusting all duties purely executive to officers arranged in proper departments . . . it seems certain that greater responsibility will be ensured."

The executive power of the mayor was intended to be somewhat increased by the charter, but the

---

[1] Laws, 1834, Chap. 133.

appointment of officers still remained with the council.

It was, further, the design of the convention that the separate executive departments should be thoroughly under the oversight of the municipal legislature and responsible to it. The council was to provide for official accountability, while a detailed statement of the city receipts and expenditures was to be published annually. Most important of all was the provision which now first introduced a regular appropriation system: —

"Annual and occasional appropriations shall be made by proper ordinances of the common council, for every branch and object of city expenditure; nor shall any money be drawn from the city treasury, except the same shall have previously been appropriated to the purposes for which it is drawn." The spirit of this section is evident from the declaration of the convention: —

"It will bring the whole disbursements of the city annually before the Corporation and their constituents, and by shewing the several heads of expense distinctly, will indicate the proper place and mode of reform or retrenchment. . . . Besides, every man's experience will teach him that when a limited sum of money, esteemed adequate to any given object, is set apart for it, the same is much more likely to be used discreetly, and made to go as far as possible in effecting its end, than if it were allowed, without limit, under a general order to complete the work, or make the necessary purchase, whatever they might cost. A contrary practice under our present system, of appointing committees 'with power' to carry into effect resolutions of the Board, without any previous specific appropriation, is believed to be a source of no small part of our city debt and taxes."

From all this it is perfectly clear that the ideas of the worthy delegates to the convention of 1829 were all moulded on the conventional example of the federal and state governments. The two mutually restraining houses, the veto by the mayor, the separation of executive and legislative functions, the appropriation system — all were copied closely. The question whether the different character of municipal affairs might not justify considerable differences in the form of government, was not raised. It was apparently not even because specially grievous fault was found in the actual working of the existing system, — for the charges against it, after all, are neither bitter nor specific, — but far more on theoretical grounds, that these changes were urged. Be this as it may, it is certain that the objects sought by the charter of 1830 were almost entirely frustrated in practice. The utterances of the convention are chiefly interesting as showing how early and how strong was the movement towards following national precedent, a movement which continued till nineteen years later a law more effective to accomplish this end was secured.

§ 9. *The Budget.*

In accordance with the requirement of the charter, the common council early passed an ordinance providing for a system of appropriations.[1] Although the council took office in May, appropriations were to be made for the calendar year. The members therefore would acquire some experience before being called upon to vote the budget. The various executive officers were required to furnish the comptroller "a detailed statement, as near as may be, of the sums which will be required for each distinct object of expenditure." On the basis of these, the comptroller was to present to both boards, in December, a general estimate for the year, together with an estimate of the probable miscellaneous revenues and of the amount that must be raised by taxation, in order that application might be made to the legislature for the annual law, which should fix the limit of the levy.

Considerable diversity appears in the methods of action on the budget in different years. The estimates were always at once referred to the joint finance committee, which reported to the council early in January, when the tax law was at once framed and forwarded to Albany. In drawing up this bill, the council of course ought to have felt that it was limiting practically even the details of the appropriation, although these were

---

[1] See Laws and Ordinances of New York city, revised 1834, p. 109.

sometimes not fixed by ordinance till later, temporary appropriations being quite often made pending further discussion, as is now the custom of the British Parliament. In at least two cases, indeed, 1840[1] and 1843,[2] the council appears to have considered that the voting of the appropriations was a mere formality after the decision as to the tax levy; for the original appropriations covered barely half of the amount of the estimates, and it was left for the new council, which took office May 1, to vote supplies for the rest of the year. The purpose of this action may have been to put the responsibility on the incoming board.

The fact that such procedure as this was considered a legitimate fulfilment of the requirement of annual appropriations shows how loose was the interpretation of the charter. Such action, however, would not have been specially harmful had the estimates in accordance with which the taxes were raised been in fact always treated as limitations on expenditure. But there was an unfortunate freedom also in construing the permission to pass 'occasional appropriations,' the purpose of which was merely to allow for extraordinary contingencies. Gradually grew up a most vicious system of additional appropriations, very similar

---

[1] Proceedings of the Council approved by the Mayor, vol. 7 (1839-40), p. 111; vol. 8, pp. 6, 23, 44, 65, 70.

[2] Report of Comptroller, etc., Documents of the Aldermen, vol. 10 (1843-44), p. 44, table.

in effect to the deficiency appropriations which so often constitute a serious abuse in our national and state finances. Fixed limits of income were thus disregarded in expenditure, and the necessary result was a floating debt in the shape of revenue bonds, created in violation of the charter provision which forbade the city to incur debt without legislative authority, except in "anticipation of the revenue of the year in which such loan is made." The first serious appearance of this evil was in 1836, when in addition to the original budget of $1,271,350 additional appropriations aggregating $207,263 were made.[1] It was partly this disregard of law which rendered necessary in 1840 the issue of $400,000 of funding stock.[2]

Additional appropriations were less extensive for a few years after this, but in 1843 they began again to constitute a decided abuse. It seems to have been at times the motive of the city fathers either to give a false appearance of economy before the April election, or at least to embarrass their successors in office; for the tax levies were unduly cut down and an altogether disproportionate share of their amount was spent by the outgoing board before May 1. This motive is distinctly charged by Mayor Morris in 1843.[3] In that year the esti-

---

[1] Proceedings of the Council approved by the Mayor, vol. 3, p. 252 (with subtraction of "street opening"); vol. 4, pp. 45, 120, 150.

[2] See *post*, p. 56.

[3] Message, Proceedings of the Aldermen, vol. 25, p. 68.

mates of the comptroller were reduced in making the application for the tax levy from $960,000 to $850,500, while $387,582 of this was already spent up to May 9. The original budget had been only partial, and the incoming council was compelled to pass appropriations considerably in excess even of the comptroller's estimates. Further illustration of the irregularity of the budgetary system might be taken from almost any year after this. It seems to have merited the condemnation made by Comptroller John Ewen in 1846:[1]—

"The amounts are frequently exceeded in large sums, requiring additional appropriations. . . . As a consequence, a temporary debt must be accumulated at the end of the year, either to be funded, or to increase the following year's taxes. The provision of the Charter prohibiting any sums from being drawn from the Treasury, unless an appropriation shall first be made, is rendered nugatory, if those charged with expenditures may at pleasure exceed the amount estimated for the expenditures of the year, and thereby render an appropriation absolutely necessary to discharge the obligation thus created. In such case the Common Council does not exercise the control over the Treasury intended by the Charter, but acts merely ministerially, in passing whatever ap-

---

[1] Communication to the Council, Proceedings of the Aldermen, vol. 30, p. 135.

propriations may be represented to be necessary, and to whatever extent, although exceeding the amounts provided in the taxes of the year."

The practice of raising additional taxes for deficiencies, alluded to by Mr. Ewen, began in 1846[1] and continued yearly up to 1857. In 1850 no less than $290,840 was added to the tax levy to cover the shortage of the preceding year.

Besides the evil of additional appropriations, the lack of clearness in the budget and the frequent changes in the method of grouping the expenditures show the undeveloped character of the system. A similar criticism applies to the methods of accounting and to the financial reports. It was at this time the custom to vote appropriations for the so-called 'trust accounts,' *i.e.* for the redemption of revenue bonds, for expenditures to be recovered by assessments, etc.; and these were often included with the other appropriations in a single alphabetical list. During the '40's, moreover, a division of the budget was usually made between appropriations authorized by existing law and those requiring special action of the legislature. These three groups being sometimes separated, sometimes combined, the totals being quite as often omitted as given in the ordinances and in the reports, and the additional appropriations still further complicating the problem, it must have been very difficult for a lay-

[1] Laws, 1846, Chap. 67 (the tax law).

man to understand the city finances.[1] The budget, however, was much less detailed than now; about forty items, alphabetically arranged, made up the list of ordinary appropriations.

§ 10. *The City Debt.*

Although the loan of $900,000 which, in 1812, began the history of the New York debt had seemed to the people of that day a considerable burden, public indebtedness scarcely became a really important factor in the city finances till the construction of the great Croton aqueduct. In 1830 the entire funded debt was only a little over half a million, less than half of one per cent of the assessed valuation of the city, and the interest on it constituted but a small element in the budget. By the close of 1849 the debt had multiplied nearly thirty-fold, amounting to almost 6 per cent of the assessed valuation, and the annual interest was equal to about 40 per cent of the total expenditures on other ordinary accounts. The funded debt in 1830 was $2.88 *per capita;* in 1849 it was nearly $30 *per capita.*

The subject of a proper water supply for the city had been almost constantly agitated since the Revolution.[2] In contrast with the hesitation now shown by our cities in undertaking lighting, street

---

[1] This confusion also prevents the presentation of financial tables for these years in as full form as is possible later on.

[2] Where no other authority is cited, this sketch is based on King's *Memoir of the Croton Aqueduct*, New York, 1843, which quotes all original documents of importance.

railway, and other 'socialistic' enterprises at public expense, sentiment in New York (and indeed the same was true elsewhere throughout the country) was from the very first strongly in favor of municipal ownership of waterworks. Nevertheless, no satisfactory plan was discovered, and finally, in 1799, the privilege of furnishing water was given to a private company, in which, however, the city held some stock. The citizens suffered much under this arrangement, for the company merely pumped an insufficient supply from a large well. Numerous projects were discussed from time to time, most of which contemplated the Bronx as a source. At last in 1833 a commission was created for investigating the subject. It reported in favor of the Croton river as a supply, and in 1835 presented a more detailed plan, estimating the cost at $5,500,000. The city council endorsed the report and submitted to the voters the question whether the work should be undertaken. The magnitude of the enterprise might well have appalled the people; possibly had they known how far the estimates would be exceeded, they would have rejected the scheme. The vote was 17,330 yeas, 5963 nays, and the largest majorities in favor of the aqueduct were found to be in the wards most heavily assessed.

The great work was placed in the hands of commissioners appointed by the governor — an early instance of state control over an essentially local enterprise. The chief reason advanced for this arrangement was that the aqueduct required the appropriation of land outside New York county. There were not a few conflicts of authority between this board and the city council, the right of the state commissioners to lay distributing pipes in the city being especially called in question.[1] Party politics were only a trifle less prominent in the matter than in the management of the second great aqueduct a decade ago. When the Whigs gained power in 1839, the entire membership of the commission was changed; five years later a Democratic administration reinstated the original appointees. In spite of all this, there was comparatively little complaint as to the honesty or efficiency of the management of either set of commissioners. Owing to speculation in the lands condemned for the works, to the disturbed financial condition of the times, and to the substitution of the High Bridge over the Harlem for an inverted siphon, the cost of the aqueduct was considerably enhanced, and its completion was delayed. The outlay for the aqueduct proper, including the Murray Hill reservoir, was $8,917,501, while $2,097,251 was spent on distributing pipes during the period we are studying.[2]

---

[1] See concerning this controversy, and concerning the general work of the water commissioners, report of special committee, Documents of the Aldermen, vol. 7, No. 32.

[2] Manual, 1850, p. 259.

The laws authorizing bonds for the aqueduct had made no special provision for their interest or redemption; and in fact, during the years in which the work was in progress, the interest on money already borrowed was met by further long-time bonds, no less than $1,577,459 being issued for this purpose. In view of these circumstances, and of the depressed financial condition of the time, the credit of the city naturally began to suffer. Eight and a half millions of bonds had been floated at 5 per cent before 1841; but the last loans had fallen considerably below par, so that the real interest had averaged $7\frac{1}{2}$ per cent.[1] When, accordingly, the issue of $3,500,000 more was authorized, part of this sum was borrowed on temporary notes, in anticipation of funding when credit should improve. This funding was actually accomplished several years later, at 5 per cent interest.[2] Two influences combined to bring about this more satisfactory state of city credit. In 1842[3] the collection of taxes to pay interest on the bonds was at last commenced, and in the next year a general reorganization of the sinking fund was made by an ordinance,[4] which the state legis-

---

[1] A full account of these loans is given in a communication of the comptroller, Documents of the Aldermen, vol. 8, No. 13.

[2] Compare Comp. Rep., 1844, p. 11; 1847, p. 21; Manual, 1850, p. 258.

[3] Valentine, p. 524.

[4] Proceedings of the Council approved by the Mayor, vol. 11, p. 153.

lature, in 1845,[1] declared could not be amended except by its consent.

The main modification of the debt system which this measure introduced was the creation of a separate 'sinking fund' for interest. The redemption fund was continued with practically the same revenues as before, but a policy of rapid disposition of the lands held by the city, for the benefit of the fund, was inaugurated. To the interest fund were pledged practically all the remaining revenues not derived from taxation. By far the most important were the Croton water rents, which grew so rapidly that in 1850 they amounted to $458,951,[2] four-sevenths of the total income of the interest fund. The receipts from docks, which increased from $34,397 in 1844 to $108,583 in 1850, with those from ferries and from excise licenses, made up the greater part of its other revenues. The ordinance required that, in case the interest on the debt could not be met from these sources, the balance must be raised by taxation. The water rents were naturally small at the start, and considerable sums had to be contributed from taxes, but by 1851 the fund was able to pay the interest unaided.

No provision was made in this ordinance of 1844 for any mutual adjustment between the

[1] Laws, 1845, Chap. 225.
[2] Comp. Rep., 1858, pp. 58, 59. For further figures for 1850, see Table IV, Appendix.

redemption and interest funds, or between them and the general account. The system was rigid and mechanical, and frequent interferences of law have since been necessary to adjust it.

Besides the water debt, four other comparatively insignificant loans were contracted between 1830 and 1849. 'Public building stock' was issued in 1835–38,[1] for the Tombs prison and other minor building projects. Three hundred and seventy-five thousand dollars of bonds were required to pay for buildings blown up to prevent the spread of the great fire of 1835;[2] while, to aid temporarily the banks and insurance companies weakened by the disaster, the city borrowed over a million more.[3]

In 1840 it became necessary once more to fund the floating obligations of the city.[4] These had been swollen, as we have seen, by the additional appropriations, and had been further increased by several, apparently scarcely legal, expenditures for permanent public works.[5] By these means the floating debt had risen to no less than $1,636,475 in 1839,[6] a considerable part of this being borrowed from

[1] $500,000; Comp. Rep., 1838, p. 8.
[2] Manual, 1850, p. 257.
[3] $1,071,242 up to 1837. Comp. Rep., 1836, p. 110.
[4] By an issue of $400,000, payable in eight annual instalments, beginning 1841. Laws, 1840, Chap. 327; cf. Comp. Rep., 1839, p. 10.
[5] Black, p. 60.
[6] Comp. Rep., 1839, p. 9.

moneys received on the water loan, pending their actual outlay. In partial explanation of these large figures, it must be remembered that at this time taxes were paid less promptly than now, since there was no penalty for non-payment till February 1; and that, moreover, no provision existed for the addition of percentages to the yearly taxes to cover deficiencies in collection. 'Public building stock, number 2,' the issue of which began in 1846, was intended to pay for various new buildings on Randall's island.[1] Partly with a view to protect the holders of water stock, partly because the expenditures for which they were designed could scarcely, with propriety, be thrown upon the distant future, both these last-mentioned loans were made payable, from taxation, in annual instalments beginning immediately after the contraction of the debt.

The net result of the debt operations[2] during the twenty years we have been considering was that, at the close of 1849, the outstanding bonds, redeemable from the sinking fund, amounted to $14,876,783, and those payable from taxation to $365,000, while revenue bonds, which had been again rapidly growing since 1840, amounted to $2,223,453. The sinking fund had accumulated $3,690,866, leaving the net indebtedness of the city $13,774,370.

[1] Laws, 1845, Chap. 253. $350,000 outstanding at the end of 1849.
[2] Manual, 1850, pp. 250 ff. See, also, Appendix, Table V.

§ 11. *Special Assessments.*

The construction of local improvements by assessment was greatly extended during this period, especially in the decade 1830-1840. A large number of streets, laid out by the commissioners of 1807, were now first opened and improved. The amount of assessment expenditures was vastly greater, relatively to those on ordinary account, at that time than it is now. For the ten years beginning 1830 they averaged annually almost exactly half a million dollars, while the average amount of taxes levied was only $968,000. In 1837 the outlay on these accounts reached $1,113,838, almost equalling the entire sum raised by taxation.[1] Fifty years later, in the decade beginning 1880, the expenditures from assessments averaged only about three times as much as in the earlier period, while the annual tax levy had multiplied fully thirty-fold. The use of assessments, however, was considerably less from 1840 to 1849 than during the preceding years.

No changes of importance were made in the administration of the system during this time. There did not exist a separate assessment fund, but works were paid for out of the general treasury account, into which assessments were turned as collected. On the whole, the system worked fairly well in spite of somewhat rudimentary methods, and we hear little of losses to the city by failure to collect assessments.

[1] Comp. Rep., 1837, p. 17.

There was considerable opposition to the 'betterment' principle throughout the first half of the century.[1] It was repeatedly but unsuccessfully assailed in the courts as unconstitutional. Moreover, an attempt was made in the constitutional convention of 1846 to abolish assessments entirely, but it met with comparatively little support. The final word of the courts justifying the system under the constitution as then adopted, was spoken in 1851, in the case of The People *vs.* The Mayor, etc., of Brooklyn.[2]

§ 12. *General Character of the Period. Conclusion.*

The charter of 1830 failed signally to bring about the radical changes for which it was designed. This was partly due to imperfection in its provisions, but more to the wilful disregard of their spirit, and even of their letter, by the city council. We have seen how little real effect in regulating expenditure was accomplished by the introduction of the budget. The other reforms sought proved equally unsuccessful. The fact that the members of the two boards of the council were elected in equal number, from the same districts (one from each ward), by the same voters, and for the same term, defeated, to large extent, the object of making them a check upon one another. By allowing the passage of measures

---

[1] Rosewater, *Special Assessments*, pp. 27–29.
[2] 4 N. Y. 419.

over the mayor's disapproval by mere majority vote, the veto power was made of little avail. By leaving to the council the appointment of all executive officers, except the mayor, and giving them no definite term of office, the new charter enabled the legislative boards still to exercise very great control over administrative affairs.

Despite these defective features of the law, it would have been possible in considerable degree to effect that separation of powers which had been designed, had it not been for the unwillingness of the council to part with the large administrative control it had so long enjoyed. The city fathers of 1831, declared Mayor Morris eleven years later,[1] had mostly held office under the old régime, and wilfully or by mere force of custom, they followed precedent rather than the spirit of the new charter. They did, to be sure, organize somewhat more carefully the various executive departments, but they left to them practically nothing but clerical duties. The aldermen and assistants themselves, through joint committees, dictated even the details of administration, the very name of 'executive committees' which these officially retained showing how little they confined themselves to legislative functions.[2] Repeated and bitter complaints were

[1] Message, 1843, Proceedings of the Aldermen, vol. 25, pp. 62, 63.

[2] See Ordinances, revised 1845. There were twenty-one such committees then.

made by the mayors as to the maladministration of these committees and their lack of responsibility to the chief executive or to the council itself, and there was certainly some basis for their criticisms. An attempt was made in 1841 [1] to lessen this irresponsibility by requiring committees to make reports of their every meeting to the council, but this ordinance was soon repealed or fell into disuse; while even during its continuance Mayor Morris declared that there were practically given over to "these Executive Committees the legislative powers of the Common Council; so that in fact the Common Council became subdivided into a number of sub-legislatures," whose acts, never submitted to the mayor, were subject to no supervision whatever.[2] He further dwelt at length on the corruption of the council, and especially on the custom of letting contracts to its members and their friends — charges which he bore out by citing specific cases. The large-hearted aldermen and assistants of those days deemed it a matter of principle to show Gotham as a hospitable and jovial city, and many a case of wine or box of cigars, many a sumptuous banquet even, was found charged to the account of 'contingencies for the Common Council'; while quite as cheerfully read the bills for carriage hire that were paid from the city treasury.

[1] See Ordinances, revised 1845, p. 6.
[2] Message above cited.

Had the city council been free from partisan influences, and had the officials who carried out the will of the committees been men of thorough training and practically permanent in their positions, the council's administration might have approached in excellence more nearly to that of modern English cities. But unfortunately all this was far from being the case. The interference of party politics was constant.[1] In the first election for a mayor (1834), excitement reached a pitch beyond anything we witness in these days. In the sixth ward a mob seized the polls and destroyed the ballots, and the militia had to be called out.[2] Later campaigns were hardly less violent.[3] Party domination in the city changed frequently. The council's absolute power of appointment was exercised strictly from partisan motives. An illustration of the absurd extent to which the patronage system was sanctioned is found in the police act of 1844,[4] which provided that the alderman, assistant alderman, and assessors of each ward should jointly nominate the captain, assistant captain, and all the policemen for that ward. Under such circum-

---

[1] See, *e.g.*, Mayor Harper's message, 1844, Proceedings of the Aldermen, vol. 27, p. 11.

[2] *Memorial History of New York*, vol. 3, p. 340.

[3] Thus we hear of heavy election frauds in 1837, and of threats of violence in 1838, as well as of special precautionary measures in 1839. Communication from the mayor, etc., Documents of the Aldermen, vol. 5, No. 29.

[4] Laws, 1844, Chap. 315.

stances, declared Mayor Havemeyer,[1] elections to the council "cannot but be regarded in some degree as a pecuniary prize. . . . A change in the political complexion of the Common Council is generally followed by a change of all the officers in the government, from the highest to the most subordinate; and this change has now become almost annual."

And yet, however serious were the charges by contemporaries against the council's administration, we may not at once conclude that it was excessively bad as compared with other periods. The people who at that time reviled government by the common council, could not compare it with government by irresponsible executive officers such as came later. Imperfect as was the municipal administration from 1830 to 1849, it is very doubtful whether it would have been better had the restriction in the powers of the council planned by the city convention of 1829 been actually accomplished.

From the purely financial standpoint, the two main features of the period we have been considering were the introduction of specific appropriations, and the construction of the Croton aqueduct. The budget, indeed, was far from carefully managed, but foundations for a more satisfactory system had been laid; while the aqueduct was an enterprise of which the city was justly proud.

[1] Message, 1845, Proceedings of the Aldermen, vol. 29, p. 27. The changes in the list of city officers given in the Manuals seem to bear out these statements.

There was general increase of city expenditures during the twenty years from 1830 to 1850. New York was beginning now to take on more of its modern metropolitan character. Its population increased from 197,112 in 1830, to 515,547 in 1850. New municipal activities arose, and expenditures naturally grew in greater ratio than population. The total outlay for ordinary purposes increased from $676,618 in 1830, to $3,368,163 in 1850, besides $584,085 for interest paid from the sinking fund in the latter year.[1] It appears, however, that after the people came to realize the burden of the water debt, they retrenched in every possible way. A comparison of the specific expenditures for 1830, 1840, and 1850, shows that during the latter decade of the period, those forms of expenditure that had been inherited from the earlier days — cleaning streets, almshouse, docks, etc. — grew but slowly. On the other hand, aside from the great increase of interest payments, the expenditure for public schools and police now first took on large proportions, the former increasing from $25,995 in 1830, to $374,553 in 1850, the latter from $99,521 to $487,541. Education at public expense is, of course, of comparatively recent introduction. The establishment of a day police was the outcome of direst necessity, the disorders at election time having especially emphasized the need. For some years the 'watch' continued to be much more im-

[1] Comp. Rep., 1830 and 1850.

portant than the police, but finally the government of the two was merged, and the guarding of public safety by day soon became of equal consequence with that by night. Another considerable addition to the burden of taxation was the state mill tax, first levied in 1842. These added expenditures, together with the devotion of all the revenues from miscellaneous sources to the sinking funds, caused a rapid increase in the tax rate from 1830 to 1850,[1] and mutterings of discontent began to be heard.

[1] Forty-two cents in 1830, 54.7 in 1840, 113.75 in 1850, the assessed valuation having meantime increased about 130 per cent. Report of Senate (Fassett) Committee on Cities, New York Senate Documents, 1891, No. 80, p. 2266.

CHAPTER IV

THE PERIOD OF LEGISLATIVE INTERFERENCE

1850-1869

Up to 1849 New York was practically governed by its common council. The executive branch had little power. Moreover, with some exceptions, the state legislature left the council free to act as it deemed best — it was largely a time of municipal home rule. All this became almost completely changed before the close of the period on which we now enter. The first step in the process, the removal of purely executive powers from the council, was accomplished almost at one blow in 1849; the motive therefor was chiefly desire for better government. The transfer of control over the city to state authorities was more gradual. It was brought about in three ways: (1) by usurpation by the state of the appointment of many important executive officers; (2) by the creation of a separate board of county supervisors, so constituted as to be largely in sympathy with the state administration; and (3) by direct interference of the legislature, especially in the budget. The motive for this state control was to a considerable degree partisan, and must be sought in connection with the peculiar political conditions before and during the war time.

§ 13. *The Charter of* 1849.

For some years before 1849 general and growing dissatisfaction had been felt over the failure to accomplish that division of powers in the government contemplated by the charter of 1830. The dissatisfaction became so strong by 1846 that a convention of delegates elected by the people was held for revising the charter. This body proposed more specific provisions for enforcing the separation of powers, and stricter checks upon the common council.[1] But the absorption of popular attention in the beginning of the Mexican War, in the congressional election, and in the state constitutional convention then in session, withdrew interest almost entirely from the city convention. Accordingly the poll on the adoption of the charter was decidedly small, and there was a slight majority against it.[2] Yet the work of the convention had not been without effect. Many of its proposed measures were copied word for word in the charter actually adopted in 1849, while others were incorporated in the amendments of 1853. One provision suggested by the convention, which never found its way into actual law, is important

---

[1] The charter proposed and the address to the people are given in the Journal of the Convention, 1846, pp. 698 ff.

[2] 5863 for, 7195 against. 32,919 votes were cast at the same election on the state constitution. *New York Tribune*, November 7, 1846.

as showing the feeling regarding the abuse of additional appropriations and consequent temporary loans, as well as the desire to bring the creation of funded debt under the immediate control of the people rather than under the less discriminating supervision of the legislature: —

"No money shall be borrowed on the credit of the corporation unless the common council shall by law direct the same in anticipation of the revenue for the year in which the same shall be borrowed, *and shall provide, in the same law, for repaying the same out of such revenue;*[1] but money may be raised by loan whenever the law providing for the same shall be passed in each board by a majority of all the members elected, and shall be approved by the electors at any charter election."

The charter of 1849,[2] which was destined to work a revolution in city affairs, was passed by the legislature and then submitted to popular vote. Owing, doubtless, to the development of public sentiment and to the absence of distracting political conditions, it met a much more favorable reception than the proposed charter of 1846. The vote was 19,339 for, 1478 against, the charter.[3] Partisan motives had little to do with the adoption of this law. It had been urgently pushed by a non-partisan reform organization, and the practical unanimity of the vote shows how general was the belief that it was a real forward step.

[1] The italics are mine.   [2] Laws, 1849, Chap. 187.
[3] *New York Tribune*, April 14, 1849.

The fundamental feature of the new law was the establishment of independent administrative departments, and the almost entire removal of executive power from the council. The purpose of following closely the federal and state constitutions, which had not been fulfilled under the act of 1830, was at last carried out. "Neither the common council," declared the charter, "nor any committee or member thereof, shall perform any executive business whatever"; while, to prevent that collusion between the two boards of which complaint had often been made, they were given "concurrent powers and a negative on each other's proceedings," and were forbidden to appoint joint committees save one on accounts. Heretofore the council had been left to create such executive departments as it would, and to appoint their officers, but the charter of 1849 expressly established ten departments, whose heads were to be elected by the people for a three years' term. The movement of the democratic spirit is strikingly illustrated in the change from the custom of half a century before, when all the executive officers of the city, including the mayor, were appointive, to this law, which gave directly to the people the selection of a dozen executive officers besides the common council. These departments, which were chiefly single headed, were required to make annual reports to the council.

Only a few provisions regulating the finances

appear in the charter of 1849. The evil of allowing members of the council to be interested in public contracts, which, though forbidden by the former law, had yet flourished considerably, was more emphatically defined and prohibited. The regulation of the budget was still left rather indefinite, though clauses were added declaring that appropriations must be based on "specific and detailed statements in writing of the several heads of departments," and that "no expense shall be incurred by any of the departments or officers thereof, whether the object of expenditure shall have been ordered by the common council or not, unless an appropriation shall have previously been made." This last emphatic provision seems to imply that additional appropriations had been sometimes forced upon the council by executive officers after the expense had been actually incurred.[1] These but slightly more detailed restrictions had little effect in bringing about a more systematic or satisfactory budget system.

§ 14. *The Charter Amendments of* 1853.

Further amendments to the charter, chiefly intended to check certain abuses of power by the city council, were made by a law of 1853. As in 1849, this act was the result of general popular agitation, irrespective of party.

As is usually the result when improvement is sought by changes in outer organization only,

---

[1] This charge had been made also by Mr. Ewen. *ante,* p. 49.

without a change in popular spirit, the high hopes based upon the charter of four years before had been signally disappointed. The city fathers, in spite of the restriction of their domain, had found scope for an amazing amount of corruption. We have seen that already during the decade preceding the charter of 1849 the council was far from spotless, and we should hardly have looked for improvement in its character after the loss of prestige caused by that measure. It was precisely at this time that municipal franchises, ever a prolific source of jobbery, began to take on new importance. Though the Harlem railway had been established considerably earlier, no other street railways were introduced till 1851. The franchises were, at this period, granted by the council with no legislative regulation. No less than four important roads were authorized in 1851-2, without a cent of compensation to the city, and charges of corruption grew rife. The popular indignation finally burst over the attempt to grant, despite the mayor's veto, the right to lay tracks in Broadway, an attempt which only an injunction prevented from accomplishment. This was a scheme of the same Jacob Sharp, who, fully thirty-two years later, by still more gigantic corruption, actually secured this franchise. The city comptroller, Mr. A. C. Flagg, voiced emphatically even at this early day the opinion that the city should receive large pay for street railway and similar privileges.

In connection with the ferries, also, there had been no little corruption, while fraud and bribery in letting city contracts combined to make the council of 1851-2, the 'Forty Thieves,' a byword for many years.[1]

Another influence which led to the reform movement of 1853 was a great abuse of the appropriating power in the previous year. The evil of additional appropriations had been by no means effectually attacked by the charter of 1849. The original budget for 1852, which had been cut down but slightly from the departmental and comptroller's estimates, called for a tax levy of $3,380,511; but no less than $828,100 of additional appropriations were voted in the latter part of the year. Most of this amount had to be incorporated with the taxes of 1853,[2] swelling the tax rate to 123 cents, as compared with 97 cents the year before. This sudden leap in taxes was the signal for general indignation.

Mr. Flagg, the new comptroller, exposed these various evils unsparingly, and was hailed loudly as the champion of reform. A great mass meeting, presided over by Peter Cooper, was held.[3]

[1] For general account of these various frauds, see Comp. Rep., 1852, pp. 12 ff., 1853, pp. 17 ff.; *New York Tribune*, December 29, 1852, June 6, 8, 1853; *New York Times*, February 9, 1890; Report of Special Committee consisting of New York Members, on the Charter of 1853, Assembly Documents, 1853, No. 82.

[2] Comp. Rep., 1851, p. 20; 1852, p. 20.

[3] *New York Tribune*, March 7, 1853. See also second meeting, *ibid.*, June 6.

The speakers charged both political parties with corruption, and declared that good government demanded the active interest of the better classes at the primaries and polls; nevertheless, they felt that considerable improvement might be effected by further safeguards about the action of the council. The legislature adopted essentially the amendments proposed by the reformers,[1] and submitted them to the vote of the city — the last change in the charter for which popular sanction was sought. The large and nearly unanimous vote[2] in favor of the law shows how strong was the public sentiment.

Considerable but apparently unwarranted expectation of reform was based on an increase in the number of the lower board of the council. Sixty 'councilmen,' elected from as many districts, were to take the place of the assistant aldermen. A provision by which half of the aldermen should be elected each alternate year, instead of all together, was designed to place a still further check within the council itself. Moreover, a two-thirds vote was now first required to override the mayor's disapproval.

The specific evils that had been so conspicuous were vigorously attacked. The law prescribed that all leases of ferries, docks, etc., and all sales of land and of franchises, must be at auction to

---

[1] Laws, 1853, Chap. 217.
[2] 36,672 to 3351. *New York Tribune*, June 8, 1853, p. 4.

the highest bidder, and for not over ten years; that all work and supplies valued at over $250 should be furnished by contract on competitive bids; and that no additional allowances beyond the legal amount should be made on any contract. Severe penalties were fixed for giving or accepting bribes. The establishment of a special auditing bureau in the finance department was expected to prevent many fraudulent payments. The patronage of the council had been greatly diminished by the charter of 1849, yet the absurd law giving its members the appointment of policemen had still persisted; this power was now conferred on the mayor, recorder, and city judge. Although the abuse of appropriations had been so marked in 1852, the only direct attempt to improve the budgetary system was the futile one of requiring appropriations to be first voted by the board of councilmen. The change in the composition of the council was largely counted upon for improving the financial management.

Once more were the expectations of the city reformers cast to the ground. The new regulations had but little salutary effect. Only one street railway franchise, that of the Ninth Avenue Railway, was granted up to 1860, at which date the legislature abrogated the right of the council to authorize railways;[1] and there appears to have been no competition at the auction and no payment

[1] Laws, 1860, Chap. 10.

to the city. Perhaps the influence of the requirement that leases of ferries and docks be made at auction may be traced in the increase in the revenue from the former from $66,900 in 1853 to $105,459 in 1855, and from the latter from $125,361 to $160,602.[1] The provision regarding contracts, it was charged in 1857, was often evaded by splitting up jobs into parts whose value would fall below $250.[2] Though the looseness in the budget never became quite as conspicuous as in 1852, additional appropriations continued extensively for several years. The law of 1853 certainly brought about almost no improvement in the character of the common council or in the economy of the government. The large appropriations of 1853, $5,069,650, had caused loud complaint; yet only three years later more than two millions had been added to the budget. As had indeed been recognized by the reformers, the chief requisite for good government was not better forms but better men; and to secure these was made well-nigh impossible, not only by the difficulty under any circumstances of careful discrimination in the selection of so many officers by popular vote, but more especially by reason of the low character of the political majority in the city.

[1] Comp. Rep., 1858, p. 60.
[2] Report of Committee on Cities and Villages, Assembly Documents, 1857, No. 125, p. 5.

§ 15. *Charter Changes of* 1857, *etc.*

It was the failure of all these proposed reforms, together with the growing partisan motive to which color was lent by the peculiar political circumstances of the time, that finally led to the inauguration of the system of state interference. Unfortunate as was this violation of home rule, the necessities of the time perhaps partly justified it, and the better elements in the city undoubtedly approved it. New York city was then strongly inclined to a pro-slavery and disloyal position; the Democratic party, which was in large majority, represented mainly the worst elements in the population. The outside state, on the other hand, was strongly Republican and opposed to slavery. The Democrats in the city were using the public patronage, the control of election machinery, and every other influence, legitimate or illegitimate, to carry the state elections; they were not only misruling the metropolis: they were using it as a tool to capture the state government. It was no wonder that the Republicans, and the better classes in the city generally, desired some means to save the people from the spoilers, nor that the Republican majority in the legislature was very ready to come to their aid by transferring the administration as far as possible to its own control.[1]

In 1856 the legislature for the first time amended

---

[1] See Report of Committee on Cities and Villages, Assembly Documents, 1857, No. 125, p. 2.

materially the tax law proposed by the city. In the following year, chiefly for partisan ends, a general charter was passed,[1] combining and amending all earlier laws except the property grants of the colonial charters. The composition of the council was changed with a view to giving more representation to the minority party. Aldermen were to be chosen no longer from wards, but from districts named in the law, and doubtless considerably gerrymandered; while six councilmen were to be elected from each senatorial district on general ticket, without provision, however, for cumulation of votes or any other mode of minority election. The custom of choosing all the chief executive officers directly by the people, which had been bitterly attacked, not only as little calculated to favor discriminating selection, but also as making the departments unduly independent and irresponsible, was done away; and all of the department heads except the comptroller and city counsel were made appointive by the mayor, with the confirmation of the aldermen. The term of the comptroller was extended to four years with a view to making him more familiar with the finances. Detailed regulations to prevent evasion of the law regarding municipal contracts were the only new provisions of a distinctly financial character.

Another measure passed in 1857[2] sought even

[1] Laws, 1857, Chap. 446.   [2] *Ibid.*, 1857, Chap. 590.

more openly than the charter to give power to the minority party in the city. This was the separation of the city and county governments and the creation of a board of supervisors — an absolutely unnecessary division of authority from any standpoint except that of party expediency. The device by which minority representation was secured is peculiar. There were to be twelve supervisors elected, and each voter might put six names upon his ballot; the six persons receiving the highest number of votes were to be declared elected, and afterwards "the mayor of the city shall *appoint* as supervisors the six persons receiving severally" the next highest number of votes.[1]

But this was not all. The Republicans began at the same time the policy, so bitterly detested by the political majority in the city, of placing some of the most important local departments under the control of legislative commissions. The Central Park[2] and the police[3] departments were the first to be so usurped. The park had already been laid out under a law of 1853, but its improvement had only just begun. Eleven commissioners, named by the legislature itself, were now given exclusive power over it; they could require the city even to issue bonds in such amounts as they saw fit, subject only to limitations set by the act.

---

[1] The method of election was somewhat changed in 1858 (Chap. 321), but the practical working remained the same.

[2] Laws, 1857, Chap. 771.   [3] *Ibid.*, Chap. 569.

State control of the police department was deemed specially desirable because of the real danger from disloyal disturbances, as well as of the important influence exerted by the police in elections. To effect this purpose within constitutional bounds the legislature employed the device, also made use of in other parts of the state, of forming a 'district' by the combination of separate jurisdictions. The counties of New York, Kings, Westchester, and Richmond were united into the 'Metropolitan police district,' under the management of a board consisting of the mayors of New York and Brooklyn, and five commissioners appointed by the governor. Three years later [1] direct local influence in the board was withdrawn entirely, its membership being reduced to three commissioners chosen by the governor. It was eight years later before the system of legislative commissions received further extension. Then the 'Metropolitan fire department'[2] and the 'Metropolitan board of health'[3] were established. These departments comprised only New York and Brooklyn, but had much the same character and powers as the police board.

A strong attempt, led by the Democrats, was made in the constitutional convention of 1867 to abolish all these legislative commissions, but the convention rejected the proposed amendments;

---

[1] Laws, 1860, Chap. 209.   [2] *Ibid.*, 1865, Chap. 249.
[3] *Ibid.*, 1866, Chap. 74.

and, in fact, there was no change in the system till the charter of 1870 summarily ended it.

Numerous other instances of interference with city affairs by the Republican legislature might be cited. In 1860[1] the commissioners of the reorganized department of charities and correction were made appointive by the city comptroller, the explanation of this singular arrangement being merely that the comptroller was then a Republican, while the mayor was a Democrat. Again, when, in 1861, through a division in the Democratic party, George Opdyke, a Republican, had been chosen mayor, a law was passed making the term of all heads of departments four instead of two years, and the change applied to the appointees whom he had placed in office.[2] Another act created a commission,[3] named by the legislature, to revise the city charter; but, probably because of the general absorption in war affairs, no interest in its work could be obtained, and it finally adjourned without submitting any propositions.

§ 16. *The Budget and the Independent Departments.*

Having sketched the political conditions of this period and the consequent changes in the general character of the city government, we must retrace our steps to consider more fully the municipal finances and the effect of these same conditions upon them.

---

[1] Laws, 1860, Chap. 510. [2] *Ibid.*, 1863, Chap. 68.
[3] *Ibid.*, 1861, Chap. 268.

Formally, the procedure for the regulation of city expenditures remained nearly the same from 1850 to 1869 as in the preceding period. The council now took office January 1, so that the complications due to the change of administration in the middle of the year disappear. Occasionally the outgoing council voted the budget in December, but more usually the new council passed upon it in the beginning of the year. The actual spirit and working of the appropriation system, however, was almost completely changed by the reorganization of the municipal government, by the establishment of departments independent of the council, and by the direct interference of the legislature in the budget.

The first city departments to be removed from the financial control of the council were not the legislative commissions just described. Almost from the beginning of the system of free public schools, the department of education both in New York city and elsewhere has been very largely independent of the general local administration, and more directly under state supervision. As early as 1844[1] the council in New York ceased to have any control over the expenditure for schools; the city was required by law to raise a definite tax for maintaining the system, and in addition such a sum for new buildings as the board of education should determine. Similarly, in 1849,[2] the 'alms-

---

[1] Laws, 1844, Chap. 320.   [2] *Ibid.*, 1849, Chap. 246.

house department,' which governed all charitable and correctional institutions, was empowered to determine the amount of taxes that should be raised for its support. This department was then under the control of ten 'governors' elected directly by the people, on a system of minority representation.

The independence of these two departments does not appear to have engendered extravagance. Though the expenditures for schools increased very rapidly, owing to the comparative newness of the system, there was still general satisfaction with the work of the board of education.[1] The expenses of the almshouse department actually decreased under the law of 1849.[2] Nevertheless, it was felt that too much freedom was granted to these branches of the government; and the act of 1853, while it refused to increase the power of the distrusted common council, provided that the annual appropriations for schools and for charities and correction should be submitted to a commission consisting of the mayor, comptroller, recorder, and the presidents of the aldermen and councilmen.[3] This body, however, had only advisory power, for the departments themselves could override its action by two-thirds vote. If the expectation was to keep down expenditures by this supervision, it was certainly disappointed. The appropriations for

[1] See Comp. Rep., 1851, p. 14; 1852, p. 17; 1853, p. 14.
[2] $399,787 in 1848, $385,000 in 1853. *Ibid.*, 1848, p. 25; 1853, p. 37.
[3] Laws, 1853, Chap. 217.

the city schools, which had been about $600,000 in 1853, were multiplied fivefold in 1869.[1] The almshouse appropriations likewise took at first a sudden upward leap, but under the law of 1860, which gave the appointment of the heads of the department to the comptroller, it appears to have been economically administered,[2] and the board was generally commended for its work.

The expenditures of the 'legislative commissions' were even less subject to local control. The financial management of the Metropolitan police district was considerably divided among different authorities.[3] The salaries of officers and men, and largely, too, their number, were fixed by the legislative act. The amounts needed for miscellaneous expenses, which were but small as compared with the pay of the force, were estimated by a commission consisting of the police board itself and the comptrollers of New York and Brooklyn; they were then submitted to an advisory board composed of the presidents of the boards of supervisors of the counties of New York, Kings, Westchester, and Richmond, and the president of the board of aldermen of Brooklyn, with

[1] These and the following figures from Comp. Rep., 1858, p. 76; 1860, p. 82; Manual, 1870, p. 717. The various sums must of course be considered in comparison with the increase in the general budget and in other departments, remembering the inflation of the currency from 1864 to 1869.

[2] Appropriations, 1856, $925,000; 1860, $639,150; 1869, $953,000.

[3] Laws, 1860, Chap. 259, § 11.

three representatives of the smaller villages; but the final decision rested with the first commission.[1] The disordered condition of the times required a very large police force, and the expenditure increased rapidly. From 1850 to 1854, under direct city control, the police appropriations had nearly doubled, but during the following three years there had been actual decrease. It was accordingly easy for the opponents of the new system of state control to complain when the outlay rose from $825,500 in 1857 to $1,355,175 in 1860, and to $2,638,291 in 1869. Part of the increase in the later years, however, was due to the inflation of the currency; and the general opinion of the time, even among the more candid opponents of the legislative commissions, did not charge the department with special corruption or extravagance.

The current expenditures of the Central Park commission, to be met from taxes, were of less importance than those for permanent improvements, payable from bonds. As to both forms of expenditure, the only restrictions upon the commission were those set by the legislature itself.[2] Concerning this department, likewise, we find few complaints of mismanagement or extravagance. The control of the appropriations of the Metropolitan fire and health departments was quite similar to

[1] Under the law of 1860, § 60. Under the original law this larger board had the final appropriating power.
[2] Laws, 1857, Chap. 771; 1860, Chap. 85.

that of the police appropriations. The institution, by the new law of 1865, of a paid fire department, instead of the inefficient volunteer companies, naturally necessitated large added expenditure. The cost of fire machines and apparatus, buildings, etc., in 1864, had been $140,000; the appropriations for the new service by 1869 reached $907,940.[1]

On account of its bi-partisan composition, the board of supervisors was often classed by the enemies of the system with the hated 'radical' legislative commissions. Over the purely county expenditures this board had budgetary power precisely similar to that of the council in the city, and equally subject to control by the state government. The extent of its discretion was, however, comparatively small at first. With county appropriations were grouped the immense sums for state taxes and police, over which the supervisors had no real authority. These items, together with the fixed salaries of the judiciary — a rapidly increasing factor — and the large payments on the county war debt which soon began, swelled the county budget so that it nearly equalled that of the city. But while the total county appropriations for 1864 were $6,204,037, the part of these classed as 'for the support of the county government' was only $839,844,[2] while a large proportion of this amount was practically fixed in advance

---

[1] Comp. Rep., 1864, p. 68; Manual, 1870, p. 717.

[2] Comp. (county) Rep., 1864, p. 14.

by law. But there were already developing within the board of supervisors the germs of enormous corruption. As early as 1861, William M. Tweed, the future prince of 'bosses,' had commenced the formation of the 'supervisors' ring'; and about the close of the war, county expenditures for armories and drill rooms, for printing, 'lighting and cleaning, and supplies,' and other purposes, began to be exploited very extensively. Appropriations 'for the support of the county government' reached $3,609,075 in 1869,[1] an increase of nearly 450 per cent in five years. The device of the Republicans to secure, through the supervisors, control of part of the local government, had proved an expensive luxury. But the further discussion of this subject belongs to the history of the Tweed Ring.

After this review of the financial position of the independent departments, the repeated and bitter complaints of the members of the Democratic city council concerning this subtraction from their authority may be understood. In their rancor, however, they were wont to be hardly fair in their comparisons, and to class the board of education, the department of charities and correction, the commission on street cleaning, and even the supervisors, under the title of 'radical commissions.' It would not be worth while to follow the arithmetical contortions by which the finance committee

[1] Comp. (county) Rep., 1870, p. 7.

of the aldermen in 1868 sought to make it appear that of the $23,293,564 estimated for the city and county budgets, the 'total for the state' was $15,026,988, for the county $3,263,758, and for the city $5,002,818, of which latter sum it was declared that "the entire amount of *taxation* which can be chargeable to the present common council" was $1,710,709.[1] A more correct grouping of these figures is as follows: —

ESTIMATED APPROPRIATIONS, 1868

State taxes	$5,564,426
City departments not appointed by the state government but independent of the city council, viz.:	

Board of education $2,900,000
    Charities and correction . . 960,000
    Street cleaning contract . . . 504,696
	4,364,696

Commissions appointed by the state, viz.:	

Metropolitan police $2,861,871
    Metropolitan fire department . 893,000
    Metropolitan board of health . 177,588
    Central Park commission . . 219,060
	4,151,519

College of New York and asylums, required .	390,797
County expenditures, including interest . . .	3,263,758
Interest and redemption of city debt	1,847,111
Expenditures under direct control of council .	3,710,709
Total	$23,293,016 [2]

[1] Proceedings of the Aldermen, vol. 109, pp. 114–116. It must be remembered that these are estimates, not the final appropriations. The council subtracted the $2,000,000 of the general fund to arrive at the result indicated.

[2] The slight discrepancy is due to typographical errors in the original figures.

Even this classification, however, shows the comparatively small field left to the council in appropriating the city moneys, and, as we shall now see, even here its action had practically no weight, being subject to continual change by the state legislature.

§ 17. *Legislative Interference in the Budget.*

Up to the middle of the century, the yearly tax laws had been almost purely formal; changes were seldom if ever made in the sums requested by the city, and the laws did not fix specific appropriations. But, as might be anticipated, now that interference in general municipal affairs had begun, the legislature soon seized the opportunity which the tax law system made ready to its grasp. By the most flagrant violation of the home rule principle which the state has ever witnessed, the ordinary expenditures of the metropolis came to be minutely regulated by the legislature.

The first law which practically incorporated in itself the city budget, by fixing in detail the items for which the tax should be levied, was that of 1851.[1] No change, however, was made by the legislature in the sums determined by the city authorities. In 1853,[2] and regularly thereafter, a section was added to the tax law providing that no portion of the respective amounts should be applied to any other object than that specified, thus preventing transfers of appropriations. Curiously enough,

[1] Laws, 1851, Chap. 258. [2] *Ibid.*, 1853, Chap. 232.

there was still no definite prohibition of appropriations in excess of the sums authorized, and the practice of making additional appropriations continued up to 1856.[1] We have already noticed the flagrant case of 1852.[2] The charter amendments of 1853 did not avail to check the evil. For 1854 in 11 of the 50 heads of account, the appropriations made by the council exceeded the limit set by the tax law, the amount of these additions being equal to no less than 13 per cent of the levy. The deficiency for the year that had to be met by taxes in 1855 was $481,612. No new provision of law to prevent additional appropriations was adopted till 1860, but, perhaps from the influence of public sentiment, they practically ceased in 1856.

It was in this latter year that the legislature first made modifications in the tax law submitted by the city council. The assembly committee on cities took testimony of several witnesses, and changes, chiefly reductions, were made in 10 items, the total for general purposes being thus decreased from $3,485,944 to $3,247,189.[3] From this time on, such amendments to the tax levies

[1] Compare items in table of taxes levied yearly in Comp. Rep., 1856, p. 40, with the tables of appropriations in the separate annual reports.

[2] *Ante*, p. 72.

[3] Documents of the Assembly, 1856, No. 193; Proceedings of the Council approved by the Mayor, vol. 24, p. 19; Laws, 1856, Chap. 176.

occur yearly, and ever in greater degree. Moreover, the legislature, now finding that the city fathers were disposed to use as extensively and as corruptly as possible what little authority remained to them, kept tightening the reins of financial procedure. The Republican city comptroller, Mr. Haws, in 1859 began the practice of carrying on unexpended balances of appropriations to the same purposes in the following year, charging that the custom of allowing them to lapse was illegal and calculated to favor mismanagement. This change was made mandatory by a law of 1860;[1] but at the same time the council was allowed to transfer moneys from specific appropriations that were more than sufficient, to meet deficiencies in others. This permission proved a dangerous loophole for the assaults of the common council on the treasury. Sums known to be more than required were sometimes appropriated for proper purposes, and it was regularly to the more questionable objects that balances were transferred. Thus, in 1863, transfers in the city budget were made from 16 items, involving an amount of $279,935 out of a total appropriation of $7,374,861.[2] Most of this sum went to cleaning streets, a notoriously mismanaged department, to 'advertising,'

---

[1] Laws, 1860, Chap. 509.

[2] Manual, 1864, pp. 168-173. See, also, concerning this general subject, An Appeal by the Citizens' Association of New York against the Abuses in the Local Government, New York, 1866, p. 20.

and to 'city contingencies,' the transfers to these three heads amounting to more than half as much as the original appropriations for them.

In view of the abuse of 1863, the legislature in the next year forbade transfers, and enacted an apparently iron-clad section intended to make the figures of the tax law absolutely unchangeable. But another device for evasion was ready to hand. Since 1859 the tax laws had yearly authorized the levy of additional taxes to pay any judgments recovered against the city after their passage. Under this provision large contracts were made in 1864 and 1865 with the express understanding that the city would confess judgment without defence for the amount due. The greater part of these expenditures, moreover, were for the same questionable purposes to which transfers had been chiefly made. In 1864 the total amount spent on city account for advertising, printing, and stationery was $522,066, of which no less than $311,578 was paid on judgments.[1] In this same year the entire expense of street cleaning was collected by suit. The legislature had authorized the levy of $300,000 for cleaning the streets, but a bid to do the work for that sum was rejected, no appropriation

---

[1] Report of the Comptroller of New York in reply to a resolution, New York Senate Documents, 1867, No. 66, pp. 53, 63, 71. Compare Comp. Rep., 1864, pp. 68, 207. See, also, concerning the evil in general, the above-cited pamphlet of the Citizens' Association, p. 20.

whatever was made, and the streets were cleaned throughout the year by days' work. The laborers assigned their claims to bankers, who collected from the city on judgments $758,772 during the year. In both these instances the limit that the legislature had fixed on expenditure was exceeded fully 150 per cent by this simple device.[1] Once more rallying to the contest, the legislature, in the tax laws beginning with 1866,[2] forbade the payment of any judgment for a debt beyond the amount of the appropriation under which it properly belonged. This provision, however, was largely disobeyed. In fact, the Ring was now rising into power both in the city and in the legislature, and legal restrictions of all sorts were soon utterly disregarded.

The evident disposition to loose financial management, thus manifested on the part of the local authorities, constituted at least some justification for the growing tendency of the state legislature to modify extensively the annual tax levies. During the '60's this interference became so great that practically the entire appropriating power was usurped, as may be seen by the following table showing the appropriations on city account from 1860 to 1869, as originally made by the council

---

[1] Proceedings of Select Committee on Street Cleaning Frauds, New York Senate Documents, 1865, No. 38. See especially pp. 92, 531, 592.

[2] Laws, 1866, Chap. 876, § 10.

and as they stood at the end of the year after the legislature had acted upon them:[1] —

APPROPRIATIONS ON CITY ACCOUNT

	Original	Final
1860	$5,928,292	$6,571,965
1861	7,412,967	6,837,315
1862	5,681,267	6,248,164
1863	7,753,065	7,374,861
1864	7,795,104	8,671,664
1865	9,256,498	11,297,618
1866	10,216,993	10,593,148
1867	11,105,875	12,599,359
1868	11,329,393	13,173,046

The extensive additions, on the one hand, thus regularly made by the state laws,[2] were often, perhaps usually, for really necessary purposes which the local authorities, by neglect or for partisan reasons, had omitted from the budgets. The city magistrates were specially prone to refuse appropriations asked by the various independent departments, or required for special enterprises under legislative acts. As the council often neglected to vote such items, even after their inclusion in

[1] The comptroller's reports give yearly the dates of the various appropriations made during the year so that these can be distinguished.

[2] The deductions in 1861 and 1863 were due to quite exceptional causes.

the tax law, it became the custom to authorize and direct the mayor and comptroller in such case to make the appropriation.[1] On the other hand, the legislature, while so largely increasing the gross budget, quite uniformly cut down the items already voted by the council. How powerfully this general readjustment affected the budget may be perceived from the appropriations of 1867,[2] the changes on May 11 and the amount added by the mayor and comptroller being due mainly to the effect of the tax law: —

Amount appropriated by ordinance, March 15	$11,105,875
Less reduced by ordinance, May 11	592,500
	$10,513,375
Added by ordinance, May 11	1,180,767
Added by mayor and comptroller	905,217
Final appropriation	$12,599,359

The legislature added 14 items, increased 13, reduced 14, and struck out 1,[3] these constituting altogether a very large proportion of the entire number of items. It is hardly remarkable, in view of such circumstances, that in two years[4] the city council seemed to accept the futility of its own action, and made only partial appropriations till after the tax law was adopted.

[1] Laws, 1864, Chap. 405, § 6.
[2] Comp. Rep., 1867, p. 13.
[3] Report of the Finance Committee of the Aldermen, Proceedings of the Aldermen, vol. 109, p. 107.
[4] 1864, Comp. Rep., p. 12; 1866, *ibid.*, p. 12.

The Citizens' Association, an organization of certain friends of good government, mostly Republicans, of which Peter Cooper was president, was active at Albany during the years following the war in securing changes in the tax laws.[1] It boasts of having brought about very great saving, through obtaining reductions in items approved by the council, and still more through defeating attempts frequently made by city officers to have their appropriations increased in ways contemplated not even by the council. The most flagrant instance of such action of the executive departments occurred in 1869.[2] The proposed levy had been considerably cut down in the bill recommended by the senate and assembly committees; but Mayor Hall, with a number of other city officials, went to Albany, and by their effective lobbying brought it about that, when the bill came up for final passage, a substitute, vastly increasing the appropriations, was suddenly sprung upon the assembly and rushed through without reading. The senate refused to concur, and only after two conferences had been held was a bill passed, in the very last hour of the session, which, though greatly reducing the sums named in the substitute bill, still

---

[1] See the annual reports and various other pamphlets published by the association, 1864 to 1874, collected in one volume by the association. The statements made are not always trustworthy.

[2] Pamphlet of the association, reprinted from *New York Times*, June 4, 1869.

made considerable increase over the comptroller's estimates.[1]

This narrative is further interesting as showing the way in which the city tax laws, involving such immense sums of money, were regularly 'jammed' through, with no opportunity for proper consideration. It need not be said that in the last two or three years of the decade, when the legislature was becoming exceedingly corrupt, and when Tweed was already gaining wide control over it, the passage of the annual levy was the occasion of no small amount of bribery and corruption. The budget system of New York city, if system such a monstrosity could be called, was fast making ready for the gigantic frauds of 1869 to 1871.

If other illustration were needed of the little

[1] The association gives the following figures: —

	COMPTROLLER'S ESTIMATES	ASSEMBLY SUBSTITUTE	LAW AS ADOPTED
City	$4,896,477	$7,167,363	$5,595,236
County	1,442,845	3,950,550	2,550,550

It is impossible to trace out from official records just how these amounts were arrived at, as they include sums to be raised by bonds, and are otherwise complicated. Apparently there is some exaggeration, but the account of the procedure is substantially correct; and the substitute levies amounted to actually fully $600,000 more for the city and $300,000 more for the county, as to taxes alone, than those in the law as passed. See Assembly Journal, 1869, pp. 2053, 2108, 2147, 2161; Laws, 1869, Chaps. 875, 876.

heed paid by the legislature to the action of the local authorities in fixing the local expenditures, the fact might be cited that in 1867 it was enacted that thereafter the estimates should be prepared by the mayor and comptroller, and after being presented to the council should be forwarded to the legislature within three weeks, whether the council had voted upon them or not.[1] A marked change, this, from the days when the annual tax laws had been intended simply to place the seal of state authority on municipal acts. This tendency to increase the power of the mayor and comptroller in the appropriations, which has been noted also in another connection, continued till the practice merged, under the charter of 1870, into the new system of control by the board of estimate and apportionment, which meant at first control by the four arch conspirators of the Tweed Ring.

In the tax law of 1867, a section was adopted requiring a three-fourths vote of the council upon any appropriation or expenditure, only a majority having been necessary before. This change, which has persisted till the present time, was designed to give added restrictive power to the members of the Republican minority in the council; but we are told that a few of these were thereupon bought up without difficulty.

§ 18. *The City Debt.*

Although the beginning of 1870 is the time set

[1] Laws, 1867, Chap. 586, § 10.

for the close of the period now under consideration, because that was the date of the Tweed charter, the Ring rule was already firmly established during 1869, and most of the great additions to the city debt in that year properly belong to the Ring period. A just summary of the results of the financial management for the two decades will consider the state of the debt at the close of 1868. Even up to that time there had been a very rapid growth in the burden of indebtedness. Two great factors had contributed to this increase — the opening and improvement of Central Park, and the bounties paid to soldiers during the Civil War. Several smaller bond issues should, however, be briefly mentioned.

There was issued during the early '50's $500,000 more of 'public building stock' for various buildings, and an equal amount for the construction of docks and slips, for which the increasing annual outlay from regular appropriations had become a considerable burden.[1] Improvements of the water system still required large bond issues, though these scarcely aggregated as much as did the water stocks redeemed during this period. The construction of new reservoirs in Central Park, begun in 1856, was the most extensive of these enterprises,[2] but later on the erection of the high service water-

[1] Comp. Rep., 1855, pp. 45, 47. Payable in annual instalments.
[2] Total cost, $3,708,000. Comp. Rep., 1860, p. 46, p. 98, Table; Laws, 1860, Chap. 372; Manual, 1869, p. 719.

works at Carmansville for supplying the upper part of the city, and of new reservoirs for storage in Putnam county, called for considerable sums.[1] The aggregate of water bonds issued from 1850 to 1869 was $5,420,800.

The pressing need for a large park[2] to supplement the few small squares in the lower part of the city first found influential expression in a special message of Mayor Kingsland in 1851. The council, declaring that "the subject has awakened in the minds of our fellow-citizens an uncommon interest," requested the legislature to authorize the city to take a certain piece of land, known as Jones' Wood, bordering on the East river. The suggested law was passed, but before it could be put into execution there began an agitation for a larger space. A committee of the council recommended the site of the present Central Park, as being both much larger, and, on account of its very rocky and uneven character, almost worthless for dwelling or business purposes. They estimated that from this latter circumstance the cost of the land would be but $1,407,325.[3] During the long process of assessing the value of the lands taken,

[1] Laws, 1863, Chap. 95; 1865, Chaps. 285, 581; 1867, Chap. 251; Comp. Rep., 1864, p. 92; Manual, 1869, p. 719.

[2] Sketch based on documents quoted in First Annual Report on the Improvement of the Central Park, pp. 77 ff; Documents of the Aldermen, 1857, No. 5.

[3] *Ibid.*, p. 155. The change was sanctioned by Chap. 616, Laws of 1853.

however, it became apparent that the cost would far outrun this sum, and strong pressure was brought to bear to reduce the size of the park. The council actually passed a resolution that it be terminated on the south at 72d Street, but this was vetoed by the mayor. The final assessment of damages, made in 1856, fixed the sum at $5,073,443, of which $1,658,395 was charged upon the adjoining property for the benefit thereto; while to meet the remainder (with sundry other expenses) bonds to the amount of $3,740,300 were issued.[1] The improvement of the park began in 1857 under the state commission heretofore described, and by means of successive bond issues was pushed steadily forward during all the next decade, the total expenditure on the debt account, to the close of 1868, being $5,435,121.[2] Bonds to the amount of a million were also issued in 1861 for the extension of the park from 106th to 110th Street. The total debt for the park January 1, 1869, was $10,048,571.[3]

All of the park bonds were redeemable from the sinking fund, which already promised to be more than sufficient for the purpose, — the interest, however, not being payable from the interest sinking fund, but from taxation. It is difficult to understand the reason for the exception regarding the

[1] Comp. Rep., 1859, p. 35.
[2] Thirteenth Annual Report of Commissioners of Central Park, p. 79.   [3] Manual, 1869, p. 720.

interest, which further complicated the elaborate debt system; unless, perhaps, it was intended ultimately to abandon the interest fund altogether, which would indeed have been a rational thing to do had it been undertaken entirely and at once. The arrangement could scarcely be designed to protect the holders of earlier stocks, for the interest fund, swollen by the rapid growth of the water rents, had already at the time of the issue of the first park stocks accumulated a surplus of considerable amount [1]; so that, in 1859, a law, the first of the several patches on the sinking fund system, was secured, allowing the transfer of the existing and any future surplus to the redemption fund.[2] This change added half a million yearly to the income of the redemption fund, and within three years it was perceived that there would be an unnecessary accumulation in the latter fund. Another act, accordingly, permitted the transfer of the annual surplus of the interest fund to the 'general fund' for the reduction of taxes, an arrangement that lasted till 1878.[3] When it is remembered that all the great issues of bonds after 1860, aside from those for water and parks, were made payable principal and interest from taxation, it will be

---

[1] The annual income of the redemption fund had risen from $497,638 in 1850 to $879,744 in 1858, that of the interest fund from $757,153 to $1,159,388. Comp. Rep., 1858, pp. 45 ff.

[2] Laws, 1859, Chap. 406; Comp. Rep., 1858, p. 13. The surplus was then $2,579,534.   [3] Laws, 1862, Chap. 163.

understood how exceedingly bungling the debt system had become. The simile of taking money from one pocket to place it in another is hardly adequate to characterize it.

Meantime, in 1860, just as had been the case twenty years before, careless management of the budget had required the issue of bonds ($2,748,000) to fund deficiencies.[1] The shortage was due perhaps less to the additional appropriations of the earlier '50's than to the failure to collect in full the amount of taxes levied, no provision existing till 1861[2] for adding a small percentage to the required amount to cover the loss due to non-collection. A large amount of uncollectable special assessments contributed to the deficiency. In this same year, too, the county began the construction of its famous court house, and first entered the field, in which it was destined to play so conspicuous a part, as a debt-creating body. By 1869 $2,600,000 had been borrowed for this building.[3]

The immense proportions of the loans made for paying war bounties were partly due to the strong anti-Union sentiment of large classes in the metropolis, partly to the poverty of many citizens. Probably in few places throughout New York or other states was there so great *per capita* expenditure for this purpose. From the very beginning of the war the city council commenced to give aid

---

[1] Comp. Rep., 1860, pp. 35, 47, 48.
[2] Laws, 1861, Chap. 240.   [3] Manual, 1869, p. 722.

to the families of volunteers, and when the drafts began, enormous outlay for bounties and substitutes was necessary to prevent the repetition of the terrible riots of 1863. Toward the close of the war, the county authorities took even a greater part in paying bounties than the city authorities. There was considerable discord among the city fathers, many of whom showed disloyal tendencies; and it was doubtless on this account that the board of supervisors, half of whom were Republicans, took the matter up.[1] The first debt created by that body was to pay for damages to property in the riot of July, 1863, but immediately thereafter a committee of the supervisors was authorized to procure substitutes for the firemen, policemen, and state militia-men in the city, and also at discretion to pay bounties or procure substitutes for other drafted men. These county bounties were sometimes granted in addition to the amount paid to the same persons by the city, the usual sum allowed by the county being $300. About one-fourth of the recruits furnished by New York city during the entire war were recipients of bounties from one authority or the other.[2]

Early in 1865 the legislature passed a law providing that the state should refund bounties there-

---

[1] Proceedings of the Supervisors, 1863, vol. 2, p. 213.
[2] Proceedings of the Supervisors, 1863, vol. 2, pp. 215, 624; Report of Special Committee on Volunteering, Documents of the Supervisors, 1864, pp. 356, 359.

after paid by all local authorities, but the great bulk of the war expenditures of New York city had already been incurred.[1] At its highest point the war debt of the metropolis stood at $14,597,300 — considerably more than the original cost of the Croton aqueduct.[2] Of this amount the county had borrowed about two-thirds, the city the remainder. The bond issues composing this debt were numerous and complex. Often they were made temporarily at first, in anticipation of legislative authority. Owing to these circumstances there was some difficulty in placing loans at all; nevertheless by fixing interest at 6 per cent the city succeeded in selling bonds at par till the end, although, of course, the inflation of the currency really constituted a depreciation in the price of stocks. These great bond issues were all made payable from taxation, chiefly in equal annual instalments, beginning during the war itself and running as far as the present year, 1897.

One other enterprise that ultimately added largely to the permanent debt was begun in this period. The county authorities undertook, in 1865 to 1869, the opening and improvement of the great public drive in the upper part of the island, now known as 'The Boulevard.' Part of its cost was met by special assessments, but nearly an equal sum

---

[1] Laws, 1865, Chap. 29. New York county received about $2,500,000. Comp. Co. Rep., 1869, p. 33.

[2] Manual, 1869, p. 722.

was paid by the city at large.[1] The bonds issued for this purpose amounted to $851,700 up to 1869.[2]

A few other small bond issues during this period, which are indicated below, need scarcely be described in detail. The following is a summary of the issues of funded debt from 1850 to 1868 inclusive: —

Debt Issues, 1850-1868

Debt outstanding January 1, 1850 .		$15,241,783
Issued to January 1, 1869, for —		
Water supply	$ 5,420,800	
Central Park	10,048,571	
Real estate (West Washington Market and Fort Gansevoort property, 1860-1863) . . .	1,133,437	
Public buildings	822,000	
Court-house	2,600,000	
Improving Boulevard . . .	851,700	
Floating debt	2,748,000	
War purposes (amount January 1, 1869)[3]	13,593,600	
Refunding taxes on U. S. bonds (amount January 1, 1869)[3] .	1,364,800	
Docks	500,000	
Miscellaneous	229,000	$39,311,908
		54,553,691
Bonds redeemed 1850-1869, except war and tax-refunding bonds . .		9,966,833
Funded debt, January 1, 1869 . .		$44,586,858

[1] See *post*, p. 109-110.   [2] Manual, 1869, p. 722.

[3] The complicated refundings of the war bonds, and likewise the amount of these, and of the bonds for refunding taxes, which had been paid prior to 1869, have been disregarded. These annual payments may properly be considered part of ordinary current outlay.

About one-third of the $44,586,858 thus outstanding was county debt. Nearly one-half was payable from taxation, the remainder from the sinking fund, which already amounted to $16,501,109. Besides the funded debt, $4,395,872 of assessment bonds were now outstanding, and $3,222,700 of revenue bonds. The net debt of all classes was thus $35,704,321.[1] The gross funded debt had increased 292 per cent between 1850 and 1868, the net debt 259 per cent, while even up to 1870 the population had increased only 193 per cent.

It must have been evident from the figures of 1868 that the sinking fund would be far more than sufficient to meet the part of the debt for which it was pledged. Already it was equal to nearly three-fourths of that debt, fully two millions a year were being added to it from the revenues, while many of the bonds to which it was applicable would not fall due for over twenty years. No special attempts had been made to increase the revenues of either the interest or the redemption fund during the '60's; but the natural development of the city caused them to augment in a greater ratio than had been anticipated. While the interest fund would have been quite inadequate to the interest on the entire debt, the redemption fund could without prejudice have paid all the bonds that were annually maturing after the war, and no

[1] Manual, 1869, pp. 722 ff.

small burden would have been removed from the taxpayers.

§ 19. *Special Assessments, Taxes, and Accounts.*

During the decade from 1850 to 1860, the improvement of streets by special assessments was carried on to a relatively very great extent, the average annual outlay to be met in this way being equal to fully one-fourth of that from taxation. In 1855, $2,378,817 was spent on assessment enterprises, the tax levy being only $5,843,822.[1] In the following decade, however, up to and including 1867, the assessment expenditure failed decidedly to keep pace with the enormous increase in the tax budget; but after the latter year the omnivorous Ring seized upon this system as a means of further plunder, and swelled the assessment lists to a vast degree.

Several noteworthy changes were introduced in the system during this period. Up to 1852 it had been the custom to require the contractors for street improvements to wait for their pay until the collection of the assessments, and a somewhat similar practice was in vogue regarding payments for land taken in opening streets. Contractors thus needed to possess large capital to conduct business, and this fact tended to concentrate the work in the hands of a few firms, and to destroy competition.[2] To remedy this evil

---

[1] Comp. Rep., 1855, pp. 28, 111.

[2] For description of the system, see Comp. Rep., 1853, p. 9.

a law[1] was secured in 1852, which instituted the practice of issuing assessment bonds in anticipation of the collection of assessments, from the proceeds of which bonds contractors were paid. The term of these bonds in practice was at first only from one to three years. At an early period a distinction was established between 'assessment bonds' for street openings and 'street improvement bonds.'

Under the new arrangement the management of the system for some years continued to be, even more than before, loose and unmethodical, and losses from uncollected assessments and other causes began to fall on the city. The amount of assessment bonds increased steadily, reaching $1,898,200 in 1860.[2] When Mr. Haws became comptroller in 1859, he found the accounts relating to assessments in hopeless confusion. It finally developed that there was a deficiency of nearly a million in the assessment and street improvement funds, and it was in part to cover this that the floating debt stock of 1860 was issued.[3] Just how all this deficiency had arisen, not even the financial officers understood. It was at least not due, as were largely the great losses of later years, to remissions of assessments by the courts on the ground of fraud and irregularity.

This evil of remissions by the courts, however,

---

[1] Laws, 1852, Chap. 397. [2] Comp. Rep., 1860, p. 55.
[3] Comp. Rep., 1858, pp. 25 ff; 1860, p. 48.

found its basis in a law of 1858.[1] With the perfectly proper purpose of preventing injustice and fraud in charging the cost of improvements upon property owners, it was provided that in case any 'fraud or legal irregularity' were alleged to have been committed, the party aggrieved could appeal to the supreme court, and if the charge were sustained, the assessment should be vacated. Unfortunately the too indefinite wording of this law, together with the absence of sufficiently stringent provisions for the reassessment of a fair charge for the benefit actually received, or for curing irregularities, made an opening for evasion of just obligations. But it was not till the time of the Tweed Ring that this abuse became serious.[2]

In 1861[3] a further act of some importance took away from the common council the power of confirming the assessment lists for street improvements; and conferred it upon a 'board of revision and correction of assessments,' consisting of the mayor, comptroller, corporation counsel, and recorder — a body that continues to possess this important power to the present time. In 1865,[4] in connection with the law requiring the Central Park commission to lay out the Boulevard, the

---

[1] Laws, 1858, c. 338.

[2] Usually the vacations amounted to not over $20,000 a year up to 1868. Communication from Comptroller of New York, etc., New York Senate Documents, 1873, No. 105, p. 2.

[3] Laws, 1861, Chap. 308.   [4] *Ibid.*, 1865, Chap. 565.

entire control of opening and improving streets above 155th was conferred upon that board — a change doubtless dictated by the usual partisan motive. A noteworthy feature of this law was that, in the case of streets in this district, more than a mile in length, only one-half of the cost of opening or improvement could be assessed on the adjoining property, the remainder falling on the general treasury. This provision was of special importance regarding the cost of the Boulevard itself. In 1869[1] the same restriction, so far as opening of streets was concerned, was made applicable to all streets, of whatever length, not laid out by the commissioners of 1807; and the burden thus thrown on the city as a whole, which was met by 'city improvement stock,' soon became a heavy one.

A few changes of some importance, which have persisted to the present time, were made during this period in the system of taxation and of accounts. At the outset the date at which the penalty for non-payment of taxes should be added was pushed back from February 1 to December 1,[2] — a change which helped materially in securing prompt payment. In 1861[3] a still more important provision was enacted, requiring a certain percentage to be added to the tax levy yearly to cover deficiencies in collection. The need for this meas-

[1] Laws, 1869, Chap. 920. [2] *Ibid.*, 1850, Chap. 121.
[3] *Ibid.*, 1861, Chap. 240.

ure had been emphasized in the preceding year by the necessity of issuing the large amount of funding bonds[1] to cover the deficiency which had accumulated. This deficiency had been caused partly, to be sure, by careless management, which had allowed revenue bonds to be issued where assessment bonds should have been used, but largely by failure to collect taxes levied. Under the improved system established by these two laws, Comptroller Haws succeeded, by careful administration, in reducing the amount of revenue bonds outstanding at the close of the year from nearly five millions in 1859 to zero in 1863; and throughout the decade the amount unpaid at the end of each year was never considerable.

Besides other innovations introduced by Comptroller Haws, a complete reorganization of the system of book-keeping was effected. To describe in detail the irregularity and unintelligibility of the earlier accounts, or the nature of the changes now made, would prove tedious. Suffice it to say that, while the broad outlines of the accounting system had been but little modified since a very early period, and were decidedly antiquated, each comptroller had made minor changes, especially in the extent and form of the published reports, so that it must have been well-nigh impossible for a citizen to get any definite view of the city's financial progress from year to year. The large and unex-

[1] *Ante*, p. 102. Comp. Rep., 1858, p. 18; 1859, p. 25.

plained discrepancies and irregularities that Mr. Haws discovered further indicate the looseness of the management. The system of accounts and reports introduced by him remains essentially the basis of that existing at the present day. If the previous administrations had usually failed to give sufficient information, Mr. Haws and his immediate successors almost erred in the opposite direction. The minutest details were published in the comptroller's reports themselves, which were thus swollen to volumes, printed in fine type, of about 300 and 200 pages for the city and county respectively. The quarterly reports and other financial publications grew similarly in detail.

§ 20. *General Progress of Expenditures.*

Almost no other city has ever witnessed so rapid a growth of yearly expenditures in a like time as did New York from 1850 to 1870. Although the population had less than doubled, increasing from 515,000 in 1850 to 942,000 in 1870, the annual municipal appropriations had multiplied more than eight-fold, from $3,230,180 in 1850 to $26,485,847 in 1869. The only halt in the steady increase of expenditure during these two decades was in the four years from 1859 to 1862, when the appropriations, less state taxes, actually diminished slightly; there is reason to believe that Mr. Haws's conscientious administration as comptroller contributed largely to this result. The marked growth of the budgets during and after the war can be partly accounted for by the inflation of the paper currency. Gold was quoted at an average of nearly 200 in 1864, so that the hard-money equivalent of the appropriations for that year would be only about half of their nominal amount. The price of gold was still about 135 in 1869, and the purchasing power of the appropriations of that year was doubtless less than $20,000,000 in gold. Salaries of all kinds had been increased as an immediate consequence of the inflation. It also, beyond question, had an indirect influence on the expenditures by its effect in producing a general fictitious prosperity and inducing speculation. In the universal rush of business, and the general looseness of business methods, it was natural that the financial affairs of the city should participate. In particular, the real estate speculation had not a little to do with the immense augmentation of the street improvements from 1868 to 1873.

The table in the appendix (III) shows by departments the progress of expenditure between 1850 and 1869. Excluding the amount required for state taxes, which had grown enormously, the greatest leap had been in the debt charges. The amount paid for interest and redemption out of regular taxes was nearly four millions in 1869, almost a fifth of the total budget expenditure for city and county purposes; while if the amount being annually added to the sinking funds be also included, the yearly debt payments were now fully a third of the city's burdens. The appropriations for police, public schools, and fire protection required greater increases than the average because of the comparative newness of those departments in the city, and in the case of the police because of the special need of protection during the war time. The judiciary had been supported chiefly by the state in 1850: it was a large local expense in 1869. The expenditure for parks constituted a new item of the budget, amounting to $250,000 in 1869. Most of the vast increase in donations to asylums and other private institutions was through requirements of state law, though the reckless generosity of Tweed swelled the amount in the last year or two of this period. A very large part of the increased outlay for advertising, printing, and stationery was the result of fraud and corruption; the amount spent for these purposes in 1869, though it appeared as $443,768 on the regular appropriation account, was in reality fully four times that sum, the remainder being charged to 'adjusted claims,' judgments, etc. The immense amount of the newly introduced expenditures for armories and drill rooms, $1,450,000 in 1869, was also due largely to corrupt influences.[1]

§ 21. *General Character of Government. Conclusion.*

It is very difficult to form a just judgment concerning the character of the municipal government

---

[1] Concerning these various Ring frauds, see *post*, p. 137 ff.

in general during the two decades from 1850 to 1869, so extraordinary were the circumstances under which it was conducted. The enormous increase in the budget might seem to be in itself a sufficient condemnation of the entire system of independent departments and state interference. And yet the extravagance and corruption displayed by the city fathers in the narrow bounds still left them, and above all their disloyal inclinations, give reason for hesitation in concluding that greater economy or better administration would have been secured by a continuance of the system of unmolested council government which had existed before 1849. We have indeed noticed that real needs had swollen the expenditures of some of the independent departments, while others had kept their outlay well within limits.

Probably a municipal government has never existed more conglomerate and unsystematic than that of New York city during the sixties. There were three legislative bodies, elected in different manners and for different terms, besides an independent board of education elected by the people. Half a dozen important departments were governed by commissions appointed by the governor, each, almost, composed of a different number of members and holding for a different term of years, and all usually opposed in politics to the locally chosen officers. Another department was headed by commissioners appointed by the comptroller. The street department, on the contrary, was administered by a single commissioner appointed by the mayor, to whom likewise, as it were by chance, the choice of two or three other officers was still entrusted. The three executive officers whom the people elected (the mayor, comptroller and corporation counsel) each held for a different term, and therefore were often conflicting in politics. What with all this, it is no wonder that James Parton, writing at that day, exclaimed,[1] "Was there ever such a hodge-podge of a government before in the world!" This confusion was worse confounded by the continual direct interference of the legislature, deposing officers and changing terms of office, and fixing the expenditures of the city in their minutest details with most absolute disregard of the will of the local authorities. Yet for this state of affairs there was excuse if not justification. It was almost entirely the manifold result of the one consistent policy of transferring power from the Democratic majority in the city to the Republican majority in the state. And, utterly opposed to ordinary political principles as was this policy, many of the best citizens of state and city defended it as an unavoidable necessity. Even the writer whom we have just quoted declares that,[2] "to that temporary transfer of power from a completely corrupt to an incompletely cor-

---

[1] "The Government of the City of New York," *North American Review*, vol. 103 (1866), p. 456. [2] *Ibid.*, p. 455.

rupt organization, we owe it that the city of New York is still, in some degree, inhabitable." The policy was strongly defended too by the Citizens' Association,[1] which, while some of its officers later came under the influence of the Ring, undoubtedly long represented the highest elements in the metropolis.

Among all the legislative commissions the police board alone had some degree of reasonableness from a broader standpoint than that of temporary expediency. The police in most European countries are directly under central control, for the preservation of peace may often be a matter of by no means local importance. Moreover, the times presented peculiar exigencies in New York city. The danger of disloyal outbreaks, such as might threaten the very stability of the state government itself, reached a climax during the war. No wonder the Unionists in the state felt justified in almost any measures, when a mayor of New York was boldly proclaiming sympathy for the South[2] and confidence in its success, and even advocating secession on the part of the metropolis itself. It is perhaps not too much to say, in the words of a prominent member of the constitutional convention of 1867,[3]

---

[1] See, *e.g.*, their communication to the Constitutional Convention of 1867, Documents of the Convention, No. 126.

[2] Mayor Wood, 1861, Message.

[3] Mr. M. I. Townsend. Proceedings and Debates of the Constitutional Convention, p. 2955.

that, when this hostile spirit culminated in the great draft riot of July, 1863, had it not been for the fact that "the control of its police was in loyal hands, in all human probability, what was a mere mob, continued for three days, employed in riot, arson, and bloodshed, would have been a revolution." The same need for state control of the police had made itself felt at this period in Buffalo and other large cities.

Whether, in view of the corrupt nature of the municipal rulers and the disloyal character of great masses of the population, the legislature was justified in going so much further in domineering the city as it did, is harder to say. It is possible, though by no means axiomatic, that by leaving the city to itself the very seriousness of the disease would have forced the citizens to rise up and effect a cure from the root, instead of applying the mere external palliations, themselves attended with injurious effects, that state interference could offer.

CHAPTER V

THE TWEED RING

The long period of disorder in the municipal government which we have just been considering was fermenting within itself the germs of still greater evils. Perhaps it would be too severe to say that the gigantic phenomenon of the Tweed Ring was merely the logical outcome of the conditions of the time and the character of the people, for surely there must have been some element of chance in bringing together at the proper moment such adepts in corruption as were the leaders in that conspiracy. But while for more than a decade state interference had been called in to remedy the misrule of the city, the purely local authorities, perhaps partly as the very result of that interference, had been steadily growing more corrupt; so that the way was prepared for an unprecedented era of misgovernment, the moment central influence should cease to be exercised or should be exercised in the opposite direction. With the close of the war and the absorption of the people in the general rush of business and speculation, the spirit of patriotism, which had so largely animated the state administration, decayed. The long Republican rule in the legislature finally gave way; Tammany Hall, which represented all that was worst in politics, obtained control, and instead of a restraining influence, the legislature now became an obedient and powerful tool in the hands of the city's spoilers.

§ 22. *Origin and Growth of the Ring to* 1870.[1]

William M. Tweed, born in 1823, had been in city office from his very youth. First the foreman of a fire engine company, he next became a member of that famous city council of 1851–1852, and indeed was a leader in its corrupt schemes of franchise selling and contract jobbery. He succeeded then in getting elected to Congress for one term. In 1857 he was chosen one of the newly created board of county supervisors, a position which he held till 1870. It was here that, as early as 1860, Tweed and two others combined to secure, by various means, percentages upon bills approved by the board. Others were gradually added to the 'Supervisors' Ring' till six or seven of the twelve members belonged to it. The methods of peculation up to 1868 were somewhat irregular as compared with the later systematic frauds; the amount

---

[1] For the general historical statements in this chapter, I have followed to considerable extent the articles of Charles F. Wingate, "An Episode in Municipal Government," *North American Review*, vols. 119, 120, 121, 123. All financial statements are taken from official documents duly cited.

added to bills for the benefit of the Ring was usually only 15 per cent, while the bills themselves had some basis.

Meantime Tweed had been gaining power in another direction. Tammany Hall, which had been divided and had lost influence just before the war, was reorganized with the basest elements in control. Tweed became chairman of the general committee in 1863, and remained such till his fall, a party dictator of the most absolute type. It was the control thus obtained over the votes of a vast section of the people that was long the chief defence of the Ring. In the same year Tweed became deputy street commissioner, with entire power, as his chief had been elected a state senator. This position, too, he retained till 1870, in spite of his own election to the senate in 1868. The work of this department, especially in assessment enterprises, grew amazingly under his administration, and not only were great opportunities for private gain afforded, but the patronage of the department was of immense importance in strengthening the Tammany 'machine.'

The Supervisors' Ring was too large and unwieldy, and its hold on the city treasury was too indirect, to permit the wholesale plundering that Tweed desired. A narrower and more efficacious Ring must be formed. Peter B. Sweeney, the city chamberlain and county treasurer, and Richard B. Connolly, the comptroller, possessed just those financial powers which were needed, and with these Tweed now made an alliance. James Watson, auditor in the comptroller's office, had also to receive a minor position in the new Ring. Tweed's membership in the legislature enabled him to insert in the tax levy of 1868[1] a section authorizing the comptroller, "in order to save the expense of litigation," to audit and pay all claims outstanding against both city and county, borrowing the necessary money on revenue bonds payable the following year. It is not apparent that the dangerous nature of this power was perceived by the legislature, yet surely this unlimited power of 'audit' marks a wide deviation from the policy which, only a year before, had enacted that not even judgments obtained by due process of law should be paid when they exceeded the amount of the appropriation concerned. In fact, by the practice of special audits thus begun, the whole system of specific appropriations was made wellnigh meaningless. The amount of claims 'adjusted' under this law during 1868 was $2,776,900,[2] and on most of these 45 per cent only went to the claimant, 55 per cent to the city officials.[3]

[1] Laws, 1868, Chap. 853, § 7; 854, § 3.

[2] Proceedings of the Joint Investigating Committee of Supervisors, Aldermen, and Associated Citizens, 1872, pp. 115, 117, 'revenue bonds.'

[3] Report of the Special Committee of the Aldermen appointed to investigate the Ring Frauds, 1878, p. 397. For a more detailed account of these fraudulent bills, see *post*, § 26.

In the fall of 1868 came the general election. Tammany needed especially to elect the governor and the mayor, as well as to obtain stronger representation in the legislature. Tweed knew how much was at stake for him and mustered his forces accordingly. Probably no other election was ever held in a Northern state where all manner of frauds were so rampant.[1] An important factor in the result was the enormous foreign vote, swollen by wholesale naturalizations on the part of the corrupt judges, Barnard, Cardozo, and McCunn, whom the Ring had placed in power.[2] Most of the newspapers at this time, and till the fall of the Ring, were in its support, the immense expenditures for city advertising and printing being a powerful instrument in purchasing their favor. By such means as these, John T. Hoffman was elected governor, and A. Oakey Hall was chosen mayor, while the Tammany membership in the legislature was so increased that, by the aid of the considerable element of corrupt Republicans, Tweed could carry his will easily.

With this added power came added peculation.

[1] See Report of the Select Committee on the Alleged New York Election Frauds. United States House of Representatives, Reports of Committees, 1868–69, Nos. 31, 41.

[2] The number of aliens admitted to citizenship in New York city during 1868 was 41,112, as compared with an average of 9207 for the preceding ten years; and the great majority of these were admitted in the single month preceding election. Wingate, *North American Review*, vol. 119, p. 401.

To have followed the original 'adjusted claims' law and placed the burden of the expenditures under it immediately on the already hard-pressed taxpayers, would have raised an outcry. Throughout its career the policy of the Ring was to keep down present taxes at the expense of the future, and to deceive the people as to the real cost of government. Accordingly, the new tax law[1] provided that the revenue bonds already issued and the future expenditures for adjusted claims should be funded by 'accumulated debt bonds,' payable in 1884 and 1888. The fraudulent auditing went on steadily, and though this power was taken from the comptroller in April, 1870, it was not till $6,500,000 had been added to the city debt, and $6,000,000 to the county debt.[2] Of moneys paid on these claims, the proportion that went to the Ring was usually 65 per cent.[3] The same policy of fictitiously reducing taxes led to the postponement of all payments on the war debt for 1869 and 1870, as well as of that proportion of state taxes destined to redeem the state war debt, by the issue of 'tax relief bonds' to the amount of $5,767,000.[4]

---

[1] Laws, 1869, Chap. 875, § 5; 876, § 4.
[2] Joint Investigating Committee, pp. 119, 121.
[3] Special Committee of Aldermen, p. 397.
[4] Payable in ten and twenty years, respectively. Laws, 1869, Chap. 876, § 2; 1870, Chap. 383, § 9; Joint Investigating Committee, p. 123.

§ 23. *Charter and Other Laws of* 1870.

The Ring, despite its triumph in the election of 1868, felt by no means secure. The evident misgovernment of 1869 had aroused ominous mutterings. Moreover, in the ranks of Tammany itself was growing a strong disaffection, headed by James O'Brien, sheriff of the county. The Ring hardly dared risk another mayoralty election. An attempt must be made to perpetuate its power by state law, regardless of the people's will. A new charter was needed. In 1870, for the first time in twenty-four years, the Democrats had a majority in the legislature. But the opposition within the party, which took the name of the 'Young Democracy,' threatened to defeat Ring legislation. The first, or Frear, charter introduced by the Ring was rejected by a large majority, and it seemed likely that another bill framed by the opposition Democrats would be adopted. Meantime Tweed had been removed from his powerful position as deputy street commissioner, and a strong movement was also being made to depose him from the leadership of Tammany.

The Ring was in dire straits, but it did not relinquish the conflict. Money was its chief weapon. Tweed testified afterward that he paid no less than $600,000 to one agent to be used in buying up members of the legislature,[1] the chief design being to secure Republican aid in passing the new meas-

[1] Special Committee of Aldermen, pp. 73, 84–87.

ure which Tweed now introduced. Strange to say, even the Citizens' Association, which for so many years had opposed corruption, was brought into the support of the Ring charter and the Ring rule; its treacherous paid secretary and one or two other leading members having been gained over by fat offices or more direct bribes.[1] Not a few worthy citizens and newspapers were deluded by certain fair seeming features into favoring the Ring bills. When, accordingly, the charter introduced by the Young Democracy came up for third reading, a sudden shifting of votes defeated it, and not long after the charter introduced by Tweed was adopted, thirty out of the thirty-two senators voting in its favor.[2] An act abolishing the old county board of supervisors, and tax levies for the city and county, were then passed.[3]

These acts delivered the control of the city absolutely to the inner circle of the Ring. The legislative commissions, and the board of county supervisors, which had subtracted so much from its authority, were all done away — a change which won the favor of many people by no means sympathizing with the Ring in general. The heads of all the city departments were made appointive by the mayor for terms of usually five to eight years.

[1] Special Committee of Aldermen, p. 223.
[2] *Ibid.*, p. 87. The charter is Chap. 137, Laws, 1870.
[3] Laws, 1870, Chaps. 190, 382, 383. The tax laws had important charter features.

In case of the death or removal of the mayor, his appointing power would devolve on the comptroller, whom he himself had chosen. The right of removing city officers formerly possessed by the governor was abrogated, and likewise the impeaching power of the council except as to the mayor. The mayor could remove officers only by complicated legal process. The tenure of the Tammany officials was thus not to be dependent on the will of the mayor, or on the will of the people — at least for years to come. The inner Ring assured its own power still further. The great department of public works was, almost alone of the departments, ruled by a single officer instead of by a commission, and that position, of course, was taken by Tweed. Hall reappointed Connolly as comptroller, and Sweeney was made president of the park department.

Already during the later sixties the mayor and comptroller had been given large powers as regards appropriations, to the detriment of the council's authority. The budget had heretofore, however, been subject to very great modification by the legislature. But in accordance with the new general policy that body now withdrew its supervision. The tax law of 1870, which was the last to prescribe the details of the appropriations, provided that thereafter the chief departments should submit their annual estimates to a board consisting of the mayor, comptroller, and the chief officer of the department concerned, whose appropriating power should be final — a further step toward the present system of appropriations by the board of estimate and apportionment. A peculiar provision regarding the administration and finances of the dock department, which has persisted to this day, was the most noteworthy of the other financial features of the charter.

Notwithstanding the great opportunities for plunder that its added power under the new charter would give in the ordinary administration of affairs, the Ring was not content. The enormous outlay for carrying the elections and corrupting the legislature must be reimbursed in shorter order, and with usury. Accordingly, as if with a view to winding up the affairs of the old county organization, a section was put into the county tax law [1] authorizing the mayor, comptroller, and president of the supervisors (Tweed) to 'audit' all then existing liabilities of the county, and to pay them by revenue bonds, nominally redeemable from the taxes of 1871, though, as in 1868 and 1869, there was no real purpose that they should become an immediate addition to taxes. This famous 'ad interim' board of audit never held a single formal meeting, though a fictitious record of one was afterwards made up.[2] The county auditor, Watson, collected the bills, many of which were prob-

---

[1] Laws, 1870, Chap. 382, § 4.
[2] Special Committee of Aldermen, pp. 76, 141.

ably invented after the passage of the law, and Tweed as chairman approved them. The board merely continued the process of fraud that had been going on before under the comptroller's audits of 1868 and 1869. Tweed received 25 per cent of the face of the bills audited, Connolly 20, Sweeney 10, Watson 5, and Hall (probably) 5.[1] The total amount of 'county liabilities' paid under this arrangement was $6,413,737.[2]

§ 24. *Events of* 1871. *The 'Two per Cent Law.'*

At the general election in the fall of 1870 Tammany had but little difficulty in reëlecting the governor and the mayor. In the campaign the Democrats were helped materially by a device of Sweeney's to mislead the people as to the financial condition of the city. The regular comptroller's report for 1869 had been prepared, but its revelations were felt to be too compromising, and it was never given to the public, a fact that caused not a little unfavorable comment. To allay suspicion, half a dozen very prominent and wealthy citizens, headed by John Jacob Astor, were invited to come to the comptroller's office and investigate the accounts. In the few hours which they gave to the examination, with the supervising aid of the wily comptroller, these gentlemen could by no

[1] Special Committee of Aldermen, pp. 77, 397. There was never absolute proof, save from Tweed's testimony, that Hall received a part, but the circumstantial evidence was strong.

[2] Minutes of the Board of Estimate and Apportionment, vol. 1, p. 46.

means arrive at a thorough understanding of the situation; but in some way they were influenced or deceived into reporting that "the financial affairs of the city under the charge of the comptroller are administered in a correct and faithful manner." The committee stated that the city debt would be extinguished, at the rate it had been provided for during Connolly's administration, within twelve years.

The Ring had even more absolute sway in the legislature of 1871 than in that of 1870. Little more legislation was needed to complete its grasp on every branch of the city government, but that legislation was forthcoming. The financial measures enacted continued the general policy of lightening present taxes by deferring current obligations to the distant future. Laws for the 'consolidation' of the city and county debt authorized the issue of thirty-year stock to redeem *all* bonds of the city and county maturing in 1871.[1] Under this authority were refunded the entire amount of county revenue bonds issued to meet the audits of the 'ad interim' board, $2,500,000 of city revenue bonds which the Ring's entire disregard of appropriations had left outstanding at the close of 1870, and all the payments due on the city, county, and state war debts, together with over a million due gas companies.[2] At the time when

---

[1] Laws, 1871, Chaps. 322, 323.
[2] Minutes Board of Estimate and Apportionment, vol. I, p. 46.

the Ring was ousted, September 16, 1871, the amount of bonds of this class already issued was over ten millions, and other obligations for which they could be issued were still unfunded.[1]

The tax levy, familiarly known as the 'two per cent law,' had a similar purpose of deluding taxpayers. It provided that the total tax in the city and county for each year 1871 and 1872 should not exceed two per cent on the valuation of 1871, save that the excess of state taxes over those of 1870 might be added to this sum.[2] The act did not, as had every previous tax law since 1851, prescribe the amounts that should be allowed to the various purposes, but the sole appropriating power for the future was conferred on a board, the first to receive the present title of 'board of estimate and apportionment,' composed of the mayor (at this time Hall), the comptroller (Connolly), the commissioner of public works (Tweed), and the president of the department of parks (Sweeny). These officers — precisely the Ring leaders — were selected, as Hall (one would suppose ironically) explained in his message of June, 1871,[3] because they each had "held a variety of elective and appointive offices in the city and county during the past twenty years, were the

---

[1] Joint Inv. Com., pp. 123, 138, 144, 148. The total ultimately reached $13,138,000. *City Record*, 1873, p. 274.

[2] Laws, 1871, Chap. 583.

[3] Message, p. 7.

seniors in public service, . . . and were therefore presumed to be best and thoroughly acquainted with the wants and exigencies of that service." Even if we were to grant the expediency of entrusting the appropriating power to a small body of executive officers, it would be unnecessary to dwell on the absurdity of selecting, as two of the members of such a board, heads of departments whose duties neither allowed the time nor furnished the occasion for studying the general financial affairs and needs, and who moreover themselves were to spend a large proportion of the money appropriated.

The action of the new board in revising the appropriations for 1871, which had already been accomplished during the month of May, had been hardly such as Hall described in his message; but as the proceedings had not been public, he did not expect refutation. The two per cent limit, together with the excess of state taxes, allowed a levy of $23,362,527, to which $3,157,573 could be added for the amount of properly current expenses to be met by consolidated stock. The general fund, which included all other revenues aside from taxes, had been overdrawn more than $2,600,000 in 1870,[1] and if, as was proper, this deficiency should be repaid, could now contribute nothing; otherwise it could be counted on for not over $2,000,000, which would increase the total limit of the budget

[1] Comp. Rep., 1870, p. 13, omitting 'tax relief fund.'

to $28,520,100.[1] In spite of this absolute legal restriction, the appropriations made in May by the board of estimate and apportionment were $31,478,148. Even with this large sum a great decrease was necessary in the appropriations already voted by the mayor and comptroller under the law of 1870. The recklessness of the board in making reductions that it never intended to observe is seen in the fact that, after deducting fixed sums and reducing certain salaries, the remaining departmental estimates were simply cut in half,[2] regardless of their merits or of the amounts that had already been spent. So great, indeed, had already been the expenditure, that it would have been difficult, even with real economy, to keep the further outlay within the bounds of the budget. As a matter of fact, expenditures went on regardless of appropriations. It was but two months after the revision of the budget that the *New York Times* made its exposures and the public began to be deeply aroused. In September a citizen named Foley secured an injunction to prevent further payments by the comptroller, charging that the two per cent law was being violated. In view of this threatening situation, with the hope possibly of once more deceiving the people as to the state of the finances, the board of estimate now

---

[1] Joint Inv. Com., pp. 138 ff.
[2] Minutes Board of Estimate and Apportionment, vol. 1, pp. 183, 185, 197, 200.

proceeded to go through the absurd form of reducing the appropriations to the precise limit of law.[1] But it was too late to prevent the impending ruin. Only a few days later the comptroller's office was occupied by the reformers, and the true financial condition of the city was soon made public. Practically every appropriation, the distribution of whose expenditure through the year was at all discretionary, had been already exhausted at this date,[2] and an immense amount of liabilities was left behind.[3] Such was the work of the first board of estimate and apportionment.

§ 25. *Fall of the Ring.*

But we must go back a little to trace more fully the movement that culminated in this capture of the Ring's stronghold, the comptroller's office. In spite of many rumblings of the approaching earthquake, the Ring felt thoroughly confident of its position up to the middle of 1871. Nor were Tweed and his associates even seriously disturbed by the severe comments on the rapid increase of the debt that were made when the mayor's message, which should have been issued in January, appeared in June, 1871, with an appendix containing what purported to be a comptroller's report for 1870, which gave in very incomplete fashion

---

[1] Minutes Board of Estimate and Apportionment, vol. I, pp. 361-363.

[2] See tables, Joint Inv. Com., pp. 142-149.

[3] *Ibid.*, p. 23.

a statement of the city finances. They were not aware of a danger long impending, which suddenly appeared when, in the closing days of July, the *Times* published the secret accounts known as 'county liabilities,' including among other payments those made under the 'ad interim' board of audit of 1870. The Ring had taken care to conceal its account books from all save a few trusted clerks in the finance department; but by accident a friend of O'Brien's, the leader of the Young Democracy, who was in the office, succeeded in making a copy of this account, which he turned over to his chief. It was some time before O'Brien was sufficiently exasperated with Tweed to put this in possession of the *Times*. The figures showed no more than that large sums had been paid in a very short time to two or three firms for work and furniture for the new court house and other county buildings, but the vastness of the amounts created more than a suspicion that the bills were fraudulent. The city was powerfully stirred by the revelations. Nevertheless the Ring was not entirely hopeless; if we may trust the opinion of Samuel J. Tilden, it fully expected to carry the elections of 1871, while its opponents were exceedingly fearful that it would do so.[1] To attack the Ring by means of the corrupt courts was wellnigh useless; while to secure the removal of its members under the new charter had been made

---

[1] Tilden, *The New York City Ring*, 1873, p. 36.

almost impossible. Mr. Tilden, however, began to move energetically to overthrow the Tammany wing in the Democratic state convention. At last, moreover, public sentiment was so aroused that an immense mass meeting was held September 4, at which the famous Committee of Seventy was created. The Ring leaders now felt that affairs were growing desperate, and Tweed and Sweeny devised as a last expedient the scheme of sacrificing the comptroller, who alone was to be declared responsible for all fraud and mismanagement. Connolly was publicly asked to resign, but refused to do so and consulted Mr. Tilden, apparently with a view to making him his counsel if litigation should ensue. The latter saw that it was of the utmost importance to prevent the Ring from placing another of its own creatures in Connolly's position, and succeeded in persuading him to appoint, under an old law, a deputy with full power.[1] Mr. A. H. Green, who had been for many years at the head of the Central Park commission, was chosen and installed September 16.

During these negotiations the Ring had seized the opportunity to destroy a great deal of damaging evidence — accounts, vouchers, etc. — in the comptroller's office. Notwithstanding this fact, with the financial centre lost, the Ring was at once shut off from further operations, and there was opportunity, even with the evidence still at hand, to ferret

[1] Tilden, *The New York City Ring*, 1873, pp. 42-44.

out the frauds. The first certain proof of criminal action was secured by Mr. Tilden, who by tracing through bank accounts the payments made to the suspected contractors, discovered the manner in which definite and large percentages of them had gone to different members of the Ring. Even before the November election the former dictators of New York were known fugitives from justice. It is no part of our task to follow them further — to tell how the various plunderers escaped punishment by flight or otherwise, save Tweed alone, who died in a felon's cell. It is of interest to us only to know that civil judgments for large sums were obtained against several of the Ring members and contractors, but that of the many millions — perhaps not less than $50,000,000 — that had been stolen outright, only $1,152,373 was paid back to the city, at least up to 1878.[1]

§ 26. *General Character of Ring Financial Management.*

Although much concerning the financial methods and frauds of the Ring has been already given in connection with its more general history, it is desirable to describe them somewhat more fully and systematically. Accuracy here is made difficult by the incompleteness of the official statements that were published.

Attention has already been called to the fact that it was far more upon the permanent debt

[1] Special Committee of Aldermen, p. 827.

than upon the annual budgets that the extravagance and peculation of the Ring made itself felt. The appropriations for 1869 show the Ring's influence only to a minor degree. In the next year, however, there was a sudden leap of over $4,000,000 in the budget, even if state taxes be excluded from the calculation, and the total appropriations reached $30,906,263. We have noticed that the gross original appropriations made in May, 1871, under the two per cent law, were even larger than those of 1870, though they were somewhat less if state taxes are excluded. The reduction in September was only a farce. The appropriations were already exhausted, but the city government had to go on under the reformers for the remaining months. The actual expenditures on appropriation account for 1871 were no less than $36,567,825,[1] over eight millions more than the limit set by the tax law. Had *all* these expenditures been included in the tax levy, even allowing $2,000,000 from the general fund, the tax rate would have been fully 3.2 cents instead of 2 cents on the dollar. It is, to be sure, true that a large proportion of the increase of current expenditures under the Ring rule was not in operating expenses, but in the heavy interest payments required by the ever-swelling debt. Nevertheless, the table of appropriations for 1871,[2] even after the reduction in September, shows that

---

[1] Communication from the Comptroller, *City Record*, 1873, p. 42.
[2] Joint Inv. Com., pp. 142–149.

it was the worst forms of expenditure, — for printing and advertising, the department of public works, etc., — that were relatively the largest. The allowance for education was actually reduced by nearly one-third from the appropriation of 1869.

But the figures in the appropriation account alone give no idea of the actual payments from the treasury for what should properly have been current expenditures from taxation. For example, the sums really spent for advertising, printing, and stationery, and for armories, were partly covered by the appropriations for judgments, but still more by bonds issued under the special audits. The amount reported in the appropriation tables as spent for advertising, printing, and stationery in 1869 was only $443,768. The investigating committee of 1871 found that the actual payments for those purposes in that year were $1,926,335; while from January 1, 1869, to September 16, 1871, they reached the vast sum of $7,168,212,[1] and, as if this were not enough, the new administration found further claims aggregating millions that had been left unsettled. These figures may be compared with the total expended for the same objects in 1895, $265,861.[2] From 1869 to 1871 nearly three and a half millions were paid to the *Transcript*, the New York Printing Company, and the Manfacturing Stationers, in each of which Tweed was a partner. The *Transcript*, and indeed all of the

[1] Joint Inv. Com., pp. 68–73. [2] Comp. Rep., 1895, p. 112.

papers that received the largest share of city patronage, were almost unknown sheets whose chief means of support was the public advertising. The New York Printing Company was confessedly formed to thrive on the municipal business alone. Tweed testified[1] that for some years it paid annual dividends of from $250,000 to $350,000 on a capital of $10,000. A number of more important newspapers also received a considerable amount of patronage, which must have influenced their position regarding the Ring not a little.

The immense expenditures for armories and drill rooms consisted partly of exorbitant rents, but more largely of payments for 'furniture and repairs,' mostly made to the same few contractors who were employed on the court house. The total amount paid on armories during the three years of Ring domination was $3,791,594, of which $3,221,865 was for furniture, repairs, and plumbing that experts estimated to be worth little over $200,000.[2] When these figures are compared with the armory expenditures of 1895,[3] less than $200,000 (including interest on bonds issued for building armories), some idea of the character of the Ring expenditures may be obtained.

But it was in connection with the new court

---

[1] Special Committee of Aldermen, p. 160.

[2] Joint Inv. Com., pp. 44, 46.

[3] Comp. Rep., 1895, pp. 92, 147 (interest reckoned at four per cent).

house that the most gigantic frauds were perpetrated. This building was very nearly completed in 1867, lacking only plastering and plumbing, and the cost up to that time was $2,600,000, ample enough surely. In 1871 the expenditure charged on the books to the construction of the building was $5,734,144, and that to furnishing it $2,400,558. Besides, there was charged to the construction and furnishing of 'county buildings, courts, and offices' $5,282,229, most of which, as there were few such offices outside the court house, must be reckoned with the cost of that building, making twelve or thirteen millions in all for this by no means imposing structure. $641,900 was spent for carpets, $1,937,545 for plastering and frescoing, $2,960,187 for furniture and cabinet work. Experts estimated the value of such items, for which had been nominally paid $7,289,466, as about $624,000.[1] On nearly all the bills for these immense expenditures on armories and court house, the Ring leaders drew 65 per cent of the amount paid. The bills were for the most part presented by three great contractors, or in the name of men of straw connected with them;[2] their full amount was paid to the persons presenting the claims, and the recipients then turned over the proper percentage to the various members of the Ring. A. J. Garvey,

---

[1] Figures in this paragraph all from Joint Inv. Com., pp. 56-65, 190.

[2] Special Committee of Aldermen, p. 570.

who did plastering and frescoing, drew over three millions from 1869 to 1871; Keyser & Co., plumbers, nearly that sum; while to J. A. Ingersoll, under three fictitious names, was paid no less than $4,844,971. Several other dealers, who received large sums, were really mere creatures of Ingersoll.

But it is needless to pursue further the familiar details of these frauds or to consider the less extensive peculations in other departments. Enough has been said to illustrate the Ring's financial methods in swelling the debt and the budget.

§ 27. *Special Assessments.*

One other important feature of the Ring finances should, however, be **mentioned**. The opening and improving of streets was carried on to an unprecedented extent, and became a means both of direct plunder and indirect gain. Reference has been made to the law of 1869 allowing half the cost of practically all opening enterprises to be charged on the city as a whole.[1] Although such a provision had been perhaps proper enough as regards the Boulevard, which was intended for the benefit of the general public, its further extension could be designed only to permit the Ring to gather spoils while the time remained, by opening streets before they were demanded and escaping the outcry of the adjoining property owners by the removal of part of their burdens. The number of

[1] See *ante*, p. 110.

new streets opened was very great, the payments on the regular account alone during the two years 1869 and 1870, aggregating over eleven millions.[1] The amount of 'city improvement stock' issued in three years to meet the city's share in these expenditures was $3,791,200.[2] Moreover, several large enterprises, such as the widening of Broadway and of Sixth Avenue, were authorized by special acts of the legislature, and part of their cost also was defrayed by the creation of permanent debt to the amount of $1,606,939.[3] Almost as extensive were the operations of the Ring in paving and otherwise improving streets, all of whose cost was nominally to be borne by the abutting owners. Nearly $7,400,000 was spent on these works in 1869 and 1870.[4] Furthermore, a great number of assessment enterprises begun by the Ring had of necessity to be carried out by their successors, so that the expenditures on both these accounts were hardly less in 1872 and 1873.

These various enterprises, especially the pavements, were made a source of direct jobbery by the Ring. Testimony is unanimous as to the wretched character of much of the work done. A large proportion of the pavements laid were of

[1] Manual, 1870, p. 719; Comp. Rep. 1870, p. 10.
[2] Joint Inv. Com., p. 122.
[3] *Ibid.*, p. 122, 'street improvement' and 'street opening and improvement' bonds.
[4] Manual, 1870, p. 719; Comp. Rep., 1870, p. 10, including special items for 6th, 7th, and St. Nicholas Avenues.

wood, a smaller part of worthless concrete. A less immediate form of profit resulted to the Ring from 'inside' speculation in property affected. The most striking instance of this was in connection with the widening of Broadway from 34th to 59th Street. One might mention by way of illustration that satellites of the Ring in three cases, just before the award of damages was made, bought lots on Broadway costing them respectively $24,500, $27,500, and $28,000. A part only of these lots was taken by the widening, yet the amounts paid for damages were respectively $25,100, $30,355, and $40,380, while the owners retained fronts which, considering the improvement effected by the widening itself, were worth probably fully the original cost.[1]

It is charged also that members of the Ring sometimes intentionally made technical errors in levying assessments upon lands in which they were directly or indirectly interested, in order that these might afterward be vacated and the cost of the improvement thrown upon the general public. Whether this was the purpose or not, an immense number of assessments, in fact, were set aside during these years, partly because of mere trivial irregularities, such as the failure to advertise in some one of the many corporation papers, partly on account of just complaints of fraud and worthless work. The vacations of assessments reached

[1] Wingate, *North American Review*, vol. 120, p. 131.

over half a million in 1871, and nearly a million in the following year,[1] while for several years thereafter fully as extensive losses fell annually upon the city, largely as an inheritance from the assessment enterprises begun by the Ring.

The extent of these operations, as well as of their abuse, may be well estimated by the increase in outstanding assessment bonds. The amount of these at the close of 1868, already swollen by the Boulevard opening, had been little over four million dollars. When the Ring was displaced, in 1871, they had risen to $12,592,500,[2] in spite of the issue of long-time bonds for part of the cost of street openings and improvements; while, chiefly as the result of the Ring's policy, this class of indebtedness still kept growing, reaching in 1876 the enormous sum of $22,371,400.[3] We shall see that a large proportion of this amount ultimately had to be added to the funded debt.

§ 28. *The City Debt.*

Throughout the fight against the Ring, up to the discovery of the fraudulent payments of 'county liabilities,' the strongest argument had

---

[1] 1870, $337,626; 1871, $521,042; 1872, $967,791. Communication from the Comptroller, New York Senate Documents, 1873, No. 105, p. 2.

[2] Joint Inv. Com., pp. 115, 117, 123, 124, counting 'assessment fund bonds' of 1869-71, as they should be, with the temporary debt.

[3] Comp. Rep., 1894, p. 137.

been the rapid increase of the city debt. And well might this cause alarm. The total funded debt at the close of 1868 was $44,586,858, the debt of all classes, less the sinking fund, $35,704,321.[1] At the close of 1870 the funded debt had risen to $68,998,146, while, owing to the slow increase of the sinking fund and the rapid growth of revenue and assessment bonds, the net indebtedness had more than doubled in two years. No wonder there was an outcry when this fact was made public in June, 1871. When the Ring was overthrown in September, the funded debt had taken another bound to $81,351,158, and the net bonded debt of all classes was $97,287,525, only ten millions less than triple the debt 32 months before. Moreover, the Ring left countless liabilities behind it. The amount of permanent stocks actually issued between the fall of the Ring and September 1, 1874, to meet obligations incurred by the Ring, was no less than $19,885,591.[2] The funded bonds issued directly by the Ring from 1869 to 1871 were $41,724,624, so that the total addition to the permanent debt due to this brief reign of corruption was over sixty-one millions. Possibly ten millions more of the assessment bonds still unfunded in 1874 may likewise be fairly charged directly to the Ring.

[1] Figures all from Joint Inv. Com., pp. 111-124.
[2] A. H. Green, *Municipal Debt of New York*, 1874, pp. 15, 16.

The issues of stocks that had contributed most largely to this enormous increase of forty-one million dollars from 1869 to 1871 have been already described; namely, those caused by the special audits, the postponement of maturing war debt, and the payment of the city's share of street enterprises. Several other minor additions had been made.[1] Besides further bonds to complete improvements in the water supply already commenced, a million was added to the debt in 1871 by the laying of water mains,[2] undertaken on an unprecedented scale. The improvement of Central Park was still going on, and in the year 1870 especially Sweeney managed to use a large sum, $616,600. Other bond issues were for the construction of lunatic asylum buildings, for the payment of some rather fraudulent charges for suburban firemen and the improvement of the fire telegraph, and for the first instalment on the Brooklyn bridge. Of all the immense expenditures actually made on the court house during the Ring rule, only $600,000 was met by stocks nominally intended for that purpose. The peculiar arrangement of the dock department, under the charter of 1870, required all its expenditures to be paid out of bonds, but only half a million had been issued up to the fall of the Ring. The following table, showing the funded debt contracted from January 1, 1869, to Septem-

---

[1] Figures in general from the tables just cited.
[2] Laws, 1871, Chap. 213.

ber 16, 1871, will serve as a summary of the Ring's debt operations:[1]

Debt Created by Tweed Ring

Water supply, four issues		$2,536,000
Central Park improvement		1,041,600
Public buildings —		
County court house	$600,000	
Ninth district court house	300,000	
Lunatic asylum	700,000	
Market	181,000	
Repairs to buildings (county)	100,000	1,881,000
Street improvement		5,653,139
Dock bonds		500,000
Fire department		921,952
Brooklyn bridge		450,000
War purposes		90,000
Repayment of taxes		58,932
Funding old and floating debt —		
'Accumulated debt'	12,500,000	
Consolidated stock (partly for postponed war debt)	10,325,000	
Tax relief bonds	5,767,000	28,592,000
Total issues		$41,724,624
Debt, January 1, 1869		44,586,858
		$86,311,482
Redemptions, 1869–71		4,960,324
Funded debt, September 16, 1871		$81,351,158

[1] Joint Inv. Com., pp. 113–125, correcting typographical errors, and omitting 'assessment fund bonds of 1869–71,' wrongly classed as funded debt.

Of all these vast additions to the debt, only those for Croton water and park improvement were made payable from the sinking fund, although that fund was evidently much more than sufficient to redeem the bonds already charged to it,[1] and indeed already equalled at the close of the Ring period four-fifths of those bonds. The slowness of the increase in the sinking fund, — barely three millions in the three years, despite the fact that there had been almost no payments from it, — was a source of just complaint at the time.

It is a matter of some wonder that in the face of its enormous borrowing the city was able to obtain credit at all. None of its bonds sold below par, but to effect this the rate of interest had to be high even for those times. The large blocks of consolidated stock could be floated at 6 per cent only by making them payable, principal and interest, in gold. On nearly all the other bonds issued from 1869 to 1871, as well as on the temporary debt, the rate was 7 per cent.[2] It is needless to comment on the magnitude of the interest burden thus imposed on the city; in 1876 no less than $9,503,188, out of total appropriations of $34,934,801, went to the payment of interest,[3]

---

[1] Total debt payable from sinking fund September 16, 1871, $24,532,216; accumulations of fund, $19,422,333.

[2] See Report of the Comptroller on the bonded Indebtedness, *City Record*, 1873, p. 274.

[3] Comp. Rep., 1884, p. 88, Table.

while even to this day that legacy of misgovernment contributes largely to the annual budget.

§ 29. *Finances during the Period of Reconstruction.*

The mere expulsion from the city government of Connolly, Tweed, and Sweeney (Hall remained in office to the end of his term), and the stoppage of downright robbery, by no means meant that good government was now assured. A large number of Tammany officials, accustomed to extravagance and sinecures, still held positions for long terms. In every department scores of loafers were drawing salaries. To straighten out the general confusion of the administration, to reduce the scale of expenditures, to settle the numberless claims against the city, was a gigantic task. Mr. Andrew H. Green, who was duly appointed comptroller soon after his installation as deputy, was in many ways the best possible man for this arduous position. His integrity was admitted on all sides, and it was a vice which certainly, under the circumstances, approached closely to a virtue, that he was inclined to run things with a high hand, and to treat all claimants somewhat cavalierly, so that some, even of those who recognized fully his great services, were inclined to criticise his harshness.[1] Not a few of the old claims presented had some degree of fairness; they were for work or materials actually furnished at the instance of some one of the

[1] *E.g. New York Tribune*, December 9, 1876, p. 4.

many departments which, quite regardless of legal limits, had been allowed to create all manner of liabilities. Others were purely fraudulent. At the close of 1874 Mr. Green stated that the amount which had been saved to the city since his accession, by the defeat of suits against the city and by final settlement of claims without suit, was $3,313,545; while of the nearly $7,000,000 of bills that still remained unadjusted, the city, he declared, could be compelled to pay but a small proportion,[1] a prophecy which was apparently fulfilled.[2] The comptroller, moreover, had no small part in the gradual weeding out of surplus employees and the retrenchment in the extravagant customs that existed everywhere.

The budget system was necessarily very irregular for some years after the ousting of the Ring. Early in 1872 a special act[3] of the legislature authorized temporary appropriations to be made. The 2 per cent limit that had been fixed for this year also by the tax law of 1871 was clearly insufficient, in view of the great increase of fixed charges. Accordingly the limit was extended to $2\frac{3}{4}$ per cent on the valuation of 1871, besides the excess of state taxes,[4] the allowable expenditure

---

[1] Communication from the Comptroller, *City Record*, 1875, pp. 361 ff.

[2] As appears from records of further bond issues for claims.

[3] Laws, 1872, Chaps. 9, 29.

[4] *Ibid.*, Chap. 444.

being thus fixed at $32,437,525.[1] The board of estimate and apportionment, still constituted according to the Ring charter amendments of 1871,[2] apportioned this full sum in May.

This tax law of 1872 was the last of the long series of direct annual restrictions on the city levy. Some further legislative action regarding the budget was, however, necessary from 1873 to 1875. For the former year no regular appropriation had been made at first, the evident intention being to wait till, as the result of the election and by legal enactment, the board of estimate and apportionment should be reconstituted. Under the new charter of 1873, the president of the department of taxes and assessments and the president of the aldermen were put in the place of the commissioner of public works and the president of the park department as members of this body. By special legislative authority,[3] the new board in June adopted a budget amounting to a sum considerably less[4] than the comptroller had estimated as necessary six months before, the reduction being accomplished by the postponement for one year of the large payment for the

---

[1] Including $2,000,000 from general fund, Minutes Board of Estimate and Apportionment, vol. 2, p. 534.

[2] Hall was excluded from action in the temporary appropriations, but was given his usual power as to the vote in May.

[3] Laws, 1873, Chaps. 758, 779.

[4] *City Record*, 1873, pp. 25, 26. Compare Minutes Board of Estimate and Apportionment, 1872-73.

city's share in the cost of sinking the railway tracks in Fourth Avenue ($1,598,767), as well as by general retrenchment. Further, with a view to equalizing the burdens of taxation, the proportion of the city in the large deficiency which about this time was discovered in the state sinking fund, — another result of the general demoralization of politics at the Ring period, — was made payable in ten annual instalments, beginning 1874, instead of all being added to the taxes of 1873.[1] A similar revision of the original appropriations was also sanctioned by law in 1874.[2] The further postponement of certain payments, the entire consolidation of the city and county,[3] which did away with a number of superfluous offices, and continued reduction in the scale of expenditure of the departments generally, made it possible to decrease the total budget from $39,218,945 to $34,822,391, the tax levy being lowered from the very high rate of 3.40 per cent to 2.80 per cent.[4] In the following year a law[5] allowing still another postponement of the cost of the Fourth Avenue improvement constituted the last of these special measures for adjusting the extraordinary burdens resulting from the Ring's mismanagement.

[1] The amount of bonds required for this purpose was $3,899,494. Laws, 1873, Chap. 95; Report of the Commissioners of Accounts, *City Record*, 1875, p. 1190.
[2] Laws, 1874, Chaps. 303, 308.   [3] Laws, 1874, Chap. 304.
[4] *City Record*, 1874, pp. 61, 699, 821 ff.
[5] Laws, 1875, Chap. 492.

PART II

THE PRESENT WORKING OF THE FINANCIAL SYSTEM

CHAPTER VI

INTRODUCTION

In turning now to a more minute study of the finances of the present period of city history, which began with the fall of the Tweed Ring, we need first of all to glance at the history of the adoption and at the general character of the charter of 1873 now in force, as well as of the Greater New York charter soon to take effect; in order that the bearing of the general municipal organization upon the financial system may be understood. Owing to the exceeding complexity of the city's book-keeping, we need likewise to take a rapid general survey of the system of finance, as an aid to comprehending the details which follow.

§ 30. *Adoption and Character of the Charter of 1873.*

So powerful was the revulsion against the Democrats resulting from the exposure of the

Tweed Ring, that by the election of November, 1871, their former majority in the legislature was changed to a Republican majority of over three to one.[1] It was but natural that legislative action should be taken toward a new frame of government for the city. The Committee of Seventy, comprising many of the best citizens of both parties, devised a charter[2] whose purpose appears to have been purely to secure better government, although the method by which chiefly this was to be brought about, minority representation, was necessarily favorable to the Republican party in the city. Although the Seventy's proposed charter can scarcely be said to have contributed largely toward moulding the form of government actually enacted in 1873, nevertheless their propositions have no little interest as showing the best thought of the time as to reform methods, struck out in the very presence of the evils whose remedy was sought.

The great evil of the Tweed charter had been the well-nigh absolute independence and irresponsibility of the executive departments. The mayor had almost no control over the administration, while the council had practically no power as re-

---

[1] Tribune Almanac, 1872, p. 67.

[2] Published in pamphlet form, 1872. It constitutes Assembly Bill, No. 118, of 1872. The names of the committee who drafted the charter included several well-known citizens and publicists of high reputation. See *New York Times*, January 17, 1872, p. 1.

gards either appropriations or appointments. The absence of responsibility and of publicity regarding financial matters had proved especially dangerous. It was perhaps natural, accordingly, that the powerful reaction against the Ring system should lead the Seventy to propose a change in the relations of the executive and legislative branches nearly as radical as that made in 1849, and precisely its opposite. Council government, which had existed up to the middle of the century, was to be reinstated in somewhat modified degree. The low character which the city council had taken on was to be raised, and proper restraint within its own ranks was to be secured, by increasing the number of members to forty-five, but more especially by the plan of minority representation, which found a precedent, though scarcely a favorable one, in the old system of electing county supervisors. On the other hand, the check of a second body in the council seemed to the committee unnecessary. It was probably more than any other motive the desire to render possible a curious and scarcely wise extension of minority representation into the executive branch of the government, that led to the proposal of commission heads in all departments, even including that of finance. These boards were to be composed, with one or two exceptions, of five members, one appointed by the mayor, the others elected by the council, each member of which could cast four votes, cumulating them as he saw fit. In entire contrast with the long terms under the existing law, the tenure of office of all executive officers was reduced uniformly to one year, which was also to be the term of the aldermen. The government was thus to be brought into close touch with the will of the people. The mayor could remove summarily his appointees and the council theirs, while the mayor, on assigning cause to the council, could remove any officer.

The provision for the budget made by this proposed charter resembles somewhat that under the Greater New York charter, but was perhaps superior to it. The comptroller and the four other 'commissioners of the treasury' were primarily to prepare the budget. The aldermen should possess the sole appropriating power; but could only decrease and not increase the estimates of the finance commission, a provision apparently copied from European parliamentary customs. The commissioners of the treasury were authorized to take part in the debates of the council regarding the appropriations. Full financial reports of all departments were to be made monthly to the finance commissioners, who in turn were to publish a monthly report. An amendment to the bill,[1] made in the senate, contained an interesting provision that the city accounts should be audited annually by a committee appointed by the council. Many detailed regulations were inserted, designed

[1] Assembly Bill, No. 750, § 72.

to prevent corruption of all sorts, the most important being the provision that any officer might be summarily examined before a court on the application of a commissioner of the treasury, or of any three aldermen, a provision which was practically copied into the law of 1873. The sanction of the legislature was still to be required in order to contract permanent debt; otherwise the city should be left free from state control.

This important bill passed the legislature by large majorities, though of the Democrats only a few reformers from New York city voted for it.[1] But Governor Hoffman, who appears to have been somewhat under Tammany influence, vetoed the measure.[2] In a previous annual message he had favored minority representation,[3] but now he expressed grave doubts as to both its constitutionality and its expediency, characterizing the system as an uncertain experiment, and especially (with more justice) denouncing its extension to the executive departments. Still stronger objections were brought against the weakening of the mayor involved in the bestowal of such large appointing power on the council. That some, at least, of the governor's arguments appeared reasonable is perhaps indicated by the fact that a majority in the assembly voted against the bill on reconsideration.[4]

[1] *New York Times*, April 19, 1872, p. 5.
[2] Public Papers of Governor Hoffman, pp. 353 ff.
[3] *Ibid.*, p. 26.   [4] Journal of the Assembly, 1872, p. 1611.

In the year following the defeat of this measure, with both legislature and governor Republican, a renewed movement for a charter was begun. The Committee of Seventy were urged to prepare a new draft, but they were anticipated. Mayor Havemeyer, an anti-Tammany Democrat who had been elected by a fusion with the Republicans, had already suggested in his inaugural message [1] charter amendments tending to centralize executive power in the mayor. While he also spoke of the need of greater authority in the council, he scarcely pointed out specific means for securing it; but even favored the retention of the board of estimate and apportionment, though with the substitution of the president of the aldermen, and the president of the assistant aldermen, for the heads of the public works and parks departments, whose presence on the board he sharply condemned. A charter embodying many of these features [2] was prepared by the Republican central committee of the city. In general, the new proposals followed much more closely the existing charter than the radical changes sought in the bill of 1872. Various modifications in the measure were proposed in the legislature,[3] but under the influence of the Committee of Seventy several of these were omit-

---

[1] Proceedings of the Aldermen, vol. 129, pp. 17 ff.
[2] *New York Times*, January 8, 1873, p. 5. Their original bill is Assembly Bill, No. 1, 1873.
[3] Assembly Bill, No. 202, 1873.

ted and certain changes in the original bill were also effected.[1] The chief amendments which were due to their suggestions were the insertion of a provision for minority representation as regards the council; and the slight restriction on the proposed unlimited control of the budget by the board of estimate and apportionment afforded by giving the aldermen advisory power in modifying the appropriations. Whether the Seventy had entirely given up the idea of council government, or whether, finding themselves unable to secure that in its entirety, they preferred to concentrate authority and responsibility in the mayor, at any rate they now urged strenuously that he be given sole appointing power; and they actually succeeded in having the control of the aldermen in this regard reduced to mere confirmation, in place of a complicated scheme by which that body could easily have usurped almost the entire authority. The bill as thus modified was passed almost unanimously,[2] and became for twenty-three years the general basis of municipal government.[3] The Committee of Seventy publicly expressed their satisfaction with many features of the new charter, while condemning other provisions.[4]

---

[1] Resolutions of Committee of Seventy, *Times*, February 20, 1873, p. 8; April 20, p. 12.

[2] *Times*, April 17, 1873, p. 5.

[3] Laws, 1873, Chap. 335.

[4] *Times*, April 20, 1873, p. 12.

While leaving to special chapters its more detailed regulations as to finance, the general nature of the charter may be briefly described as an aid to clear understanding of financial affairs.

The common council, henceforth to consist of one board only, was not made, as the Seventy's charter had proposed, a large and all-powerful body. It was composed of twenty-one aldermen. The minority party was given the opportunity to secure representation by the provision that three members should be elected on general ticket from each of the five senate districts, each person being allowed to vote for two candidates only; and that the other six should be elected from the city at large on a similar plan. The organization of the departments followed the Tweed charter quite closely, the chief difference being that some of the commission heads were reduced from five to three members, while the term of office was made usually six years. The finance and public works departments were continued with single heads, and the comptroller was still an appointive officer. The lack of control over the executive departments on the part of either the council or the mayor, which had been the evil most severely censured in the previous law, was but little remedied. The mayor had appointed alone: now his action required confirmation by the aldermen. Instead of having to impeach the heads of departments before a court, the mayor could now remove them, but under the practically prohibitory requirement of securing the approval of the governor after the assignment of written reasons for the action. The council was still empowered to impeach the mayor only. These provisions, combined with the long terms of the department heads, left their independence and irresponsibility well-nigh as complete as before.

Nor, as we shall see hereafter, was the control of the council over appropriations practically increased by the merely advisory power in the budget which the new charter conferred. The board of estimate and apportionment was retained, though, following in part Mayor Havemeyer's suggestion, its constitution was made somewhat more rational by the substitution of the president of the board of aldermen and the president of the department of taxes and assessments for the purely administrative officers — the heads of the departments of public works and of parks. The influence of the Seventy's charter is seen in a section authorizing the appointment of three commissioners of accounts, whose duty it should be to examine and publish quarterly a detailed statement of the financial condition of the city, as well as in several other provisions for securing the accountability of municipal officers.

This, then, was the law which resulted from two years of legislative conflict and which has had naturally so much influence in the framing of the charter for the greater city. It was undoubtedly intended in many respects to be a real reform measure, and was quite generally so considered by the public, but it was after all essentially a jumble. It was a compromise, not between government by the council and government by the mayor, — which indeed are far from being inconsistent with one another, — but between the indefensible system of irresponsible executive departments which the Tweed charter had established, and the system of subordination of departments to the council, proposed by the Seventy. Moreover the tendency of the charter in practice, if not in the expectations of its framers, was far more toward the former than toward the latter system. The council acquired no real power under the new law, and it failed utterly to improve in character. The power of the mayor was almost as limited as that of the council. The only really effective control over the departments was that exercised, through its hold on the purse strings, by the board of estimate and apportionment, — that altogether anomalous body which has come to be the main governing power in the metropolis.

§ 31. *Charter Changes since* 1873.

It is not surprising that such a frame of government as this should have failed to give satisfaction. Many have been the proposed changes during the past two decades, and two or three of considerable importance have actually been accomplished.

The first general amendment was the abandonment of minority representation in 1882,[1] a change of less importance because of the insignificant power which belonged to the council. None even of the champions of good government seemed to consider the dropping of the system of any serious consequence. Probably it was less the effect of the new method of election than the new opportunities presented by the restored power to grant street railway franchises, that led to such corruption as to make the name of alderman for some years after 1882 a byword and a hissing. The panacea by which it has been sought to remedy the abuse of power by the council has been a constant reduction in its sphere of authority, until to-day words can hardly express the ridicule which is heaped upon the mere shreds of governmental control which remain to this once honorable and powerful body.

While the council has thus steadily sunk into insignificance, the demand for centralization in some form has gradually succeeded in winning far greater administrative control for the mayor, while the board of estimate and apportionment has likewise increased its financial control. For a long time after 1873 the mayors complained incessantly of their weakness. A senate investigating committee in 1881 declared that the departments were "little short of independent commissions account-

[1] Laws, 1882, Chap. 403.

able to no superior," and recommended that the mayor be given sole power of appointment and removal, without action of council or governor.[1] It was three years longer before the right to confirm appointments was taken from the council,[2] while only in 1895 did the idea of 'one-man rule' gain the ascendant sufficiently to secure to the mayor the power to remove summarily any department head, within six months after taking office.[3]

Of recent years another change has met with some favor — that of making the various departmental commissions bi-partisan, or, as is sometimes said euphemistically, 'non-partisan.' The policy throughout the state in this matter has been very wavering. The working of the system since its introduction into the police board of the metropolis[4] has scarcely been the brilliant success which was promised.

Considerable hope of better things was based upon the provision of the new constitution of 1894,[5] giving to the local authorities of cities a conditional veto over legislative acts affecting them. In the larger cities this power rests with the mayor alone. The legislature, however, can override local disapproval by a mere majority vote, and it has shown itself little inclined to pay serious attention to local wishes. The new provision is helpful in securing

---

[1] New York Senate Documents, 1881, No. 25, p. 2.
[2] Laws, 1884, Chap. 43.   [4] *Ibid.*, 1895, Chap. 569.
[3] *Ibid.*, 1895, Chap. 11.   [5] Const. 1894, Art. 12, § 2.

some measure of home rule, only as regards those bills which are passed so near the close of legislative session that no opportunity is given for repassing them after disapproval.

§ 32. *The Greater New York Charter.*

The history of the measure which is so soon to unite into one vast municipality the three millions of people dwelling about New York harbor is too recent, and its character too familiar, to need extended discussion; nor, in view of the widespread opposition to many features, is it certain that the law as passed by the legislature will long stand unchanged.

The movement for consolidation began long ago; but it was not till 1890[1] that the first definitive step was taken by the establishment of an investigating commission, partly chosen by the state and partly by the local bodies affected. This commission, which was headed by Andrew H. Green, who had already done so much for the city, after long inquiry as to the feasibility and method of the change, obtained the passage of an act in 1894, providing for the submission of the general question whether consolidation would be acceptable, to a vote of the communities concerned.[2] A poll equal to from one-half to two-thirds of the entire electorate was cast — a fair vote on such a question. Almost 60 per cent of the votes in New York city were for consolidation; but in Brooklyn, where a relatively

[1] Laws, 1890, Chap. 311.   [2] Senate Documents, 1895, No. 7.

larger vote was cast, a majority of only a few hundreds favored it. As the perplexing subject of the distribution of taxation between the two cities had not been touched on in the referendum, and as absolutely nothing concerning a frame of government had been under discussion, the election was maintained by many not to be sufficient warrant for action by the legislature without further local approval. Certainly the many complicated problems that would later arise had not been fully placed before the citizens ; and a large part of the votes, on both sides, must have been cast on sentimental or prejudiced grounds. In view of these circumstances, the legislature did not take immediate action on the recommendation of the charter commission, made to the session of 1895,[1] that the consolidation be decreed, to take effect at some definite date, and that further time for the preparation of a charter be given. In 1896,[2] however, the consolidation bill was at length passed, being largely favored by the Republicans, who were coerced by the party whip, and generally opposed by the Democrats. The veto of Mayors Strong and Wurster was overridden by the legislature. The consolidation is to take effect January 1, 1898. Meantime a commission for drafting the charter was created, composed of the mayors of New York, Brooklyn, and Long Island city, the state attorney-general, the state

[1] Senate Documents, 1895, No. 7.   [2] Laws, 1896, Chap. 488.

engineer, and 10 members appointed by the governor, among whom were included Ex-Mayors Low of Brooklyn and Gilroy of New York.

The time for the task of framing a government for so huge and so complex a city was confessedly far too short. Nevertheless the commission, after many hearings and much labor, succeeded in presenting a charter to the legislature of 1897. The Republican party machine was again back of the measure; and accordingly without serious discussion, except, perhaps, as to the composition of the police department, and practically unamended, the bill was 'jammed through.' Again did Mayor Strong interpose his veto,[1] his objections being chiefly to the two-chambered council, the bi-partisan commission head for the police department, and the want of absolute power of removal in the mayor. Almost without consideration his disapproval was voted down, and the charter was duly signed by the governor.

Although from a broad standpoint some form of consolidation of Greater New York seems, undoubtedly, not only desirable, but almost inevitable, there is no little basis for the strong opposition to the charter shown in many quarters and on many grounds.[2] The objections on the part of certain taxpayers of New York, who fear increased

[1] *New York Tribune*, April 10, 1897.
[2] The financial features of the charter are more fully described hereafter.

burdens as the result of the union, may perhaps be dismissed as narrow and selfish. It seems not unjust that the great wealth of the business district of the consolidated city should aid in the improvement of the residence district dependent upon it. On the other hand, the criticism that in its technical details the charter is confused and inconsistent is well founded, although doubtless these defects can be remedied from time to time by amendments. More general and fundamental objections, however, may be urged. The charter adopts no definite and scientific principle of government; while following too closely the compromise act which has so long governed the city, it has attempted to introduce new features, forming combinations which will, it may well be feared, prove unworkable. The somewhat more satisfactory charter of Brooklyn has contributed but little apparently to the evolution of the law of 1897.

Of great importance, indeed, if it shall prove more than an empty name, is the added degree of home rule conferred upon the city. Heretofore, every enterprise involving bond issues has required special legislative sanction, and the legislature has often regulated or usurped entirely the management of such enterprises. The city is now to have power to undertake all classes of public works and to issue bonds on its own initiative. But unfortunately this provision will not prevent future legislatures from indulging in the practice, so common in the past, of making mandatory additions to the city debt; nor can one legislature in any way bind its successors so as to prevent indefinite deductions or modifications, direct or indirect, in the power thus nominally granted. Only a constitutional amendment can be any guaranty of continued autonomy in this regard.

Nevertheless, there can be no doubt that the municipal government will hereafter have greater independent power than heretofore. A large part of this added authority is nominally given by the charter to the reorganized city council, now to be dignified by the title 'municipal assembly.' But the combination of different methods of government proposed by the commissioners is likely to prove an impossibility. Declaring that mayor-rule has worked well, they have sought to further increase his power; observing the generally high opinion in which the board of estimate is held, they have resolved to make it still stronger; but because forsooth the council ought theoretically to have some real function, the commissioners have, so they promise us, conferred new and great authority upon it also. As if this were not a sufficient subdivision of power, they have gone still further and have given to the newly constituted 'board of public improvements' considerable control over great municipal enterprises. It seems likely that the framers of the charter have overshot the mark in their attempt to establish checks and balances. Either power will be so disintegrated that responsibility cannot be properly located and that deadlocks will be of frequent occurrence; or, as is perhaps more probable, the council and board of public improvements will fail to acquire any considerable power, while the mayor and board of estimate and apportionment will continue, as in the past, to dictate all important matters. Unless a marked change in the character of the council is brought about by other influences, it is doubtful if the authority conferred upon it of finally fixing items in the budget, by decreasing but not by increasing the sums proposed by the board of estimate, will prove of special significance. Strenuous indeed were the attempts to prevail upon the charter commission to adopt once more the system of genuine council government; but the prejudice against the council was too strong. Equally urgent were the arguments against the reinstatement of two boards in the council, a system apparently discredited by the experience of New York, of Brooklyn, and of many other cities. The increase in the number of municipal assemblymen, the lengthening of the term of the upper house to four years, and even the reëstablishment of minority representation, if this last is ever accomplished by constitutional amendment, can scarcely make much improvement in the character of the council, so long as it remains practically powerless. The same is true of the interesting provision, apparently borrowed from the charter of the Committee of Seventy, allowing department heads and ex-mayors seats for debate, without vote, in the municipal assembly.

The design of the charter commission to add to the mayor's power finds expression chiefly in an increase of his term to four years. He retains the sole power of appointment, and, as before, his right of summary removal is limited to six months after taking office. In face of great opposition, the system of plural or commission heads has been retained in most of the departments, notwithstanding the more rational example furnished by the Brooklyn charter, which provides for single department heads. The bi-partisan character of the police board has likewise been continued. The change of policy regarding city franchises, which does away with the vicious practice of making perpetual grants, is probably the most noteworthy forward step in the new charter.

§ 33. *Outline of Financial System and Plan of Study.*

A city's housekeeping, like that of an individual, involves: (*a*) recurrent revenue from various sources; (*b*) recurrent expenditures for various objects; (*c*) a control of the details of such revenue and expenditure, and an adjustment between them, in the 'budget'; (*d*) expenditures for extraordinary purposes, to distribute the cost of which conveniently over a period of years requires the creation of debt; (*e*) a system of auditing and accounting. But into this simple classification of our subject the actual financial system of the metropolis will fit but roughly. An intricate historical development has indeed so complicated matters that comprehension is very difficult. Thus, what is technically called the budget does not include all classes of recurrent income and outlay, those connected with street improvements and with debt redemption especially being separated — a fact which keeps many citizens from appreciating the full magnitude of the city's annual business. The actual arrangement of the accounts as given in the comptroller's reports is as follows: —

1. The 'Appropriation Account' covers all expenditures for purposes designed to benefit the whole city, including most of the payments for interest on the debt, and part of the yearly contributions made to reduce the debt. The revenue on this account is chiefly from *ad valorem* taxes on general property, but a small nominal addition is made from lapsed appropriations, and two or three millions are derived from sundry sources constituting the 'general fund.'

2. 'Special and Trust Accounts' are next distinguished, the expenditures upon them being thrown together promiscuously, while the receipts from loans — including the immense sums borrowed temporarily each year in anticipation of taxes —

are kept separate from the numerous other receipts, of which the chief are : (*a*) from premium on bonds, the proceeds of which go to the same purposes for which the principal of the bonds is destined; (*b*) from special assessments on property directly benefited by street improvements; and (*c*) from excise and theatrical licenses. The receipts and expenditures on these last two accounts are regularly recurrent and might well be grouped with the appropriation accounts, but are distinguished because subject by law to special management and methods. All receipts and expenditures from loans ought properly to be kept in entirely separate accounts, in which, moreover, those on revenue bonds and on assessment bonds should be carefully distinguished from the others.

3. The 'Sinking Fund Accounts' include the 'sinking fund for interest' and that for redemption, to each of which certain miscellaneous sources of income, of considerable amount, are pledged. The former fund is merely a survival, now paying interest on but a fraction of the city debt and turning its large annual surplus into the redemption fund, which, besides this transfer and its own revenues, receives income directly from appropriations. The redemption fund accounts are further complicated by receipts and payments in the reinvestment of its accumulations.

4. Debt tables classifying the outstanding city bonds according to various methods complete the

essential part of the comptroller's reports, the remainder being occupied with certain comparative statements and with less important details.

One of the chief reasons for the distinction from one another of the classes of accounts mentioned is that the management of the respective branches of the finances concerned is largely in different hands. (1) The control of appropriation expenditures now belongs, practically, exclusively to the board of estimate and apportionment, an anomalous and unprecedented body of five executive officers headed by the mayor and comptroller. The city council has merely advisory power, which amounts to nothing at all, in the budget. On the other hand, neither the board of estimate nor the council has any discretionary power worthy of mention in regulating the receipts of the appropriation account; the 'general fund,' whose revenues are almost entirely fixed independently, is simply subtracted and the remainder raised by taxes, levied by a formal ordinance of the council. (2) The authorization of assessment enterprises belongs partly to the council and partly to a special *ex officio* board, while the determination of the assessments themselves is also subdivided among still other officers. The board of estimate has no voice in regulating the income from excise licenses, but is empowered to appropriate the proceeds to charitable institutions. (3) The sinking funds are controlled by a board of five commissioners, also including the mayor and comptroller. Besides formal duties of debt management, this body has considerable discretionary power in regard to certain of the special revenues appropriated to the two funds, and occasionally is given authority to determine bond issues. (4) The authorization of debt has, for the most part, up to the time of the Greater New York charter, been directly retained in the hands of the legislature, though some local control has been given to the board of estimate, and in a few cases to other city officers or boards.

While, owing to the important historical and in part logical reasons which have led to some of these complications in the city accounts, it will be impracticable to conduct our study on the simple plan first outlined, it will be possible to disregard some of the complexities. We must sharply distinguish between recurrent and extraordinary receipts and expenditures, and under the latter head the entire discussion of the debt and of the sinking funds from the debt standpoint may be united (Chap. XI). In treating recurrent receipts and expenditures, we must first, in a preliminary section, group all together in a way not done by official reports (sec. 34), with some analysis and comparative study. The receipts may then be studied under the three heads, — roughly but not strictly corresponding to the first three groups of accounts in the reports, — of taxation

(Chap. VII), special assessments (Chap. VIII), and revenues from property and franchises (Chap. IX). The expenditures on special assessment accounts will be studied in connection with the receipts from this source, so that only the appropriation expenditures remain to be discussed, the manner of determining these in the budget being especially considered (Chap. X). The methods of auditing and accounting will be reviewed in a final chapter (XII).

§ 34. *Preliminary View of Receipts and Expenditures.*

To discover the actual recurrent yearly receipts and expenditures of the metropolis, we can neither take the totals on all the accounts, nor, as is often done, the total on appropriation account alone. The total receipts of all the accounts for 1896, as given by the comptroller, are as follows: —

GROSS RECEIPTS, 1896

Taxes	$ 40,887,505
General fund	2,017,929
Appropriation account	144,251
Special and trust accounts	8,425,823
Loans	48,944,728
Total 'treasury' receipts	$ 100,420,236
Redemption fund (excluding reinvestments)	9,030,597
Interest fund	4,796,773
Grand total	$ 114,247,607

The properly recurrent receipts, however, were almost exactly half of this amount, for we must omit : (1) the small sum of lapsed appropriations constituting the 'appropriation account,' since this is only nominally income; (2) the receipts from loans, nearly half of which are from revenue bonds temporarily issued in anticipation of taxes, and redeemed before the close of the year; (3) all the receipts of special and trust accounts except those from special assessments and from licenses, the rest being either premium on bonds or small receipts as to which the city acts merely in the capacity of trustee ; and (4) various transfers, especially those from the appropriation and interest fund accounts to the redemption fund. With these changes the net annual revenues appear as follows : —

NET RECURRENT RECEIPTS. 1896

Taxes	$40,887,504
General fund	2,017,929
Special assessments	2,897,068
Excise licenses	3,857,097
Theatrical licenses	42,120
Redemption fund — net	2,879,601
Interest fund	4,796,773
Total	$57,378,092

While in New York it is customary enough to refer to the receipts from taxes and the general fund as constituting the regular city income, the other revenues above named ought properly to be included ; in most cities, indeed, all these classes of revenues are placed in a single account. From the total just given, however, $6,402,009, the amount of taxes collected for state purposes by the city, should be subtracted, leaving the net income for 1896, $50,976,083. This enormous sum is more than three times as much as the receipts of any other American city in 1890, nearly four times as much as the yearly receipts of the state of New York, and is equal to about 40 per cent of the total receipts of all our state governments.[1] The United States census (which uses a somewhat different method of computation) gives the receipts of several leading cities for 1890 as follows: —

New York	$35,740,547
Chicago	15,484,325
Philadelphia	15,431,810
Boston	14,369,350
Brooklyn	13,499,433
St. Louis	7,092,296
Baltimore	6,132,437

The amount of the annual income of the consolidated metropolis can be estimated only roughly. The total receipts of the city of Brooklyn, for 1895, aside from loans, were about $20,500,000;[2] those

---

[1] See U. S. Census, 1890, Wealth, Debt, and Taxation, vol. 2, p. 555; New York State Library Bulletin on State Finance, 1897. Comparison with census figures is somewhat misleading, as only net revenues from property, etc., deducting expenditures, are given.

[2] The accounts are very complicated, but apparently the proper total is reached by deducting from the general fund the amount from loans, leaving $19,397,751; and adding the receipts of the special fund (assessments for opening streets and for sewers),

of Long Island city, Richmond county, and the smaller municipalities, perhaps $2,000,000. The income of New York herself being about $57,500,000 yearly, a round estimate would probably place the annual revenue of the greater city at approximately eighty millions — much more than that of any other city in the world except Paris. Between eight and ten millions of this sum, however, would be intended for state taxes.

More important in many ways than the classification of city revenues above given, according to the funds to which they go, is a grouping according to their source. The three broadest classes of New York's receipts are: (1) from taxes, $40,887,504 in 1896, or 71 per cent of the total receipts; (2) from special assessments, $2,897,068, or 5 per cent; and (3) from miscellaneous sources, not coming directly from the pockets of taxpayers, $13,593,522, or 24 per cent of the recurrent income of the city. The receipts from taxes are a residual factor, depending upon the difference between appropriations and miscellaneous revenues. The receipts from special assessments are supposed to cover, and of late years practically have covered, the actual outlay for street-improvement enterprises; their amount is thus dependent on the

$80,145, of the redemption fund, $690,877, and those of the revenue fund less the transfer to the general fund, $445,126, giving a total of $20,613,900. Brooklyn Comptroller's Report, 1895, pp. 44, 91 ff. The Kings county receipts are included.

number and extent of such enterprises, which varies greatly with different conditions. It is in regard to the miscellaneous revenues that careful financial management has most scope, and it is to augment these that many municipal reformers have specially striven. The amount of these revenues in New York is already larger in proportion than in almost any other American city,[1] — its magnitude being, indeed, hardly appreciated by taxpayers, partly owing to the complications of the accounts, — but there is yet much room for improvement in managing them. Such improvement, to be sure, may not consist merely in increasing the income from these sources, for many other than purely financial motives enter in certain cases.

The miscellaneous revenues, in fact, comprise widely divergent classes. For our purpose, the most important line of division may be drawn roughly between (1) revenues merely incidental to the performance of municipal functions, and (2) revenues from city property and franchises, where the matter of income is of prime importance. To the first class, whose amount is largely determined by motives and circumstances other than purely financial, belong : (a) most of the general fund revenues, — interest on taxes and assessments, proceeds of sales of old material, street sweepings, etc., contri-

---

[1] In Chicago, the large receipts from liquor licenses bring the proportion of miscellaneous revenues ahead of that in New York. Comparisons by census figures are practically impossible.

butions by the state to the support of schools, and various smaller amounts; (*b*) receipts from fees, fines, etc.; (*c*) receipts from licenses and permits, where the chief purpose is to restrict or regulate. The motives governing the revenues composing the second class are intricate, and require special discussion. Meantime they may be classified, according to whether they involve an investment by the city or not, into revenues from property and revenues from franchises.

The miscellaneous revenues of New York for 1896 may be divided, without too great separation of items grouped by the official reports, as follows, the parentheses indicating the funds to which they mainly go:—

MISCELLANEOUS REVENUES, 1896

1. *Revenues incidental to Function*

a. Fees, fines, etc.
Courts generally (Int. fund)	$ 279,848	
County clerk and register (Gen. fund)	145,738	
Sheriff (Gen.)	116,782	
Miscellaneous (Gen.)	8,972	$ 551,341

b. Licenses and permits.
Excise (separate)	$3,857,247	
Theatrical (separate)	42,120	
Department of parks[1] (Gen.)	40,180	
Pawnbrokers (Int.)	66,000	
Street vault permits (Red.)	141,540	
Miscellaneous (Gen. Red.)	93,556	4,240,644

[1] Including rents.

c. Miscellaneous sources.

Sale street sweepings, etc. (Gen.) $	33,007	
Department of correction (Gen.)	32,981	
Charges for sewers and water-mains (Gen.)	43,959	
Other payments for service and material (Gen.)	27,054	
Interest on taxes (Gen.)	395,504	
Interest on assessments (Gen.)	213,968	
Interest on deposits (Int.)	142,064	
School money from state (Gen.)	693,771	
Miscellaneous (Gen. Red.)	5,215	1,587,524

2. *Revenues from Property and Franchises*

a. Property.

Rent of real estate (Int.) $	92,094	
Sale of real estate (Red.)	35,943	
Croton water rents (Int.)	4,073,856	
Dock rents (Red.)	2,039,015	
Market rents and fees (Red.)	285,392	
Net interest on investments (Int.)	36,585	6,562,885

b. Franchises.

Ferries (Int.)	346,598	
Street railways (Gen. Red.)	302,111	
Pipe-line, steam and gas (Gen. Red.)	2,418	651,128
Total		$13,593,522

For the purpose of a financial study, the first class of miscellaneous revenues, which comprise nearly half of the whole, may be passed over lightly. We may note, however, that, especially in regard to excise licenses, there have been many changes in policy, partly dictated by financial, partly by other motives. The most noteworthy change was made in 1896,[1] when the Raines liquor-tax law, while transferring a fourth of the revenue to the state treasury, so increased rates that the city received twice as much from this source as in the preceding year. The other class of miscellaneous revenues, which amounted to $7,214,013 last year, will require thorough study in a special chapter.

Bearing in mind what has been said as to the varying motives, subject to change, governing the management of many of the miscellaneous revenues, we may compare the receipts of the city by decennial periods. (See table on opposite page.) That the miscellaneous revenues bore a greater proportion to the tax levy in 1830 and 1850 than they do at present, was due less to their own large amount than to the limited extent of the city budget in those days; in proportion to population they are now considerably greater than ever before. The comparatively slow growth of these revenues from 1860 to 1870 was but one result of the general loose financiering of the time, while the remarkable increase since 1880 has been in part at least due to conscious effort to make city property and franchises more productive.

The annual expenditures of the city are naturally approximately equal to the receipts. As above intimated, the amount spent on street improve-

[1] Laws, 1896, Chap. 112.

COMPARATIVE RECEIPTS BY CLASSES

	1830	1840	1850	1860	1870	1880	1890	1896
Incidental revenue	$152,539	$177,266	$472,370	$814,860	$1,441,065	$2,767,153	$3,900,379	$6,379,509
Property and franchises [1]	173,260	204,420	912,513	1,287,946	2,309,972	2,929,940	5,574,508	7,214,013
Total miscellaneous revenue	325,799	381,686	1,384,883	2,102,806	3,751,037	5,697,093	9,474,887	13,593,522
Taxes (levied)	509,173	1,354,835	3,230,180	9,758,507	23,569,127	28,167,991	32,501,137	40,887,504 [2]
Per cent of miscellaneous revenue to taxes	64.1	28.2	42.9	21.5	15.9	20.2	29.1	29.9

[1] Revenues from sinking fund investments excluded (except net revenues in 1896), being chiefly paid from appropriations.

[2] Amount collected. These figures are chosen for 1896 because already cited above. The corresponding figures are not available for some earlier years.

ments, payable from assessments, does not appear in the yearly appropriations. In calculating the payments for reducing the city debt, it is evident that the proper method is to add to the sum paid from the appropriation account into the sinking fund for redemption, the sum received annually from other sources and going to swell the fund's accumulations; rather than to consider the moneys actually paid out of the fund for redeeming bonds, which often vary greatly in amount in different years, owing to the unequal maturity of the city debt.

It is unnecessary to compare the total expenditures of New York with those of other American cities, since they will naturally bear about the same relation to one another as do the receipts. Suffice it to say that, according to the census of 1890, the *per capita* expenditure of the metropolis was second only to that of Boston, and not far from double that of Chicago, Philadelphia, or Brooklyn.[1]

[1] The following are the figures given: —

PER CAPITA EXPENDITURES

City	Amount	City	Amount
New York	$24.56	Cincinnati	$18.04
Chicago	13.80	Cleveland	14.56
Philadelphia	13.10	Buffalo	22.41
Brooklyn	13.67	New Orleans	8.65
St. Louis	14.45	Pittsburgh	12.04
Boston	32.69	Detroit	16.61
Baltimore	14.02	Milwaukee	13.36
San Francisco	18.86		

U. S. Census, 1890, Wealth, Debt, and Taxation, p. 556.

CHAPTER VII

THE SYSTEM OF TAXATION

§ 35. *Outline of the Tax System.*[1]

We turn now to a more detailed study of the city receipts. By far the most important source of income is taxation based on the value of general property. More than nine-tenths of the expenditures on the 'budget' proper are met from taxes. We must accordingly study the system by which property is assessed and taxes collected, although, on account of its familiarity and its resemblance to that in force elsewhere, it possesses somewhat less interest than other financial features. Few important changes in the law governing the subject have been made since the general tax act for the city passed in 1859.[2]

At present the assessment of property in New York city is under the supervision of three 'commissioners of taxes and assessments,' appointed by the mayor for six years. They choose about fifteen deputies to do the primary work of assessment. Real estate is, as usual, assessed by the lot or piece, personal property to the individual holding it. A separate assessment of bank shares

[1] Consolidation Act, §§ 812–864. [2] Laws, 1859, Chap. 302.

is made, as in the rest of the state, for the reason that, although the tax is assessed to the separate holders, it is nevertheless collected from the banks and withheld by them from dividends. The process of determining the taxable valuations for each year is begun by the deputies in September of the preceding year and must be completed by the second Monday of January. From that time till the first of May, the assessment books are open to public inspection and subject to revision. Persons objecting to the valuation of their real estate must do so in writing, and the tax commissioners will then take the matter into more or less careful consideration. On the other hand, people remonstrating against personal assessments must appear in person before one or more of the commissioners and make affidavit, not as to the details of their personal estate, but simply, in general form, that it does not exceed such and such an amount, — in other words, they are permitted to 'swear off' their assessments in bulk. Any one aggrieved by the decision of the commissioners as to either class of assessments may obtain from the supreme court a *certiorari* to review their action. Even after payment of taxes has actually begun, the tax commissioners still have authority to remit or reduce taxes, but they do so only to a limited extent. The common council formerly possessed and often abused this power of remission, but it has now been taken away entirely from that body.

After the revision of the valuations by the commissioners of taxes and assessments, new assessment rolls are prepared and transmitted to the aldermen, who ordain the amount of tax to be levied, in a purely formal manner.[1] The addition that is made to the levy to cover deficiencies is so adjusted that the tax rate need not be fixed beyond hundredths of one per cent. Next comes the work of calculating the tax for each piece or individual. This requires considerable time, so that it is about the first of October before collection begins. Meanwhile, from the opening of the year, the government has been carried on by means of money raised on short-time 'revenue bonds,' which the city commences to pay off as soon as taxes come in. The receiver of taxes, — who does not belong to the same department as the commissioners of taxes and assessments, but is an officer of the finance department, — immediately on opening the tax books must advertise the fact that taxes are now payable. On all taxes paid before November 1, interest at six per cent from the date of payment to December 1 is deducted. If they are not paid by December 1, a penalty of one per cent is added, and if not paid before January 1, interest is charged thereafter from the first day when the tax books were opened, at seven per cent. There are marked differences in the procedure to collect delinquent personal and real estate

[1] See *post*, p. 255.

taxes, both of which are placed in the hands of a special department of arrears. If the former are unpaid after January 15 of the year following the levy, a distress warrant on the property of the person assessed is issued; if no property is found, a further mode of enforcement is by obtaining from the court an order imposing a fine sufficient to cover tax and costs. On the other hand, three years must elapse before real estate can be sold for taxes, and the procedure is more complicated.

The only important change in the tax system of the greater city will be an increase in the number of tax commissioners to five instead of three, and a reduction of their term from six to four years.

§ 36. *Practical Character of the Assessment of Property.*

The following are the assessed valuations of New York city for 1896:[1] —

ASSESSED VALUATIONS, 1896

Personal estate —		
Resident	$245,883,488	
Non-resident	46,468,081	
Shareholders of banks	82,624,193	$374,975,762
Real estate		1,731,509,143
Total		$2,106,484,905

The most striking fact about these figures, were it not, unfortunately, such a commonplace, is the

---

[1] Report of Commissioners of Taxes and Assessments, *City Record*, 1896, p. 2603.

enormous excess of the real estate assessment over that of personalty. No one can for a moment doubt that in this, the very centre of capital in America, the personal property held far exceeds in value the real estate, yet it is assessed at but a little over one-fifth as much. The evasion of personal property was relatively a great deal less up to about 1870; in 1860 it was assessed at nearly 45 per cent as much as realty.[1] Apparently, the actual shrinkage in values after the crisis of 1873 gave the impulse to a reduction in personal assessments far greater and far more prolonged than was justifiable. The real estate valuation likewise had fallen off for a time after the crash, but it so far recovered by 1880 that it amounted to two hundred millions more than in 1870. The personal assessment for 1880, on the other hand, was a full

[1] RELATIVE ASSESSMENT OF REAL AND PERSONAL PROPERTY

Year	Real	Personal	Proportion of Personal to Real — %
1830	$ 87,603,580	$ 37,684,938	43
1840	187,221,714	65,013,802	34.7
1850	207,146,176	78,939,240	38
1860	398,533,619	178,697,037	44.8
1870	742,202,525	305,317,699	41.1
1880	942,571,690	201,194,037	21.3
1890	1,398,290,007	298,688,383	21.4
1896	1,731,509,143	374,975,762	21.7

third less than in 1870; the proportion borne by the personal to the real estate valuation had decreased during the decade no less astonishingly than from 41 to 21 per cent. Since 1880 there has been some improvement. The assessment of personal property has increased at almost exactly the same rate as that of real estate; this is probably, however, considerably less than in proportion to the actual growth of personal wealth in the metropolis.

It is not because the assessors utterly ignore personalty that it thus escapes taxation. They regularly place on the rolls at the outset nearly double the number of names, and from six to ten times the amount of property ultimately retained. There is no provision in the state for listing personal property by the owner, and, in fact, no attempt is usually made to secure any sort of an inventory of the taxpayer's property. A considerable part of the process of assessing personalty is indeed mere haphazard. The deputy assessor selects names from the city directory, using "his judgment — from his experience, and from what he has passed through in regard to the affidavits of those who correct or swear off — in placing the sums opposite each individual name."[1] An enormous proportion of the assessments so made are sworn off. The figures on the following page show for certain

[1] Testimony of Tax Commissioner Coleman before the (Fassett) Committee on Cities, Senate Documents, 1891. No. 80. p. 2351.

Assessment of Personal Property

	1874	1880	1889	1896
Names on rolls at opening	25,293	22,084	26,184	35,556
Applications for reduction	12,126	15,100	13,174	19,704
Erased, not liable	10,927	7,320	11,469	13,824
Retained on rolls	14,366	14,764	14,715	21,732
Amount on rolls at opening	$483,729,399	$1,924,571,906	$1,646,986,215	?
Amount erased	286,144,788	1,778,979,476	1,442,723,339	?
Amount retained	197,583,611	145,592,430	204,262,876	?

years the results of this process.[1] The assessments of shareholders of banks are omitted, there being little opportunity for evasion here.

These enormous reductions in personal assessments contrast markedly with those in the real estate lists, where out of 161,402 pieces assessed in 1889 applications for reduction were made as to only 559. Certainly it is remarkable that out of the population of nearly two millions that New York now boasts, only 21,732 persons should be found with personal property subject to taxation. It is, moreover, the wealthiest citizens who most largely escape their just burdens. "We only catch the widows and the orphans," said Tax Commissioner Coleman in 1891,[2] since their property can be ascertained from the surrogate's office. After the death of William H. Vanderbilt several years ago, it was found that perhaps $40,000,000 of his personal estate was taxable, — he had been paying during his lifetime on $500,000, — but the heirs threatened to convert the property into non-taxable securities if the full amount were assessed, and the city officers counted themselves exceedingly fortunate to make a compromise by which the estate paid taxes on $8,000,000[3] — a sum which, added to the separate assessments of the various members of the family, made the Vanderbilts pay

---

[1] Quarterly Report Commissioners of Taxes and Assessments, *City Record*, 1889, pp. 3233, 3234; 1896, p. 2569.

[2] Fassett Committee's Report, p. 2238. [3] *Ibid.*, pp. 2354-2363.

about one-thirteenth of the resident personal taxes of New York. Many men of wealth move their residences to some of the suburbs to escape assessment, and many others by threatening to do so keep their taxes down as the result of a sort of bargain with the city. So complete a failure is the assessment of personal property that many thoughtful citizens have advocated the entire exemption of personalty from local taxation, trusting to state taxes on corporations, inheritances, etc., to reach this class of wealth. The problem of securing equitable taxation is certainly a pressing one, not only in New York city, but in other cities and in other states. Great as is the evasion of personal taxes in New York, in Brooklyn, where personalty pays barely three per cent of the entire amount of taxes, it must be even greater.

Real estate, of course, cannot escape assessment altogether unless it is exempt by law; but the charge is often made that there is material inequality in the valuations as between individuals and localities. Districts inhabited by small taxpayers, and those where real estate transfers are least numerous, are, it is declared, rated too high in proportion. On the other hand, large blocks of unimproved property held for speculation are often assessed very far below their real worth. The tax commissioners themselves [1] admit that injustice is often done, but they tell us that they can exercise

[1] Fassett Committee's Report, pp. 2197 ff.

little real control over the general plan of assessment which their deputies may individually follow, consciously or unconsciously. As each deputy has exclusively the assessment of his assigned district, the personal equation cannot fail to enter largely. Unfortunately the new charter makes no provision to secure more deliberative action in equalizing valuations between districts, or otherwise to improve the assessment system.

The gross assessed valuation of real estate in the metropolis, according to the almost universal custom, is considerably less than the true value. One motive which leads to this undervaluation is the desire to make the burden of state taxes upon the county relatively as light as possible. The same motive, of course, influences the action of assessors throughout the state; hence arises the need for an equalization between the assessments of the various counties for the purpose of apportioning state taxes. Instead of making an entirely new assessment for this purpose, the state assessors, by taking a considerable number of typical cases, endeavor to estimate the average proportion of assessed to true valuation of real estate (there is no equalization of personal property) in each county; they then add to or subtract from the local assessments such a percentage as will make this proportion uniform in the state. In the opinion of this state board, the valuations of realty made by New York city officials are about 65 per cent of the true value, and are somewhat less proportionally than the average valuations of the other counties. Accordingly, in apportioning the state tax, they have regularly for the past two decades increased considerably the local assessment — on the average nearly a tenth having been added. The proportion of increase has, however, been somewhat less since 1890 than before. In 1881 the local valuation of realty was $976,735,199, the increase by the state officials no less than $126,829,509;[1] while in 1895 only $70,458,738 was added to the original assessment of over sixteen hundred millions.[2] Despite the fact that by this action of the state assessors the metropolis is made to pay more than 45 per cent of the state taxes,[3] this probably indicates much less discrimination against the city than many New York citizens are wont to charge. The people of the rural districts are quite as strongly convinced that it is they who suffer injustice.

It is not infrequently declared by newspapers and others that the city authorities at times attempt to blind the taxpayers as to actual increase of public expenditures by unduly swelling the assessed valuation, and thus keeping down the tax-rate. This, however, is quite doubtful. The device is almost

---

[1] Mayor's Message, *City Record*, 1892, p. 21.

[2] Report of State Assessors, 1895, p. 18.

[3] *Ibid.*, p. 8. 45.966 per cent for 1895. There has been little change for twenty years.

too transparent to be effective. The approximate equality of the annual increases in assessments also argues against this charge. Moreover, as we have seen, the desire to lighten the city's burden of state taxes is a motive always tending to keep down local assessments. The study given by the state board of assessors to the valuations is scarcely so thorough but that any undue addition to the assessments by the city officers would be apt to lead to a somewhat proportionate increase in the state valuation. Although the assessment of New York city has nearly doubled since 1879, this is probably hardly more than proportional to the real growth in values.

§ 37. *Collection of Taxes.*

Under the present system, taxes have usually been collected quite completely. There have been no deficiencies necessitating the issue of funding bonds, such as occurred in the earlier days. This may be judged from the fact that the total amount of taxes collected for the period of twenty-two years ending 1895, counting interest, has come within a shade of equalling the amount of taxes levied.[1] Although, on account of the longer

---

[1] Taxes levied $700,965,113
Collected by receiver of taxes . . . $624,499,994
Collected by clerk of arrears . . .   62,715,611
                                                   $687,215,605
Interest on taxes   12,973,560
    Total collected $700,189,166
Comp. Rep., 1895, pp. 178, 180.

period that must elapse before real estate taxes can be enforced by sale, there is a considerably larger amount of these unpaid for the more recent years, they are ultimately collected much more fully than personal taxes. Indeed, if we go back eight or ten years, the amount of uncollected real estate taxes is barely a tenth of that of unpaid personal taxes, notwithstanding that the real taxes originally levied are so much the greater. About 85 per cent of the annual taxes have in recent years been collected before the close of the year, although the proportion varies considerably with different conditions. This greater promptness in collection has contributed to the noteworthy reduction in the amount of revenue bonds outstanding at the end of the year and to the reduction in the sum spent for interest on such bonds. For 1896 the taxes were collected even more promptly than usual; and the amount of revenue bonds, for the first time in over thirty years, was reduced to zero on December 31,[1] except for certain bonds not intended to be paid by the taxes of that year. A change has been frequently urged by city officers and others, by which the collection of taxes should take place much earlier in the year for whose expenditures they are intended,[2] or in the preceding year, in order to avoid borrowing money

[1] Manuscript records in comptroller's office.
[2] Comptroller Myers urged the change strongly in his report of 1892, p. 64.

for current outlay during so great a part of the time. The expensiveness of the present system is pointed out by the advocates of this modification. The amount of interest paid on revenue bonds for twenty-two years, ending 1895, was $8,045,719, the income from interest on deposits only $2,076,906, the difference representing a loss to the city of about $275,000 yearly.[1] In Brooklyn and in other cities taxes for the current year are collected in the year preceding; but notwithstanding this example, the new charter proposes no change from the present practice. If such a change were attempted, it would doubtless have to be made gradually, perhaps by pushing back the date when taxes should be due one or two months each year, in order that an altogether extraordinary burden might not be placed on the taxpayers at the time of the change.[2]

[1] Comp. Rep., 1895, p. 181.

[2] A further change in the tax system that might be suggested is the abandonment of the practice of adding a percentage to the levy for deficiencies. The amount of interest on taxes collected has been for many years approximately equal to that of these additions. There is, perhaps, some advantage in the way of clearness in the present practice of distinguishing interest on taxes from taxes collected, and turning the former into the general fund. Otherwise the two might be grouped together as tax income, and the addition for deficiencies simply dropped. This would amount to the same thing practically as the present arrangement, since the estimated receipts of the general fund, including interest on taxes, are now subtracted from the levy.

CHAPTER VIII

SPECIAL ASSESSMENTS

NEXT to general taxes, New York's most important source of revenue, although it does not enter into the regular budget account, is from special assessments for local improvements. Perhaps more than any other branch of the finances this system has given rise in the past to difficulties and abuses; but it has been materially improved and simplified since the Tweed Ring, and while the methods are still complex and inconsistent, the practical working of late years has been fairly satisfactory. It is to be feared that the somewhat important changes proposed by the charter of 1897 will not greatly improve the system.

The distinction (which will be more fully explained in section 39) between assessments for 'street openings' and for 'local or street improvements' respectively, must be borne in mind.

§ 38. *Changes in the Assessment System.*

Since the Ring days some changes in the law have been made regarding the authority to inaugurate and carry on assessment undertakings. From the institution of the system to the present time it has required an ordinance of the common council to authorize those of the second class, — street improvements, — though their conduct, and the details of the assessments, are at present left to executive officers. The theory on which this power regarding street improvements has been retained in spite of the general weakening of the council is apparently that their authorization implies a form of tax levying, and to impose taxes is considered a prerogative of the council.[1] In practice the action of that body has of late years been somewhat perfunctory. Up to 1865 the first authorization of street openings also belonged in every case to the council, but in that year [2] its powers as to streets above 155th were transferred to the Central Park commission, a change which may doubtless be explained, although hardly justified, by the fact that the same law had empowered the commission to open and improve the Boulevard, — park authorities often being given charge of boulevards and driveways. The department of parks, which succeeded the Central Park commission, was given authority also over street openings in the 23d and 24th wards, after their annexation. Meantime, by the charter of 1870 and amendments of 1871, the right to regulate street openings below 59th Street was bestowed on a 'board of street

---

[1] See Matter of Roberts, 81 N. Y. 62.
[2] Laws, 1865, Chap. 565.

opening and improvement,' consisting of the mayor, comptroller, commissioner of public works, president of the park department, and president of the board of aldermen.[1] The charter of 1873[2] took away from the council its last vestige of power in regard to street openings, giving to the commissioner of public works the entire control of these enterprises from 59th to 155th Street. This triple division of authority lasted till, in 1885,[3] the impropriety of leaving this power as regards so large a part of the city to a single executive officer, — the work of whose department in improving streets would be, moreover, largely affected by his decision as to opening them, — led to the transfer of all powers of the commissioner of public works in this respect to the board of street opening and improvement. In 1890, furthermore, the powers of the park department as to streets were given over to a commissioner of street improvements for the 23d and 24th wards, whose action as to openings is subject to the board of street opening, which thus at last has obtained exclusive control of these enterprises.

The Greater New York charter has made important changes regarding the authority to inaugurate both classes of assessment enterprises. The aim has been to grant more home rule to the dis-

---

[1] Laws, 1870, Chap. 383, § 30; 1871, Chap. 574, § 18.
[2] *Ibid.*, 1873, Chap. 335, § 73.
[3] *Ibid.*, 1885, Chap. 185.

tricts specially affected, and at the same time to make the system more secure and to establish additional checks and balances. Hereafter each of the twenty-two state senatorial districts embraced in the greater city is to have a board of local improvements, to be composed of the president of the borough in which the district may be situated and of the members of each house of the municipal assembly elected from the district, — the board thus containing either four or five members. No street enterprise affecting only a particular district can be inaugurated except upon the initiative of the district board, and where two or more districts are affected, their local boards must jointly approve. The effect of such a recommendation is to bring the enterprise before the general 'board of public improvements' instituted by the new law, which consists of a president of the board, the heads of the six departments concerned with public works, the mayor, comptroller, corporation counsel, and the president of the borough affected by the work. To this powerful body will belong all the prerogatives now possessed by the board of street opening and improvements, with still added authority. By a provision designed to secure more careful consideration and economy, an estimate of the cost of the proposed work, and a statement of the assessed value of the real estate included within the probable area of assessment, must be submitted to the board before its action.

The resolution of the board of public improvements favoring any enterprise has still to be submitted to the municipal assembly; and, in turn, any measure introduced into the assembly in favor of a public work must, before final action, be submitted to the approval of the smaller board, failing which only a five-sixths vote of the assembly can carry it into effect. The board of public improvements is authorized to frame general ordinances regulating the methods of conducting public works, which can be approved or rejected but not amended by the municipal assembly.

It seems to be the opinion of many that this new manner of regulating improvements is too complicated, and presents too many mutually restrictive bodies to work smoothly. There is danger of deadlock, and to fix responsibility will be almost impossible. Had the district and general boards been given merely advisory power, and, if local autonomy was desired, had some provision been made for direct approval or disapproval by the people affected, the system would probably have been more satisfactory.

Other changes of importance have been made since the Ring period as to the financial management of the assessment system. The law of 1869, allowing the special commissioners of estimate in each street-opening proceeding to decide that any part not exceeding one-half of the cost might be charged upon the city as a whole, remained in force for some years after the fall of the Tweed Ring, and continued to add largely to the city debt, while encouraging extravagant and premature enterprises. By the end of 1875, more than eight and a half millions of 'city improvement stock' had been issued under this law.[1] Though the abuse had been checked during that year, it might begin again at any time so long as the statute remained in force; in 1876, accordingly, it was repealed, and the option to make part of the cost of such enterprises a general charge was transferred to the board of street opening and improvement.[2] The latter body has seldom made use of this authority, except in the case of the small parks recently opened, a part of whose cost, determined by the board, has been levied upon the property benefited. A law of 1874,[3] however, is still in force, providing that in the 23d and 24th wards the cost of opening streets over a mile long must be divided equally between the abutting owners and the city as a whole. Up to 1884, less than a million of bonds had been issued under these two provisions to cover the city's proportion of street-opening expenses.[4] Since then, burdens thus thrown on the general treasury have usually been

[1] Comp. Rep., 1883, p. 48, table.
[2] Laws, 1876, Chap. 210.
[3] *Ibid.*, 1874, Chap. 604.
[4] $893,371. Comp. Rep., 1884, p. 64, — city improvement, consolidated L. and M stocks. Compare Comp. Rep., 1895, Statement D.

paid from appropriations, either directly or by the intervention of special revenue bonds.

Exceedingly heavy losses have fallen upon the city from the vacation of assessments by the courts and from failure to collect them on other grounds. These difficulties belong chiefly to street improvements, and only to a much less degree to openings, for the obvious reason that by far the greater part of the cost of lands taken in the latter proceedings is charged back upon the very persons to whom damages are awarded, so that the transaction practically amounts to the payment of small balances on one side or the other. Even after the expulsion of Tweed from the position of commissioner of public works, that commissioner, under whom a very large part of street improvements are carried on, remained subject to no control except that of the city council, which was always ready to authorize expenditure; and Tweed's immediate successor himself was far from economical.[1] Many undertakings, indeed, already begun under the Ring, had necessarily to be completed, but many new ones also were commenced. The expenditures for local improvements continued to average over three millions yearly from 1872 to 1876, while the amount of unpaid assessment bonds rose rapidly. Vacations, not only of assessments made under the former régime, but of newly confirmed lists, were very extensive. They amounted

[1] See Mayor Havemeyer's Message, *City Record*, 1874, p. 62.

to nearly a million annually in 1872 and 1873. While these vacations were often on account of just complaints of overcharge and poor work, many were still, as during the Ring period, on trivial grounds. Attempts to secure reforms in the laws, under which this was possible, "encountered at Albany the organized opposition of a knot of lawyers," who drew large profits by aiding in these raids on the city treasury.[1] Finally, in 1874,[2] acts were passed removing 'legal irregularity' as a ground for vacating assessments, and leaving only fraud and overcharge as such grounds. In 1880[3] it was further enacted that no assessment should be reduced, except "to the extent that the same may be shown, by parties complaining thereof, to have been in fact increased in dollars and cents by reason of fraud or substantial error; and in no event shall that proportion of any such assessment which is equivalent to the fair value of any actual local improvement be disturbed for any cause." All these restrictive provisions remain in force under the charter of 1897.

Meantime legislation had been necessary to adjust the heavy burdens that had fallen on the city from vacations and non-collection of assessments.

---

[1] *Ante*, p. 144. Mayor's Message, *City Record*, 1874, p. 64. Communication from Comptroller of City of New York, New York Senate Documents, 1873, No. 105.

[2] Laws, 1874, Chaps. 312, 313.

[3] *Ibid.*, 1880, Chap. 550.

Although part of these losses had already been funded from time to time by consolidated stock, the city was still, in 1878, paying interest at six and seven per cent on more than twenty millions of assessment bonds, nearly all issued for street improvements alone. Fully half of these bonds had been issued even before 1874,[1] and there was little likelihood that further collections to any considerable extent would be made for redeeming them. Accordingly, by the general debt act of 1878,[2] one of whose chief objects was the disposition of this immense floating indebtedness, $10,204,745 of assessment bonds were funded by the issue of consolidated stock;[3] while all the rest of the existing assessment debt was made redeemable from the sinking fund, to which assessments on works begun before the date of the law were to be turned over, — a provision extended by an act of 1880[4] to all bonds for enterprises commenced before that time. The more than twelve millions of bonds thus charged on the sinking fund were all paid off by 1884.[5] The act of 1880 had also established a special 'assessment commission' to

[1] Comp. (August) Rep., *City Record*, 1878, p. 1296. The 'street improvement,' 'Central Park commission,' and a considerable part of the 'department of parks' bonds had all been issued before 1873, as had a large amount of 'assessment bonds.'

[2] Laws, 1878, Chap. 383.

[3] *City Record*, 1879, p. 1342; Comp. Rep., 1880, p. 15.

[4] Laws, 1880, Chap. 550.

[5] Comp. Rep., from year to year.

adjust claims still unsettled as to prior enterprises, and fully three millions of assessments were vacated or reduced by this body during the half decade over which its work stretched. It seems probable from its *personnel* that most of these great remissions were only such as justice required. Collections on these old assessments have dragged on slowly, but at last practically the full amount not covered by the funding bonds has been collected. Of late years, under the more rigid laws, and especially by means of more rigid administration, losses to the city from the assessment system have been reduced almost to a minimum. Though city officers sometimes charge that assessments are still being set aside by the courts for improper grounds, the amount of remissions has become so small that this charge is questionable.[1] Only $17,031 of assessments were vacated in 1896. While, with the considerable increase in street enterprises

---

[1] The following are the vacations since 1880 by the assessment commission and the courts: —

Year	Amount	Year	Amount
1880	$739,301	1889	$16,084
1881	957,557	1890	(Unknown)
1882	890,150	1891	"
1883	256,324	1892	$22,640
1884	261,010	1893	73,794
1885	166,270	1894	39,297
1886	544,451	1895	26,481
1887	261,687	1896	17,031
1888	28,941		

Fassett Committee Report, p. 2482; Comp. Rep., 1892-96.

since 1890, the amount of outstanding bonds and of unpaid assessments has grown considerably, but little loss is likely to be incurred. Of the $8,916,068 of uncollected assessments at the close of 1896, more than three millions are upon property owned by the city, which, by neglect of the financial officers, have not been charged off for many years.

The constitutional amendment of 1884, limiting city indebtedness, applied to assessment bonds, and throughout 1885 this amendment was so interpreted as to prevent New York from borrowing any money except for water purposes. Some new provision regarding the assessment system was accordingly necessary, and laws[1] were secured establishing a 'fund for street and park openings,' and a 'fund for local improvements.' To replenish the latter fund it was provided that at the time of voting the annual appropriations, in case it appeared that the expense of street improvements then contracted for, and of such as the board of estimate and apportionment should "deem it necessary or desirable to undertake in such ensuing year," would be greater than the amount of assessment moneys on hand, or likely to be collected during the year, the board should appropriate a sufficient sum from the regular budget to cover the estimated deficiency. No contract for such improvements should be binding unless a

[1] Laws, 1885, Chaps. 173, 174.

certificate of the comptroller were obtained that there was already in the fund cash enough to pay the cost. The law establishing the fund for local improvements was repealed in 1886,[1] as soon as the decision of the courts made it possible again to issue assessment bonds. The repeal was strongly opposed by the board of estimate and the comptroller, who maintained,[2] not without justice, that the act had operated "to reform financial difficulties arising from conflicting and loosely adjusted provisions of law," and had placed important checks on extravagance.

The fund for street and park openings, established by the law of 1885, still persists, though the act, which originally was quite similar in general nature to the law concerning the improvement fund,—except that it gave less control to the board of estimate and apportionment,—has had two important amendments. By the first of these[3] it was made possible to issue special revenue bonds, payable in the ensuing year, whenever the accumulations in the fund from special assessments or from appropriations should be insufficient to cover the damages awarded. In 1895,[4] moreover, it was enacted that any deficiency which results from charging part of the cost of opening streets and

---

[1] Laws, 1886, Chap. 680.
[2] Letter to the governor, *City Record*, 1886, p. 1417.
[3] Laws, 1888, Chap. 222.
[4] *Ibid.*, 1895, Chap. 684.

parks upon the city as a whole, may be met by consolidated stock. Nearly $800,000 of bonds were issued in 1896 under this latter provision.[1]

A minor disadvantage that has grown out of the numerous changes, during the past twenty years, in the laws governing assessments, is that there has been and still is a very considerable complication of the accounts, which renders it difficult to learn the actual receipts and payments on assessment enterprises and the state of the finances concerning them.

§ 39. *Assessment Procedure.*

Having sketched these changes in the law since 1871, we may turn to a fuller description of the present procedure.[2] The first class of assessment enterprises, whose distinguishing feature is the appropriation of private property for public use, includes not merely the opening of streets and avenues, in whole or in part, but their extension, widening, straightening, etc., and likewise the opening or altering of parks and public places. There are at present two different ways of inaugurating such an undertaking, although, as we have seen, there will be a change under the new charter. It must be begun whenever the owners of three-fourths of the land facing the proposed street or place petition for the improvement; or it may be ordered without their petition or consent

---

[1] *City Record*, 1897, p. 96.
[2] Consolidation Act. §§ 865-914, 955-1008.

by the board of street opening and improvement (the mayor, comptroller, commissioner of public works, president of the department of public parks, and president of the aldermen). In either case application is made to the supreme court of the judicial district for the appointment of three 'commissioners of estimate and assessment,' notice of the application having been first published in the *City Record* and in four other newspapers, and posted at the site of the proposed improvement. The city authorities may nominate three persons as commissioners; one of them they may specially designate and he must be chosen. Property owners interested may each make a nomination, and if they can all agree on one person he must be appointed; otherwise, the court selects one commissioner from those so proposed, and then names the third from among the entire number of nominees by the city and the property owners.

These commissioners view the lands and assess separately the loss and the benefit to each owner through the change made, considering the effect of change of grade upon the lots, etc. With regard to certain streets above 59th in every case, and with regard to all streets laid down on any legally authorized map of the city in case no buildings are taken, the assessments for benefit may not extend beyond half-way to the next street. The assessment, moreover, must never exceed one-half the taxable valuation of the property. Subject to these limitations, the board of street opening determines what proportion, if any, of the expense of the opening or alteration shall be charged to the city; in practice the board usually levies the entire cost on the property. Having made their awards and assessments, the commissioners deposit a list of them for thirty days with the department of public works, where property owners may consult it and present objections in writing or in person. Not less than ten days after this the report, with such amendments as the commissioners see fit to make, is presented to the supreme court for confirmation. If now, at this late stage, the persons interested in a majority of the awards or assessments object to further proceedings, the entire enterprise must be discontinued — an important safeguard against premature undertakings or fraudulent adjustment of the expense. Individual property owners may also appear in court and petition for changes, and if the court believes that justice so requires, it may remand the report to the same or to new commissioners for revision. On the final confirmation of the proceedings, the title to the land affected is at once vested in the city, which is allowed four months in which to pay the damages. The legal costs and commissioners' charges for street openings were formerly very large and constituted a serious abuse, but they are now restricted by close and specific provisions of statute.

The other class of assessment enterprises — local improvements — includes grading streets, laying pavements, curbs, sidewalks, and sewers, and fencing vacant lots. The ordinance of the council required for their initiation does no more than specify the general nature of the work, without limiting the expenditure, much less fixing the details. There is no provision of law, such as is found in many states, that on petition of the property owners the work may be required, nor is their consent necessary. When, however, a street has once been paved by special assessment, it may not be repaved at the expense of the abutting property owners, unless a majority of them, who also hold a majority of the front feet, petition.

When the improvement of a street has been ordered by the council, the work falls under the charge of the department of public works, except in the 23d and 24th wards, where it is managed by a special commissioner. The work is almost invariably done by contract, and as in the case of other contracts, the comptroller is present in person or by representative at the opening of bids by the department. Payments on contracts from time to time are made out of the proceeds of 'assessment bonds,' which are later redeemed from moneys collected on assessments. These may be issued for any term not exceeding ten years, but as a matter of fact are usually payable in from one to five years, the date of maturity being partly suited to the convenience of the sinking fund, which takes most of the assessment bonds as investments.

When the work of improving a street is completed, the department in charge prepares a list and diagram of the lots affected, and presents them to the board of assessors, with a certificate of the cost, and another from the comptroller stating the amount of interest on the various instalments paid to contractors, till sixty days after the date of the certificate. The board of assessors, — which is not specially chosen for each undertaking, but a permanent body of four members appointed by the commissioners of taxes and assessments, — apportions among the property owners benefited the entire cost of the improvement, including the interest, the only restriction being that the assessment shall not exceed one-half of the taxable value of the property. In practice, the assessment district is usually confined to the lots half-way to the next street. Having made the apportionment, the assessors advertise the fact that the lists are open to inspection, and those interested may appear and remonstrate within thirty days, after which the assessments are transmitted to the 'board of revision and correction of assessments' — the comptroller, corporation counsel, and recorder[1] — for final confirmation. This

[1] Under the new charter, the president of the board of local improvements will replace the recorder.

board makes changes, usually, only when objections have been raised before the assessors, and then only when taxpayers appear personally to sustain their objections. When new remonstrants appear for the first time before the board of revision, it generally first refers their claims back to the board of assessors. Remonstrances, in fact, are made regarding a considerable proportion of assessment lists, but most of the objections are ordinarily overruled.

This system of adjusting assessments, which is practically unchanged under the new charter, is criticised as unduly complicated. Although, on account of the need of condemning private property in street-opening proceedings, it may be necessary to give some control over them to the courts, it seems needless to make such a complete difference between the procedure here and that for street improvements. The assessment of damages and benefits might be made primarily by the same officers who apportion the benefits from street improvements, subject to approval of the court, which might, if it saw fit, appoint commissioners to review the lands. It would appear more logical also that the revision of assessment lists for street improvements should belong to the regular board of taxes and assessments, subject to advice by the comptroller and the department in charge, rather than to a special *ex-officio* board. In other words, this particular form of taxation might be brought into closer relation with the general tax system.

Certain provisions as to collection apply to assessments for openings and for improvements alike. They are payable, not to the receiver of taxes, but to a special bureau of the finance department charged with the collection of assessments and of arrears of both taxes and assessments. If not paid within sixty days after confirmation, they bear interest at seven per cent. There is no provision for deferred payments except in the case of openings and improvements north of 155th Street and in the 23d and 24th wards, where by a law of 1881 [1] assessments may be paid in twenty annual instalments with interest at seven per cent. While in many cities the practice of deferring assessments is allowed to some extent, this act permitting such a large number of instalments was opposed, not without reason, by the city comptroller[2] at the time of its passage, as encouraging extravagant and speculative expenditure for local improvements. Apparently, however, no serious difficulty has arisen from it, nor do many persons care to postpone payments long at such high interest. In case of the non-payment of assessments, the same procedure for enforcing collection by sale of the property obtains as with general taxes.

The outlay on assessment accounts naturally varies far more from year to year than does that

[1] Chap. 544.   [2] Comp. Rep., 1881, p. 12.

on the regular appropriation account.[1] After the enormous assessment expenditures of the period from 1869 to 1876, there was a great falling off, the amount for 1879 being only $576,369, while during the following decade they averaged about one and one-half millions yearly. Since 1890 there has been a rather marked growth in such enterprises, the largest outlay, in 1893, reaching $4,724,339; this increase is largely due to activity in opening and improving streets in the annexed territory.[2] The proportion between outlay for street openings and for street improvements varies greatly at different times. During the Ring period the former usually exceeded the latter, and for some years after that period the street openings involved nearly as large expenditures as did the improvements; but, doubtless in part from the repeal of the law allowing half their cost to be thrown on the city as a whole, opening enterprises have since fallen off materially and are usually only from a quarter to a half as extensive in amount as street improvements.

[1] See Appendix, Tables I and II, for annual expenditure and for bonds outstanding.

[2] Assessment lists received by the board of assessors from the commissioner of the annexed territory in 1892, $252,442, from the commissioner of public works, $1,267,615; in 1893, $1,651,503 and $1,242,648; and in 1894, $1,438,755 and $2,366,287, respectively. Annual Reports of Board of Assessors, *City Record*, 1893, p. 1075; 1894, p. 1001; 1895, p. 1153.

CHAPTER IX

CITY PROPERTY AND FRANCHISES

§ 40. *Importance of Revenue from Property and Franchises.*

New York city derives nearly one-fourth of her annual income from miscellaneous sources outside of taxation and special assessments. As already explained, a considerable part of these miscellaneous revenues are of such a character that their management is either largely out of the control of the financial authorities or is subject to other than financial motives. Thus the great income from excise licenses is simply incidental to the regulation of the liquor traffic, and the excise system is, moreover, now under exclusive control of state officers. More than seven millions were, however, received in 1896 from city property and franchises, and, in the management of these, revenue is something more than an incidental feature. A study of the income from these sources is the subject of this chapter. Of the various forms of property and franchise rights enjoyed by the metropolis, several of the most important — ferries, docks, markets, and real estate — had their origin, as we have seen, far back in the colonial days, when, in accordance with the custom of the time, they were granted by the central government to the municipality. No other American city was ever so favored in this regard. Indeed a large part of the soil of Manhattan island, now so immensely valuable, was once owned by the corporation under royal grants; but most of this was sold off before the middle of the present century, to meet extraordinary outlays.

In the management of municipal property and franchises, the purpose of deriving the greatest possible income for the city is by no means in every case the sole or even the paramount motive that should control; but under present conditions the success of their administration may be judged in part by the return received. There has indeed, during the past twenty years, been a conscious effort on the part of the city to build up its revenues from these sources, and though the criticism is often and justly made that the policy is still far from satisfactory, a marked advance has actually been accomplished. The rapid increase in the main classes and in the total of the revenue from property and from franchises may be seen from the following table. The growth since 1880 is specially striking.

REVENUES FROM PROPERTY AND FRANCHISES

	1830	1840	1850	1860	1870	1880	1890	1896
Rents of real estate.	$41,319	$55,064	$85,106	$65,478	$54,589	$59,023	$109,024	$92,094
Sales of real estate .	22,290	20,863	133,115	24,692	228,095	83,335	67,586	35,943
Croton water rents .	—	—	458,951	814,711	1,185,966	1,616,009	2,840,257	4,073,856
Dock rents and fees	43,790	68,174	108,483	169,309	249,099	790,752	1,482,531	2,039,015
Market rents and fees	54,095	38,405	75,876	117,944	372,076	294,666	315,290	285,392
Ferry rents	11,766	21,914	50,982	95,812	153,147	66,693	330,344	346,598
Railway and other franchises	—	—	—	—	67,000	19,462	429,476	304,529
Total . . .	$173,260	$204,420	$912,513	$1,287,946	$2,309,972	$2,929,940	$5,574,508	$7,177,427

Nearly the whole income from the sources above named is devoted to one or other of the two sinking funds, and accordingly the commissioners of the funds are given considerable power in managing some of these revenues. There is, however, no consistency in this regard. It is unfortunate in many ways that all income from every source is not turned into a single fund and placed under the control of the body which fixes the budget. By this plan a systematic policy of cultivating the city revenues would be possible.

§ 41. *City Property — its Management and Revenues.*

The Croton waterworks represent a far greater investment and yield a far greater gross revenue than any other form of city property. The inestimable value of the bountiful and wholesome water supply which they furnish cannot be measured by the money income they bring the city. The motive of rendering good water available for every citizen at a moderate cost should prevail here; a hard bargain ought not to be driven with the people, as appears to be the case in some German cities, where the waterworks are made to pay a high rate of profit. Indeed, there is much to be said in favor of the practice in some cities (*e.g.* Manchester and other English towns), where the charge for water is reduced almost to zero, and the cost of the system is chiefly borne by general tax. In New York, however, the water plant is made nearly self-supporting. Comparatively slight discretion is required in the financial management, since the consumption of water can be increased or decreased only within rather narrow limits. The rates of water rents, which are fixed by the department of public works and have been changed but little for many years, vary with the extent and character of the consumption. Meters have been introduced gradually, and are now used in determining about half the rents collected.[1] Some discretion is, of course, required in deciding what extensions of the mains shall be made from time to time; to authorize these requires a three-fourths vote of the city council, but the aggregate expenditure is limited to $250,000 yearly, and apparently the board of estimate and apportionment may restrict the appropriation as it sees fit.

The increase in the receipts from water rents was approximately uniform up to 1880, since when it has been much faster, so that they have more than doubled in fifteen years, reaching $4,073,856 in 1896. Notwithstanding the enormous capital invested in the water system, it has proved a fairly successful undertaking from the purely commercial standpoint. We may assume the original capital outlay as approximately $72,000,000, — the total amount of bonds issued since the inception of the work.[2] If from the water revenue of 1896

---

[1] Annual Report Department of Public Works, *City Record*, 1895, p. 772.   [2] See Table V, Appendix.

we deduct the $750,000 paid from the budget for running expenses of the system,[1] and perhaps $250,000 more for the salaries of officers (inseparable from the general salaries of the department of public works), we shall have approximately three millions as the receipts for the year, which would represent a little more than four per cent on the investment. At present, to be sure, the amount paid annually for interest on water bonds (about $1,600,000) and for rapidly amortizing the water debt (about $1,700,000)[2] leaves a slight yearly deficit which must be made up from taxes; but there is reason to believe that the debt charges will gradually decrease, at least in proportion to income. Should the waterworks system thus become capable of earning a clear profit above all, a reduction in rates for service would perhaps be the best policy.

Most of the upland real estate once owned by New York had been sold off before 1850, but what was then left has for the most part been retained and brings in a slowly increasing revenue, now amounting to about $100,000 yearly. Leases of real estate, like other leases of property, must be at auction, and for not more than a ten-year period. The commissioners of the sinking fund have exclusive control of this property. Another form of city property which is of decreas-

[1] Budget, 1896; *City Record*, 1896, pp. 121, 122.
[2] *Ibid.* See, also, Comp. Rep., 1896, Statement D, Part II.

ing, rather than increasing, importance is the markets, the revenue from which actually fell from $372,076 in 1870 to $285,392 in 1896. This decrease is doubtless largely due to the fact that by changes in business methods markets have come to be of less general use, but it is likewise charged that the management is somewhat loose, and that lessees of stalls from the city often relet their holdings at great advances.

Far different has been the history of the revenues from land under water and from the dock system connected with it. Although the sale of the entire water front had been often advocated, and considerable parts had been actually disposed of before 1870, yet there remained a very large proportion belonging to the city when, in that year, a definite and comprehensive policy for a system of municipal docks was adopted. The city was even authorized to buy back wharf property held by private persons, and especially for the past three or four years considerable purchases of this sort have been made.[1] No little progress has been made in the general reconstruction of the water front; fine stone piers are taking the place of the old wooden ones, and there is promise that New York will ultimately possess the best dock system in the world, all under municipal ownership. The

[1] $3,389,060 was spent for this purpose from April 30, 1892, to April 30, 1895. Annual Report of the Dock Department, *City Record*, 1895, p. 3075.

dock revenues, moreover, have increased with great rapidity, multiplying more than eightfold since the new departure of 1870. Without attempting the impossible task of estimating the entire cost of the existing docks, a rough idea of the profitableness of this property may be formed by comparing the amount invested since 1870 with the income. The total expenditure under the new system (including cost of maintenance, which is, however, not over a fifth or sixth of the whole) to April 30, 1895, was $27,224,690. The dock revenue for the year ending that date was $1,940,079, or about $7\frac{1}{2}$ per cent on the investment thus calculated. The total income from docks for twenty-five years has nearly equalled the current and capital expenditures,[1] excluding interest on bonds. When the system is finally completed so that only repairs and renewals are necessary, it promises to yield a large net return, unless some change in policy is deemed more wise. It is possible that to protect the commerce of New York from the competition of other ports, it may be best to reduce, or even wholly to abolish, dock charges, as has been done by some other cities.

By a curious and anomalous arrangement, the entire expenditures of the dock department, for current as well as permanent purposes, are met by

[1] Annual Report of the Department of Docks, *City Record*, 1895, p. 3075. The income for the calendar year 1895 was $2,084,382.

the issue of bonds, so that the department is quite independent of the control, through the budget, of the board of estimate and apportionment. Some supervision over it is, however, retained by a provision requiring the approval of general enterprises and of bond issues by the commissioners of the sinking fund, in accordance with the policy of giving that body at least a certain degree of control over the revenues pledged to the sinking funds. The dock commissioners themselves have the immediate authority to grant leases of wharf property.[1] These must be made at public auction, except in the case of certain districts set aside for special classes of traffic, — an exception which, however, applies to more than half the leases. Indeed, there can naturally be little competition in many cases, since the companies renting wharves usually construct buildings upon or near them, and for other reasons, also, are little inclined to change their location from time to time. Much room therefore remains for careful bargaining with lessees. The city collects wharfage charges directly in a few cases, but usually farms them to the lessees, though the rates are fixed by statute. Dock leases may not exceed ten years in duration, but may contain covenants for successive renewals at advancing rates up to fifty years.

The New York and Brooklyn bridge represents

[1] Consolidation Act, § 716.

an investment of about eighteen millions, two-thirds of which was paid by the latter city. The bridge has been of immense economic value to both cities, and it is a wise policy that has reduced charges for its use to a minimum. Foot passengers now cross free, and the fee for vehicles is slight, while the charge for crossing on the cable cars, which are operated directly by the bridge board, is only three cents. Notwithstanding the low charges then in force, the bridge was able to pay $320,000 to Brooklyn and $160,000 to New York in 1895, to be applied in paying interest on bridge bonds; but since then still further reductions in rates have prevented the earning of net revenue. Some persons even advocate making all forms of transit on the bridge entirely free.

§ 42. *Revenue from Franchises.*

Although the receipts from ferries are ordinarily denominated rentals, they are more properly payments for franchise privileges, since the city has invested nothing in ferry property. As judged solely by the magnitude of the revenue derived, these are the most important form of municipal franchises in New York. By the terms of the early charters the metropolis has exclusive right, as against the other cities of the state, to collect money for the privilege of ferries terminating in the city. The entire management of ferries belongs to the commissioners of the sinking fund, who must lease them on competitive bids for not over ten years at a time. There has been marked improvement in administration of the ferries during the past fifteen years. The very low amount of rents for 1880 ($66,693)[1] was, to be sure, partly explained by the fact that large sums due from the Union Ferry Company were in litigation. The most important forward step was taken in 1883 and 1884, when the practice first became common of fixing a rather large upset price for the lease, and several ten-year leases at quite high rates were made. The advantage of setting a minimum price is apparent, since — despite the provisions frequently made that the company holding the lease must agree to sell its property at an appraised price to the next successful bidder for the same franchise — the possessor of the ferry cannot but be in a superior position over all competitors. By 1890 the income from ferries had reached $330,344,[2] while in 1896 it was $346,598. The success of the leasing of the Bay Ridge and Staten island ferries in 1894 is specially noteworthy. The competition for these was strong. The upset price fixed for the former had been 5 per cent of the gross receipts, to be not less than $15,000 yearly; the actual sale was at $15,000 annually, plus $21\frac{1}{10}$ per cent of the gross receipts, that percentage to be not less than $21,000. For the latter ferry the upset price was 5 per cent of the gross receipts

---

[1] Comp. Rep., 1880, p. 15.   [2] *Ibid.*, 1890, p. 58.

plus an annual payment of $22,500, the total not to be under $44,000 per year; the sale was at 5½ per cent and a yearly payment of $22,500, with the same required total.[1] It is probable that these percentages will in a few years exceed the minimum total amounts prescribed. As the income from these two ferries in 1892 under the previous leases was $23,476 and $28,709 respectively,[2] it will be seen that the new arrangement represents a very much higher return to the city.

The rates of ferriage are for the most part fixed, or at least limited, by law, and it is possible that, by a policy similar to that which has reduced the charges for the use of the East river bridge, the attempt should be made to lower ferry charges rather than to increase the return to the city. In any case the growing competition of the bridge traffic, especially when the second East river bridge and ultimately perhaps the proposed North river bridge are completed, will probably cut into the income of companies and city from ferries.

Partly, doubtless, because of the corruption that has been so prominent in connection with them, street railway franchises have attracted far greater attention in New York than other franchises or city properties, and the granting of them has come to be regulated by laws designed to remedy the former abuses. Although the operation of these

---

[1] *City Record*, 1894, p. 1768; Comp. Rep., 1894, pp. 192-194.
[2] Comp. Rep., 1892, p. 195.

laws can scarcely be said to have proved entirely successful, New York now receives far greater income from railways than any other American city. The new charter of 1897 has gone much further in the direction of controlling the disposal of franchises, of all sorts; but the people of New York in general have hardly as yet begun to realize that other franchises besides railways ought to yield a large revenue.

Though the Harlem railway was built as early as 1830, under a special act of the legislature, it was not till twenty years later that other railway franchises were granted. Five important lines were chartered during the fifties by the corrupt common council, with no compensation to the city.[1] The receipts of these — the Second, Third, Sixth, Eighth, and Ninth avenue lines — are probably nearly half the total received by all surface roads;[2] yet from them (except in the case of certain extensions built under the law of 1884) the city receives nothing save a small amount from car license fees, — $50 for each car, — and even the payment of these was long contested. Two of these early charters nevertheless contained provisions allowing the city to take the roads at their actual cost after a

---

[1] See *ante*, p. 71. Much of what follows is based on a communication from the comptroller of the city in New York Senate Documents, 1886, No. 40; also in *City Record*, 1886, p. 425.

[2] Precise amounts not obtainable because three lines are merged with the Metropolitan Street Railway Company. See *post*, p. 241.

certain time, and during the present year the plan of taking advantage of this provision has been actively urged, but it is not likely that it will be carried out.

The legislature in 1860 took away from the council the right to sanction further street railways, and itself granted six franchises [1] during that year and 1863, without provision for payment to the city; although in the case of two of the roads later laws allowing extensions required some small return — five per cent on the net receipts from the extension in one case, one per cent on the entire gross receipts in the other. Another charter in 1868 provided for the payment of $1000 per annum.[2] In 1869 and the first years of the seventies the legislature adopted a somewhat better policy. One franchise was granted to be sold at auction, and the city received $150,000 for it.[3] Three others were given without competition, but three per cent of the gross receipts were to be paid to

---

[1] Dry Dock, E. Broadway and Battery, Laws, 1860, Chap. 512, — five per cent required in 1866, Chap. 883; Bleecker St. and Fulton Ferry, 1860, Chap. 514, — one per cent required in 1873, Chap. 647; 42d St. and Grand St. Ferry, 1860, Chap. 515; Central Park, North and East River, 1860, Chap. 511; Harlem Bridge, Morrisania and Fordham (now merged in Union Railway Company), 1863, Chap. 361; Broadway and Seventh Ave. Some other charters were granted in 1860 and at other times, but this account regards only roads in actual operation in 1896.

[2] Houston St., West St. and Pavonia Ferry, Laws, 1868, Chap. 625.

[3] 23d St. Railway, Laws, 1869, Chap. 823.

the city.[1] The injustice of allowing the legislature thus to dispose of rights properly subject to local control led to the adoption of a constitutional amendment in 1875,[2] prohibiting all special legislation relating to street railways. The amendment, further, required the consent of the local governing body for the construction of each line, and, moreover, that of the owners of half in value of the property bounded upon, or in default thereof an order of court based on the report of three commissioners declaring that in their opinion the road ought to be built. No general law regulating street railways was, however, passed by the legislature, nor were any franchises granted in the metropolis, till 1884, when an act was passed,[3] one of whose provisions required payment to the city of not less than three per cent of the gross receipts for the first five years and five per cent thereafter. The local authorities might at discretion also provide for auction sale subject to these minimum terms. It was further required that before granting any franchise a public hearing of those interested must be held, after duly advertised notice of two weeks.

It was under this law that the famous Broadway Railway franchise was granted. Over the mayor's

---

[1] Central Crosstown, Laws, 1873, Chap. 160; Christopher and 10th St., *ibid.*, Chap. 301; 42d St., Manhattanville and St. Nicholas Ave., *ibid.*, Chap. 825.

[2] Constitution of 1846, Art. 3, § 18.   [3] Laws, 1884, Chap. 252.

veto, the council at first bestowed the privilege at the minimum terms of law, despite the fact that another company had offered a million dollars for the grant. The road, however, had some difficulty in securing connections and consent of property owners, — partly owing to the strong popular feeling, — so that it finally applied for a new charter. The council passed another ordinance, also over the mayor's veto, but this time it demanded an annual payment of $40,000 in addition to the legal requirement. Though these terms were more liberal, enormous corruption was required to secure the franchise. Later on, a large number of aldermen were indicted, and it was proved that $20,000 each had been paid to nearly every member for his vote. Nevertheless, during this same year and the two following, the city council continued to pass numerous ordinances authorizing railways, and corruption was frequently suspected.[1] Mayor Grace, however, who took advanced ground in favor of a better system, vetoed most of these ordinances, while, in the case of the half dozen passed over his vetoes, the railways were actually constructed in only three instances, and one of these is not now in operation.[2] Neither of the roads operating pays more than the minimum required by law.

[1] Compiled from Proceedings of Aldermen. The Cable Railway franchise, which was vetoed, was specially condemned.

[2] 42d St., Manhattanville and St. Nicholas Ave., and 34th St. railways are operating.

It was with a view to checking further abuse that a law was secured in 1886,[1] which prescribed that all railway franchises must be sold at auction to the bidder offering the highest percentage of gross receipts, in no case to be less than the three or five per cent minimum previously fixed. While this act, which is still in force, marks some advance over the earlier practice, it has quite failed to accomplish the desired end. In fact, it is coming gradually to be understood that street railways tend almost inevitably to consolidation, and that competition for new franchises is almost impossible. Especially within the past few years, a large majority of the numerous lines in New York have been united into the Metropolitan Street Railway Company, against which practically the only competitor for traffic or for new franchises is the Third Avenue company. For an independent company to attempt to establish a road, without the coöperation and the connections of one or the other of these great systems, would be foolhardy indeed. Accordingly, there has been little competition for the seven or eight franchises for new lines granted since 1886;[2] and in the cases where the percent-

---

[1] Laws, 1886, Chap. 642. Revised by Laws, 1890, Chap. 565.

[2] The following are the chief grants for new roads: Fulton St., Grand St. Ferry, and Metropolitan lines at the 3 per cent and 5 per cent minimum; North and East River at $\frac{1}{2}$ per cent more than the minimum; Columbus and Ninth Ave. at $\frac{1}{4}$ per cent, Lexington Ave. and Pavonia Ferry at $\frac{1}{2}$ per cent, Metropolitan Crosstown at 1 per cent, and Third Ave. extension at $38\frac{1}{2}$ per cent more than the minimum.

age offered by the successful bidder has exceeded the minimum fixed by law, it has been by only from one-eighth of one per cent to one per cent, except in the single instance when, in 1894, the Metropolitan and the Third Avenue companies came into direct competition for the control of a system in the suburban district. In this case, jealousy perhaps carried the bids beyond reasonable limits, and the latter company finally agreed to pay a cash bonus of $250,000, besides no less than $38\frac{1}{2}$ per cent of the receipts in addition to the minimum of 3-5 per cent prescribed by statute. This line is, however, still in process of building, and no return has yet been received from it. A specially noteworthy feature of this grant was that, contrary to the usual practice, the city council fixed as a pre-condition that the successful bidder must pay at least two per cent more than the legal minimum, and a bonus of $250,000. Aside from the various franchises granted under the act of 1886, that of the Union Railway Company, which operates in the annexed territory, was bestowed in 1892 by a special act of the legislature.[1] At present, this road pays nothing whatever to the city, but when its receipts reach $1700 a day, it will pay one per cent upon them.

Besides these new roads, less important extensions have been authorized from time to time, on most of whose receipts only the lowest allowable

[1] Laws, 1892, Chap. 340.

percentage is paid to the city. Of the railways bearing separate names in actual operation in New York — disregarding for the moment the fact that most of them are now united, which makes no change in the obligations of the separate parts to the city — ten pay to the city nothing on their original lines except car license fees, though one of these paid at the outset a bonus of $150,000; one pays $1000 yearly; while fourteen pay percentages of from one to six per cent on their gross receipts.[1] In the case of the Broadway and Seventh Avenue Railroad, the successor of the Broadway Railway, an ordinance of 1889, in return for added privileges, prescribed that the minimum yearly payment of five per cent should be not less than $150,000, and this large sum constituted almost half of the total receipts from railways last year. All the other roads combined paid about $105,000 as percentages and $47,000 as car license fees in 1896.

Bitter as have been the complaints over the insufficiency of the return which has been received for the immense privileges conferred on street railways in the metropolis, New York has on the whole been more fortunate in this regard than almost any other American city, except perhaps Philadelphia, St. Louis, and Baltimore. Several of our great cities receive practically nothing from railways. Never-

[1] See Comp. Rep., 1896, table of railway franchises, comparing summary above given.

theless, the percentages paid by the New York companies are utterly inadequate, so long as fares remain at the present rates. The gross receipts of the surface roads in 1896 were nearly $15,000,000,[1] so that the amount paid to the city was barely two per cent on the average. Evidently we could fully appreciate the insufficiency of this return only by knowing accurately the rate of profit that the corporations are deriving on the amount of capital actually invested. It is generally conceded that the securities of the companies are very heavily 'watered'; though the precise amount of overcapitalization is naturally impossible to ascertain, those most familiar with the subject are convinced that, on the average, the surface railways yield probably between 20 and 30 per cent on their real cost, if not even more. Mayor Grace, in vetoing the franchise of the Cable Railway in 1886, stated that in 1884 the capital of the surface railways in operation was $15,707,153, their bonded debt $11,266,665; that in that year $14\frac{1}{2}$ per cent dividends on the average had been paid on the capital and 6.8 per cent interest on the bonds. He declared it more than a fair assumption "to place the actual cost of their construction and equipment at the aggregate of their bonded indebtedness"; so that on this basis the dividends and interest paid would represent

[1] Compiled from Railroad Commissioners' Annual Report, 1895-6.

a return of 27 per cent on the *bona fide* investment.[1]

If the over-capitalization were such in 1884, the consolidations that have taken place since that day have been made the occasion of still greater watering. The Metropolitan Street Railway Company now includes or controls more than twenty lines which six or eight years ago were practically independent, but which, by a complicated series of sales, consolidations, leases, and re-leases, have been united into the greatest street railway system in the world.[2] In 1892, fifteen of these companies — the most important ones — had a capital and bonded debt of about $21,000,000 on a trackage of 142 miles, a little less than $150,000 per mile of single track.[3] In 1895–6, the Metropolitan company, which then comprised these fifteen lines only,

---

[1] Message, *City Record*, 1886, p. 720. Strong, though hardly specific, statements as to 'watering' are made in the report of the special legislative committee on Municipal Ownership, Assembly Documents, 1896, No. 53.

[2] These are: Houston St., West St. and Pavonia Ferry; Chambers and Grand St.; Broadway Surface; Broadway and Seventh Ave.; Metropolitan Crosstown; Ninth Ave.; Sixth Ave.; 23d St.; Bleecker St. and Fulton Ferry; Central Park, North and East River; 42d St. and Grand St. Ferry; Eighth Ave.; Lexington Ave. and Pavonia Ferry; Columbus and Ninth Aves.; Fulton St.; New York and Harlem; 34th St.; 34th St. and Eleventh Ave.; Christopher and 10th Sts.; Central Crosstown. See Report of Railroad Commissioners, 1895–6, and manuscript records in commissioners' office.

[3] Compiled from Railroad Commissioners' reports.

R

had increased the capitalization, — counting, as must properly be done, that of leased lines represented by rentals paid, — to $51,000,000; while the track operated had increased only to 171 miles, the average capital being thus $300,000 per mile. Since 1895 the capitalization has been raised to more than $65,000,000, the amount per mile remaining about the same.[1] There can be no doubt that this represents vastly more than the real cost of the lines. An expert has recently testified that the average cost of constructing a street railway (if built with double tracks, as are most in New York) on asphalt pavement is about $16,000 per mile of single track, and this includes the overhead trolley fixtures.[2] While the cost would naturally be higher in New York, and while the cable system, which is being largely introduced by the Metropolitan company, is more expensive, there is little question that from $50,000 to $100,000 per mile would cover amply the actual cost of the lines of the company, including their rolling stock and power plant, and that the greater part of the immense additions to the capitalization of the system since 1892 is pure 'water.'

Yet vast as is the capital of the Metropolitan, it is managing to pay a very respectable rate of interest on the whole. The net earnings for 1895–6 (taxes deducted) were $3,538,397, or

[1] More complete figures have not yet been published.
[2] Assembly Documents, 1896, No. 53.

almost seven per cent on the entire amount of securities then outstanding. The system of leasing lines and paying dividends on their capital is perhaps intended partly to blind the public as to the real rate of profit. The distribution of the net income of the company to various forms of capital was as follows : —

Interest on $9,400,000 bonds	$357,500 or 3.9 %
Dividends on $16,500,000 stock	1,252,500 or 7.65 %
Rentals on $25,634,000 securities of leased roads	1,714,049 or 6.68 %
Surplus	214,347
	$3,538,397

These figures help us to appreciate the utter insufficiency of the payments, properly designated as being in return for their franchise privileges, made to the city by street railways. It is a matter of some little importance that these railways are at least compelled to contribute a fair proportion to the general taxes. The assessment of tracks, as real estate was first attempted in 1879, and after some litigation was upheld by the courts,[1] while a law of 1881 specially authorized their assessment in this manner.[2] About the same time too the personal assessments of the companies were considerably increased. In the case of all

[1] People, *ex rel.*, N. Y. El. R. R. Co. *v.* Comrs. of Taxes, 82 N. Y. 459.

[2] Laws, 1881, Chap. 293.

the surface railways except the Broadway line, the aggregate taxes of both classes are now much more each year than the amount paid for franchise and license fees.[1] However, as all other property in the city, though it does not receive its value specially from municipal gift, has likewise to pay taxes, it is by no means just to reckon these taxes, which indeed are assessed on much less than the true value of the property, as in any sense a payment for the special privileges of the railways.

The elevated railways of New York at present pay nothing to the city except ordinary taxes. The Greenwich Street line, which was the first constructed, was required by its charter, granted by the state legislature in 1867,[2] to pay five per cent of its net receipts to the city, to be used in improving the appearance of the elevated structures and of the streets in which they stood. The percentage continued to be paid till 1890, and for some years before that time amounted to $20,526 yearly;[3] but since then the consolidated company has refused payment on this part of its lines, and the matter is dragging through litigation. The New York Elevated Railway Company, chartered by the legislature in 1871, succeeded to the possession of this original road, but it also vastly extended the

---

[1] From figures in the manuscript tax books of 1895. The Third Ave. line, which pays far the most, paid $17,807 of real, and $5183 of personal, taxes in 1895.

[2] Laws, 1867, Chap. 489.   [3] Comp. Rep., 1891, p. 33.

system, and on the added mileage never paid compensation. The same is true of the lines of the Metropolitan Elevated Railway Company. The constitutional provision of 1875 regarding street railways did not extend to elevated roads, and in the same year the legislature passed a general 'rapid transit' act,[1] which, while it requires the consent of special court commissioners for building structures, does not provide for the consent of property owners or for compensation to the municipality. All the elevated roads in the city have now, following the inevitable tendency which we saw regarding the surface lines, become consolidated into the Manhattan company, whose gross earnings are almost equal to those of all the surface roads combined. The over-capitalization of this company is probably fully as excessive as is that of the surface lines. It pays about six per cent annually on $76,596,000 of stock and bonds,[2] although, owing to the growing competition of the cable roads, it has been compelled of late to cut somewhat into its surplus to keep up its dividends. Fortunately the taxes on the elevated structures as real estate, which began at the same time as those on the surface tracks, have been relatively more important than the latter.[3] The company also pays large personal

---

[1] Laws, 1875, Chap. 606.

[2] Annual Report of the Railroad Commissioners, New York Senate Documents, 1895, No. 10, p. 716.

[3] Manuscript tax records.

taxes, the amount of both classes in 1895 being more than half a million dollars. The taxes for 1896, however, were contested by the company on the ground that the assessment, which amounts to less than half the capital of the lines, is more than the value of the road, and the courts have granted some reduction.

The policy of the city regarding lighting, steam heating, telephone, and similar franchises has hitherto been even less rational than that regarding railways. The private companies, which have entire control of all these enterprises, have never, with one exception, paid any compensation worthy of the name for their privileges.[1] In general only a nominal sum is required for each foot of street opened — three cents a foot in most cases. The Equitable Gaslight Company, however, whose charter was granted in 1883, up to 1894 paid a fair percentage of its gross receipts, the amount received by the city in that year being $18,690;[2] but here again some pretence for ceasing payment has since been devised. The charges for gas and electric lights in New York are high, and the profits of the companies on largely watered stock are great. The same powerful tendency to combination appears as with railways. A legislative committee in 1886[3] investigated the Consolidated Gas

---

[1] In 1894 the total from all, except the Equitable Company, was only $2177. Comp. Rep., pp. 21, 36.   [2] Ibid., p. 23.

[3] Report of Special Committee, New York Senate Documents. 1886, No. 47.

Company, which had been formed by the union of the New York, Manhattan, Metropolitan, Municipal, Knickerbocker, and Harlem companies; and declared that the capital of the original companies, $17,000,000, had been increased to $39,078,000 by the combination, without the addition of a single dollar of real investment, but, on the contrary, with the removal of over $2,000,000 of assets. The true value of the plants was estimated at $15,000,000 to $20,000,000. The price of gas in New York at that time was $1.75 per thousand, while in the case of many English cities, both with municipal and with private plants, the price is only from 60 to 75 cents per thousand. As a result of this investigation, a law was passed fixing the charge in the metropolis at $1.25. In 1897 a strenuous effort was made to secure a further immediate reduction to one dollar, but the bill was amended to provide that the price should be lowered five cents each year till that figure should be reached. The price of electric current has not been regulated by statute.

Fortunately there has been in the past few years a rapid growth of public opinion in favor of a more rational system of managing municipal franchises, and this has actually had some practical effect. The experience of foreign cities with railways and lighting plants, and especially the success of municipal ownership of these enterprises, has been largely cited by the advocates of reform. In Berlin, for instance, the consolidated railway company, besides having made large cash payments for the original franchises, pays 8½ per cent of its gross receipts, reimburses the city for paving and cleaning between its tracks, and in 1911 the entire system will become the property of the city without cost. In many other continental cities a similar provision for reversion of the tracks to the public exists. The absurd practice of granting perpetual franchises is almost unknown. The same is true in Great Britain. Manchester, Birmingham, and a large number of other cities own the tracks and lease them to private companies at very favorable terms; while half a dozen or more cities, the most important being Glasgow and Bradford, actually operate the systems by municipal employees, and with marked success. There is no doubt, moreover, that the usual European custom of proportioning street-car fares roughly to the distance travelled, results in a considerably lower average rate than the ordinary American five-cent fare. The lowest charge is usually two or two and a half cents, — though in some cases even less, — the highest seldom over five or six cents. Many of the English cities likewise own and operate great lighting plants, and, though furnishing service at rates much lower than are common here, succeed in earning a handsome net revenue.[1] So, too, most

---

[1] See Dr. Shaw's *Municipal Government in Great Britain*, and *Municipal Government in Continental Europe*.

German cities own their gas works. Their aim, however, seems rather to gain large profits than to furnish cheap light,—the price ranging from $1 to $1.50 per thousand.[1] Berlin earned a net return, after paying debt charges, of nearly a million dollars in 1893.

One indication of the progress of the movement toward more economical management of municipal franchises is found in the fact that the recent acts authorizing the construction of the great underground Rapid Transit system, now so much needed, have provided that the city may itself build and own the road, if it chooses to do so, although it must in that case be operated by lease to a private company. The enterprise is so vast that private capital has so far hesitated to undertake it, and it is likely that the system will actually be constructed at public expense. General sentiment appears to be favorable to this plan; but its fulfilment was temporarily checked last year by a court decision refusing to approve the propositions of the rapid transit commissioners, on the ground that the loans required for the work would carry the city debt beyond the constitutional limit. Though, in view of the rapid growth of the sinking fund, it is doubtful whether this fear was justified, yet the decision has probably had the desirable effect of compelling more careful consideration and the device of a more economical plan. The provisions

[1] See Statistisches Jahrbuch der Deutschen Städte, 1896.

of law for recompense to the city from the private company, whether it owns or merely operates the plant, are somewhat indefinite, considerable discretion being left to the rapid transit commissioners. In case the company is allowed to own the road, its franchise must not be perpetual, but no definite limit is set. If the company operates the city's plant, its lease may be for not less than thirty-five nor more than fifty years; and it must pay the interest on the bonds issued by the city for the enterprise, together with at least one per cent yearly on the cost, to be used for sinking the debt. The minimum terms thus fixed are considerably less than should be those finally demanded by the commissioners.

The Greater New York charter has sought reform regarding the disposal of franchises in two directions, — by placing additional checks on the grant itself, and by restricting the period for which the franchise may run. Hereafter every ordinance which confers a privilege involving the use of public streets or places must, after its introduction into the municipal assembly, be referred to the board of estimate and apportionment, which shall investigate as to the proper compensation to be paid; and the ordinance, which requires also a three-fourths vote of the assembly, cannot be passed except upon the terms fixed by the smaller body. If the mayor interpose his veto, a five-sixths vote is necessary to pass the ordinance.

The grant may not be for a longer period than twenty-five years, but may provide for renewals thereafter, from time to time, at a revaluation, for an aggregate of twenty-five years more. The ordinance may also prescribe that any plant established by the grantees of a franchise shall become the property of the city at the close of the term, either without further compensation or at an appraised valuation ; and property so acquired may be leased or operated by the city itself. These regulations apparently will not apply to ferry and dock leases.

These provisions, which mark a great advance over any law on the subject yet adopted in this country, with perhaps one or two exceptions, leave it discretionary with the city to prescribe any terms for franchises it sees fit ; and it is to be hoped that the growing popular sentiment will no longer be satisfied with the insufficient compensation which, under the present system of auction without real competition, has usually been received. Even if, in some cases, it seems wise to continue the competitive plan, proper minimum terms may be set for the grant. The most satisfactory change introduced by the new charter is that it does away with the evil practice of bestowing perpetual franchises. It is a fair question whether law and justice will not permit at some time the demand by the city from companies holding old grants of some more reasonable compensation than they are now making. Of course it is a matter of expediency whether public regulation, in regard to franchises both heretofore and hereafter granted, should most wisely demand greater payments to the city or lower rates and better service for the people.

CHAPTER X

THE BUDGET AND CITY EXPENDITURES

HAVING now considered the various heads of city income, we turn to city expenditures for current purposes. We have already studied, or shall later on study, the control and nature of expenditures on special assessment and sinking fund accounts, so that we may now confine ourselves for the most part to those expenditures which compose what is technically known as the budget. We need especially to consider the method and motives by which such expenditures are determined; that is, to consider the budget system. Afterward we may make a less detailed study of the items of expenditure themselves, and of the progress of expenditures during the recent period of financial history.

§ 43. *Outline of the Budget System.*

The board of estimate and apportionment, which, up to the Greater New York charter, has had practically exclusive control over the city budget, was composed, under the law of 1873, of the mayor, comptroller, president of the department of taxes and assessments, and president of the aldermen. To this board, perhaps with a view to making a majority less difficult to secure, the counsel to the corporation has recently been added.[1] He was possibly preferred for this position above other executive officers, because his own department has less to do than most with spending the money appropriated, while his opinion on legal questions and technicalities connected with the budget is also of value.

The board of estimate is required, under the charter of 1873, to make annually, on or before November 1, a provisional budget for the ensuing year, the extent to which the estimates shall enter into detail being left to its own decision. The vote of all the members is necessary to fix the gross amount of this provisional estimate, as well as that of the final one, although in each case a majority vote is sufficient to act on details. The provisional budget is based on departmental estimates, presented in duplicate to the board of estimate and to the aldermen; these are exceedingly minute, giving the salaries of each officer or employee, and the specific purpose of each expenditure. In practice the department heads explain somewhat fully the ground of each demand for increase of appropriation. The provisional estimate, as fixed by the board of estimate, with their reasons for it in detail, is submitted to the council, and simultaneously published for general information in the *City Record*. The board of aldermen must hold a special meeting

[1] Laws, 1893, Chap. 106.

to consider the appropriations. As in every action involving expenditure of money, a three-fourths vote of the members elected is required to make any change in the budget.[1] Within fifteen days the aldermen must return the budget to the smaller body, with a statement of their objections or rectifications. After this, by a provision added to the law in 1880,[2] the board of estimate must set a special time for hearing the opinions of taxpayers on the appropriations. In deciding on the final budget, which is usually voted on the last day of the year, the board must nominally consider the suggestions of the aldermen, and should it overrule them must publish its reasons for doing so in the *City Record*. As we shall see, the real influence of the council in the appropriations has been infinitesimal.

The expenditure side of the budget being thus determined, little discretion is required in providing for the receipts. As is the case in almost all our local governments, the one great source of revenue is the general property tax; there is no place accordingly for that careful deliberation as to ways and means which is customary in many national budgets, and which is coming gradually to find entrance into those of our states. New York indeed, more than any other American city, has considerable outside revenues, but by far the greater part of these are devoted to the sinking fund, and are managed quite independently of the

---

[1] Consolidation Act, § 74. [2] Laws, 1880, Chap. 521.

annual budgets. There are, however, a number of minor receipts which, as the 'general fund,' go to lower taxes, the most important of these being from interest on taxes and assessments, sales of old material, etc., and school moneys[1] contributed by the state. According to the terms of the charter the amount of the general fund, usually about $2,000,000, is to be estimated by the comptroller and reported directly to the aldermen.[2] In practice, however, the board of estimate and apportionment definitely decides how much shall be deducted from the tax levy on this score. The actual levying of the necessary taxes, to cover the remainder of the appropriations, must be by the city council, but its action in this regard is purely ministerial.

By another of the many complications in the financial system, the income from liquor and theatrical licenses does not go into the regular budget, but part of it must be separately appropriated by the board of estimate to various charitable institutions, part goes without vote to the police and firemen's pension funds, while a considerable balance is usually left for transfer to the general fund.

A further anomalous division of appropriating authority exists in the dock department, where it was first introduced by the charter of 1870. This

---

[1] Although these are in a sense income, the share paid by the city toward state school taxes is considerably greater than the amount received back.   [2] Consolidation Act, § 829.

is a provision that *all* expenditures of the department must be met by the issue of bonds. The practice is proper enough as regards permanent improvements of the dock system, but no possible justification exists for meeting, out of thirty-year bonds, the cost of ordinary repairs and running expenses, — salaries, cleaning, etc., — nor for removing the control of these expenditures from the regular appropriating board, as is done by placing the entire authority to issue dock bonds in the sinking fund commissioners. The anomaly is perhaps partly explained by the fact that the income from docks goes to the sinking fund, whose commissioners thus are interested in their management.

The Greater New York charter has retained this general budget system with only one important amendment. Hereafter there is to be no reconsideration of the appropriations by the board of estimate and apportionment after the city council has acted upon them. The present 'provisional budget' will become the final apportionment, except in so far as the municipal assembly, by a three-fourths vote, shall decrease the amounts fixed by the smaller board, the assembly having no power to increase any item. In considering the budget, the two houses of the council will meet in joint session, and they must complete their work within fifteen days. If the mayor disapprove any reduction made by the council, a five-sixths vote is necessary to override his veto. This new feature of the charter will thus give the city council absolute power, within limits, in fixing the city appropriations, instead of the merely advisory authority which it now possesses and which is, in fact, quite meaningless.

§ 44. *Absence of Power in the Common Council. Fixed Appropriations.*

If indeed we consider how the system just outlined operates in practice, and what influences actually determine the appropriations, we may at once eliminate the board of aldermen as a factor in the problem. While the existing law gives it only advisory power, it might easily happen — were the council generally respected and in other regards powerful — that its advice should be of very decided weight. But such not being the case, the board of estimate and apportionment has come to pay no heed to the action of the aldermen. Not only are their suggested 'rectifications' overruled in the final budget, but great changes are made from the provisional estimates regarding items which they have not acted upon, and new items even are often inserted. This seems clearly contrary to the spirit of the charter of 1873, which mentioned no further procedure by the board of estimate regarding the final estimate than the possible rejection of the changes of the aldermen. The common council itself has so interpreted the law, and has bitterly but vainly protested against any modification except as to such items[1] as it should have specially acted upon. But that the legislature was willing to allow the practical disregard of this provision may perhaps be inferred from the passage by that body of the amendment allowing the hearing of citizens concerning the budget *after* the action of the council.

It has been almost invariably the tendency of the aldermen, as might be expected from their general character, to increase the appropriations of the provisional estimate; from the table in the appendix[2] it will be seen that up to 1888 they added on the average about half a million annually to the total. The fact that the final estimate often exceeds the budget as revised by the aldermen might, on the surface, indicate that their additions had been concurred in by the board of estimate and apportionment; but in fact nearly every one of the 'rectifications' has always been overruled, and the increases have been made quite independently of their suggestions, for the most part in other items. Often the council's amendments have been rejected as a body; more frequently the most of them have been rejected and one or at best a few items approved in whole or in part.[3] The absence of serious consideration of the

[1] Proceedings of the Aldermen, vol. 180 (1886), p. 991.
[2] See Table IV, p. 376.
[3] *City Record*, 1878, p. 10; 1879, p. 13; 1884, p. 48; 1885, p. 18.

action of the aldermen is seen in the meaningless nature of the 'reasons' assigned by the board of estimate, as required by law, for overruling it, such as that the "increase is not necessary," or that "the appropriation in the provisional estimate is deemed sufficient."[1] The reasons given to the aldermen for the provisional appropriations themselves are quite as little justifications of them, consisting ordinarily in mere statements of the amounts requested by the department and the amounts allowed, which, it is explained, are "deemed to be sufficient."

The common council has naturally come to take less and less interest in the exercise of its merely formal authority over the city purse-strings. With rare exceptions, only a single brief session is devoted to the budget, unless, indeed, an adjourned meeting is necessary on account of a lack of the required quorum of three-fourths — as has happened several times of late years.[2] The changes proposed have grown steadily fewer and smaller. Since 1890,[3] the largest increase in the total budget proposed by the council in any year has been $131,000, of which $125,000 was for free baths — a favorite object of that body. In 1895, indeed, no definite amendment whatever was made, although the council recommended that the appropriation for the register's office be not unduly cut

---

[1] *E.g., City Record*, 1884, p. 48.
[2] *City Record*, 1889, p. 3651; 1891, p. 3491; 1892, p. 3447.
[3] Consult *City Record* index, November each year.

down. Last year the action of the aldermen on the budget for 1897 was possibly even more ludicrous; they increased the total of over forty-five millions by $1200 for an additional stenographer for their own body. It remains to be seen whether the new power, given under the charter of 1897, will prove equally futile.

The board of estimate and apportionment, then, is practically unhampered by the aldermen, but this by no means signifies that it alone has absolute control of the budget. All the charges for state taxes, interest, and debt redemption are fixed, and specific law compels their insertion.[1] These three are the largest and the most fixed of the required appropriations, but there are many others. A large sum goes to the many private charitable institutions, to which the legislature has required the city to contribute definite amounts annually. The number and salaries of all the department heads, and of their leading subordinates, of judges and officers of the city courts, are established by statute. Both the number and the salaries of the police force are prescribed, as is[2] the pay, though not the number, of the fire department. In 1886 Mayor Grace showed, in detail, that almost exactly three-fifths of the appropriations were practically out of the control of the board.[3] A somewhat

---

[1] Consolidation Act, § 194.   [2] *Ibid.*, §§ 265, 287.
[3] Message, *City Record*, 1886, p. 21. Some corrections in the figures are necessary, but the proportion is about as given. The

less, but still very considerable, proportion holds at present.

The board of estimate and apportionment often points to the amount of fixed appropriations as an explanation of the large budgets, and complains of its own weakness. Of course, precisely in so far as these required charges in fact vary from year to year, and are really responsible for fluctuations in the gross budget, this point is justifiable, but it has sometimes been urged unfairly. In fact, the board has control of practically all expenditures which can properly be subject to discretionary action from year to year. There is always in the budget of any political body a distinction, more or less clear, between appropriations that are fixed and recurrent, and those which can more readily be reduced or increased. While it would be desirable that the organization of the departments, the fixing of salaries, the determination of the number and compensation of policemen, firemen, etc., should be matters of home rule, rather than of often ill-considered legislative action, yet all

most important of the fixed appropriations which he named were: —

Interest	$7,401,300.80
Redemption	779,580.76
State taxes	4,183,708.46
Police department	3,671,792.10
Fire department	1,293,100.00
Judiciary	1,006,050.00
Charitable institutions	1,094,002.40

these might properly be prescribed by permanent ordinance, and not left open to annual changes at the time of voting the budget. Debt payments and state taxes certainly could not be changed at will, however independent were the board of estimate. There is ample opportunity, in the two-fifths of the budget where the expenditures are not fixed, for that body to show its economy and appreciation of respective needs.

In addition to these recurrent fixed sums, no year passes in which the legislature does not require the city to appropriate money for special purposes. Various public works are made mandatory, and, not infrequently, more or less doubtful claims upon the treasury are enforced by legislative act. Judgments against the city must, of course, also be paid. But these special items are, at present, seldom of large amount.

Besides the positive requirements of law regarding the budget, there are a number of limitations and prohibitions, which are, however, of less importance. Thus the city may not appropriate moneys to sectarian schools or, without legislative act, to a private institution of any sort not receiving its aid in 1874; the amount to be paid on the appropriation account in any year for street repaving is limited to $500,000, and that for laying new water mains to $250,000; and there are a number of minor restrictions.[1]

[1] Consolidation Act, §§ 194, 195.

In both its commands and its prohibitions regarding the expenditures of the city, the Greater New York charter varies little in principle from the previous law.

§ 45. *Procedure of the Board of Estimate and Apportionment.*

If the aldermen have heretofore given but a single session annually to the appropriations, it cannot be charged that the board of estimate bestows on them equally little study. To be sure, less time is perhaps devoted to the budget than a foreign parliament or the legislature of one of our states (counting in the committee work) would give to considering appropriations correspondingly large; but the margin of discretionary action is probably narrower in the city, and besides a compact board can act more rapidly than a large body. Taking at random three cases: on the budget of 1888, eight sessions of the board were devoted to the provisional, nine to the final estimate; on that of 1891, eleven to the former, and fifteen to the latter; on that of 1894, five and eight, respectively.[1] The sessions usually begin at 2 P.M.

Before the board begins its work, a preliminary study of the departmental estimates is made by the comptroller; and an outline budget, comparing the demands of the departments with the sums allowed in the preceding year, is prepared. The comptroller, in fact, being more familiar than his

[1] Compiled from *City Record.*

colleagues with the financial affairs of the city, has in many respects a rather preponderant influence in the board. The various department heads, naturally enough, request usually in their estimates somewhat larger sums than they can possibly hope to secure. They then appear before the board in person to explain the purpose of increases sought, and to hinder as far as possible reductions in their estimates. The final budget usually appropriates from one to five millions less than the departments demand. In recent years the reductions made by the board of estimate have been usually larger than before, but their amount has fluctuated less than formerly.[1]

As has been already said, the board of estimate has felt itself little bound by the provisional budget in fixing the final one. More and more the real work of considering the appropriations has been deferred till the December sessions; in fact, the provisional budget has come to serve almost no real purpose except to compel a prompt beginning. This disregard of the evident intention of the law was not indeed wholly undesirable, although, as we shall see, there have been abuses connected with it. Budgets of other financial powers are often not voted till the very last moment — sometimes during the year for which they are intended.

[1] See Table IV, Appendix. The wide difference in 1886 was due to quite exceptional conditions; it was supposed that many expenditures for permanent improvements would have to be met from taxes instead of from bonds.

During the two months between the adoption of the estimates, new needs, often new necessities, or new opportunities for retrenchment, naturally appear. For the first few years (1875 to 1878) of the present budget system, the gradual weeding out of the wasteful features left from the Ring period enabled reductions in the final as compared with the provisional estimate. Since then the final estimate has, with three exceptions (1886, 1890,[1] 1892) due to peculiar circumstances, been larger than the other by sums ranging up to over four millions in the budget of 1897, but oftener more nearly half a million.

The appropriations as voted in December are frequently not exactly the same as the ultimate appropriations.[2] After the adoption of the final

---

[1] The marked decrease in 1890 was not due to economy, but connects itself with part of the large increase of the final over the provisional estimate in 1891. The reduction was wholly in state taxes (*City Record*, 1890, p. 76), a portion of them having been contested in the courts. As usual in such suits the city was defeated, but the board of estimate in 1891 refused in the provisional budget to appropriate money to pay the judgment, proposing to carry the case higher. Mr. Coleman declared his colleagues knew perfectly well that the attempt was useless, that they were, in fact, trying to make an apparently small tax rate in order to influence the November election. (*New York Times*, November 1, 1890, p. 8.) Whether this was the motive or not, the appropriation for judgments was in fact increased in the final estimate from $100,000 to $750,000. (*City Record*, 1891, p. 64.) The reduction of the final estimate in 1886 was due to the same complication regarding the debt limit referred to on the next page.

[2] Compare Tables I and IV, Appendix.

estimate its total can be changed only by special authority from the legislature; but that body has in fact frequently increased the budget by requiring the payment of special claims, and in two exceptional cases has authorized large reductions. In 1886,[1] after the court decision allowing further contraction of debt, an act authorized the removal of several large items from the budget; while in 1889[2] the law readjusting the sinking funds made possible a reduction of over two and a half millions in debt charges. Of recent years it has been more common to provide for special expenditures authorized by the legislature by means of revenue bonds payable in the year following their issue.

More important usually than these changes in the gross budget are the transfers made within it by the board of estimate and apportionment. The charter and other acts of 1873[3] restored the power to transfer unused surpluses of appropriations, which had been taken away after the abuses of the early '60's. It was further provided that, while unexpended balances of appropriations might be carried on to the same purposes in another year, they could, if not needed either for these purposes or for transfers, be allowed to lapse into the general fund. But, the terms of these statutes being

---

[1] See *post*, p. 313.   [2] See *post*, p. 316.
[3] Laws, 1873, Chap. 757, § 20. The restriction that such transfers must be within the same department was removed in 1874, Chap. 308.

somewhat indefinite, in practice balances continued to be carried forward for many years after their original objects had been completed, and transfers from these old remnants of appropriations often constituted a serious evil. During the years 1881, 1882, and 1883, the abuse became specially grievous,[1] the transfers averaging nearly half a million each year. Balances of five, ten, or even more years' standing were transferred to purposes not only utterly foreign to their original end, but in themselves often objectionable. Other transfers, it is charged, were made from current appropriations designedly made too large. Thomas B. Asten, the only Republican on the board of estimate, declared that the power to make transfers by majority vote merely was used by his colleagues to make appropriations for purposes which he had kept out of the regular budget. Finally a proposed transfer which, though comparatively small, was particularly flagrant, led a taxpayer to seek an injunction. The point was sustained, the court declaring that the intent of the somewhat ambiguous laws was that surpluses of appropriations must

---

[1] See *New York Tribune*, February 13, 1884, pp. 3, 4. The transfers to and within the department of public works were specially commented upon. The appropriation for supplies and cleaning of public offices in 1881, $63,500, was increased $26,945 by transfers; in 1882, appropriations $70,000, transfers $21,347; 1883, appropriations $75,000, transfers $28,789. Comp. Rep., 1881, p. 41; 1882, p. 41; 1883, p. 24. Such recurring transfers of course point to hardly legitimate design.

be disposed of annually, either by being continued for the original uncompleted purpose, or by being applied to some purpose then actually deficient, or by transfer to the general fund.[1] Accordingly the board of estimate in 1884 transferred to that fund, or, in other words, cancelled, no less than $2,678,002 of accumulated balances,[2] and annually since then such surpluses, often amounting to several hundred thousand dollars, have been cancelled.[3]

It is possible that this system of transfers is still occasionally used improperly, but if so the abuses are neither frequent nor extensive. Transfers are indeed often numerous within certain departments whose functions are especially contingent, such as those of public works and street cleaning; but the gross amount involved in these changes is usually not very large. Transfers from one department to another are seldom made in more than four or five cases during the year, and to an amount hardly ever exceeding $100,000 altogether. Despite the possibility of abuse, it is doubtful if the rigidity that would come from abolishing the practice would not be a considerably greater evil.

§ 46. *Character and Motives of the Board of Estimate and Apportionment.*

What now may be said of this board of five members which controls such weighty interests?

---

[1] Bird *v.* The Mayor, 33 Hun, 396.   [2] *City Record*, 1884, p. 1130.
[3] The largest amount was in 1894, $654,248. Comp. Rep., 1894, p. 157.

What is its character and the quality of its work? What influences determine its action? Unfortunately it is impossible to answer fully and accurately.

General opinion is certainly, for the most part, fairly favorable as to the character and work of the board. It never meets the ridicule, seldom the denunciations, so freely heaped on the aldermen. Indeed we should naturally expect this superiority. In the first place, the board of estimate is composed of the most prominent officials of the city. Three of them — the mayor, comptroller, and president of the aldermen — are chosen directly by the people, and no party quite dares to put up for these positions mere ward heelers. Even Tammany Hall has given the city some well-respected members of the board. The fact that all its members have such great powers, both in their separate departments and as an appropriating body, naturally draws to it a higher class of citizens than seek the feeble power now belonging to an alderman. On the other hand, the members of the board itself have comparatively little direct interest in the appropriations; the criticism which was so pertinent regarding the body as composed under the Tweed charter no longer applies strongly. In the second place, its peculiar composition tends to prevent the domination of the board of apportionment by the mayor, as well as to hinder the exclusive and unrestricted control of any one political party over it. The comptroller and president of the aldermen are largely independent of the mayor, the former especially, by his three years' term and by his greater familiarity with the finances, having possibly even stronger influence in the budget than the chief executive. The two officers who are appointive have terms of four and six years, respectively, while the mayor (under the charter of 1873) holds but two years. There is accordingly no chance of the appropriating board at any time being composed of mere creatures of the mayor then in office, as was the case under the Tweed charter. Moreover, the dominant party in the city has not had such continuous possession of the government as to secure unmingled control of the board of estimate; this is especially due to the fact that the two wings of the Democratic party are quite as completely separated in municipal politics as either is from the Republicans. Four mayors since 1870 have been elected in opposition to Tammany Hall,[1] and four more by union of the two Democratic branches.[2] Hence it has come about that the only time when the board has not contained at least one member avowedly opposed to Tammany Hall was from 1889 to 1891, during Mayor Grant's administration, and even then Mr. Coleman[3] was far from being a strong defender

[1] Havemeyer, Cooper, Grace (second term), and Strong.
[2] Ely, Edson, Grace (first term), and Hewitt.
[3] See *New York Tribune*, May 10, 1885, pp. 1 and 4. See also *ante*, p. 266.

of that organization or from readily agreeing with his colleagues. On the expiration of the latter's term, moreover, Mayor Grant appointed Mr. E. P. Barker, a Republican, who holds office till the end of 1897.[1]

The presence of members of different parties in the board of estimate is a material safeguard, not only because unanimous action is necessary upon the gross appropriation, but quite as much because, by the familiarity of members of the minority with the administrative details, they are able to prevent actions that are fraudulent even when agreed upon by the other members. Such high-handed procedure as that of the board when the four chief Tweed Ring conspirators composed it would be quite impossible now. It is, to be sure, true that, in matters of expediency or policy, the minority can hardly force the majority to agree with it as to details; an ordinary vote is sufficient to decide these, and the necessity that some appropriations shall be made often compels the signature of the budget by the minority members even when they strongly oppose certain features. But the power of restriction is still very real. The complaint of Mr. Asten in 1884, concerning the evasion of his vote by the device of transferring balances of appropriations, shows that his single voice had been of great weight in the original budgets.

[1] *New York Tribune*, May 3, 1891, p. 3. Comptrollers Green, Campbell, and Loew were also County Democrats.

We may conclude then from the composition of the board of estimate that we must not look too confidently for traces of personal or party influences in fixing the city expenditures; yet we cannot but believe, even with little specific proof from the meagre records of the board, that the appropriations are often materially affected by such influences. In spite of the impossibility of dictation by the mayor, nevertheless when from time to time a general change in popular sentiment occurs and makes itself felt in the election of a chief executive, there cannot fail to be a considerable change in the whole spirit of the government, which will naturally extend to the appropriations. In spite of the great power held by a minority, even of one, in the board of estimate, the dominant party must at times use the budget as a political engine. There are often strong party differences among the departments, or between certain departments and the mayor; and the control of the appropriations can hardly escape being occasionally employed to favor a political friend or to punish a political foe. So, too, we should expect that the departments whose patronage counts most from the party standpoint would be sometimes favored at the expense of others. That all these evils do actually occur is vouched for by those most familiar with the inner working of the finances.

But in seeking direct proof of these facts in records, we encounter great difficulty. The minutes of the proceedings of the board of estimate, to which we might look to ascertain differences of opinion between its members, give practically no light, since formal aye and nay votes are seldom taken concerning details, nearly all decisions being reached informally. Where such votes do occasionally appear, the only indication of motive they apparently afford is that the president of the aldermen is often inclined to urge the more extravagant appropriations favored by the body which he represents. We are thrown back upon a comparison of the fluctuations in the figures of the budget from year to year, a comparison attended by many difficulties. In the first place it is to be borne in mind that the budget is voted before the beginning of the official year, and that an incoming mayor has no part in determining the appropriations for the first year of his term, while when going out he votes upon those for his successor.[1] Moreover the only just basis of comparison between gross budgets is the amount appropriated for running or contingent expenses, exclusive of the fixed outlay for state taxes, interest, and debt redemption. I do not mean that the board of estimate ought not to regard fixed charges at all in determining the other appropriations; their weight has something

---

[1] The mayor-elect and the comptroller-elect at least occasionally attend the meetings of the board, but doubtless more to become familiar with the city expenditure than to give advice.

to do with deciding how much more burden can be added. Yet the fluctuations in these charges are on the whole gradual, and the minor changes from year to year do not and should not considerably affect other appropriations. It is better that the tax rate should vary moderately than that the work of the departments should be embarrassed by frequent changes in the means at their disposal. Above all we must remember that appropriations of equal amount in different years may mean the widest possible difference in motives and in results accomplished.

Line A in diagram C of the appendix shows the annual appropriations since 1873, exclusive of state taxes and debt charges. The two fluctuations that appear most significant of the spirit of the administration are the rapid increases in 1888 and 1896, under the 'reform' mayors, Hewitt and Strong. Common opinion concerning both these administrations seems to be that they stand far above the average, and that the money spent was not spent altogether in extravagance. In the former case the appropriations for the years immediately preceding had been kept exceptionally low, apparently under the influence of Mayor Grace, who seemed specially inclined to retrenchment. In the latter case the preceding budgets had been reduced by the Tammany administration, in its general policy of delusive economy, at a great sacrifice of efficiency; the public schools especially had been seriously crippled. Too much stress cannot possibly be laid on the fact that in any government mere low expenditure is no evidence in itself of true economy. The argument of tax rate has been used by politicians till it is threadbare. Sometimes it is just; more often, perhaps, unjust. It has certainly been greatly abused in the metropolis, especially perhaps by the Tammany Democrats in the recent memorable campaign. The newspapers, in commenting on city expenditures, too often fail to go below the surface even far enough to make the distinction between fixed and contingent appropriations which we have found necessary.

It might at first blush appear likely that each administration would be inclined to make larger appropriations for the year in which it has the spending of them than for the year when its successor is in office. But this motive is naturally less strong when the same party continues in power successive terms; and even when the chief of the administration changes, several at least of the department heads usually remain unchanged. It seems doubtful if the final budget has ever been cut down for the purpose of hampering a successor. On the other hand, it is highly probable that the *provisional* estimates have at times been reduced with the purpose of influencing the elections before which they were made by the argument of tax rate, the final budget being increased after the election. Thus the final estimates made by the Tammany administration for the years 1891, 1893, and 1895 exceeded the provisional estimates, made just before the municipal elections of 1890, 1892, and 1894, by the sums of $1,360,555, $923,146, and $1,277,367, respectively.[1] The excess in each case was due chiefly, not, as has been true regarding many of the smaller increases in other years, to extraordinary and unavoidable new items coming up during the interval between the two estimates,[2] but to general increases in a large number of departments; so that one can scarcely avoid the suspicion that a partisan motive kept down the provisional estimates. Moreover, this motive was distinctly attributed to his colleagues by a member of the board of estimate itself, as regards the budget of 1891. The immense increase in the final budget for 1897, as compared with the provisional one, was largely due to added debt payments, but there were also additions for nearly all other objects. These changes, however, seem hardly due to political motives.

§ 47. *The Budget System of Greater New York.*

Though we have just seen reason to believe that the board of estimate and apportionment is not altogether free from evil influences and motives, yet it has been so much superior in character to the city council that most of New York's people have been quite willing to leave the purse in its control, rather than trust it to some worse hand.

[1] *City Record*, 1891, p. 64; 1893, p. 83; 1895, p. 108.
[2] *Ibid.*, 1897, p. 100.

Nevertheless, nearly every one who thinks about the matter at all realizes that the present budget system is both unusual and in theory unwarranted. In no other city, except the few which have followed the example of the metropolis, does a small board of executive officers have the final appropriating power. Shorn of other authority as the city council has often been elsewhere, the traditions of representative government have retained for it considerable financial control. It was partly, perhaps, because the Greater New York charter commission realized the special anomaly of the present practice, and partly because they have, in general, sought to raise the 'municipal assembly' from its present degradation, that they proposed to restore to our city fathers some real power in the appropriations. In the impression, perhaps, that they were establishing something like parliamentary or cabinet government, they have left the framing of the budget to the board of estimate and apportionment, and have given the council power only to reduce the sums proposed by the smaller body.

It seems very doubtful whether this new plan will accomplish all that is expected of it. In fact it is still an anomaly, still a mixture of systems. We are offered in no sense cabinet government, since the board of estimate, which might correspond to the cabinet, is not chosen from the council nor responsible to it; it represents in no way a policy to which the council, or the dominant party in it, is pledged. In a cabinet government there is no occasion for the legislative body to propose enterprises or increase expenditures for purposes not asked for by the responsible ministers who are carrying out its will; but the same does not hold true here. While the new charter makes no little advance by thus restoring to the council, as the representative of the people who pay the taxes, a real power to limit expenditure, it does not go far toward bringing back real council government in the city.

But, it may be interposed, no one wishes the council to govern outside its sphere as a purely legislative body and as the guardian of the purse. It is not our task here to discuss fully the general question of the relations between powers in city government. There can be no doubt, however, that much confusion of thought has arisen from the attempt to carry into municipal politics too rigid a distinction between executive and legislative functions, which cabinet governments show us are not necessarily sharply sundered even in national politics. There are some purely legislative functions in city government, and many purely executive ones, but there are not a few extremely important matters which occupy a middle ground. In those matters where the city is something more than a mere agent of state government, where its action more nearly resembles that of a private corporation, many broad questions of expediency or policy must arise — questions similar to those which the directors of a great railway or mining company have to determine. These general matters — the inauguration of public works, the establishment of parks, and many others — ought surely to be decided by a body representing the people as nearly as possible, by a body sufficiently large to feel all the local needs and wishes — in short, by the city council. The council ought logically to be not merely a restrictive power, not merely one of several checks on executive officers. It ought, subject to the advice of such officers, aided by information from them as to technical details, to be the originator, the policy maker. If it is to be this, it must have originating power in the budget also, since nearly all broad municipal problems enter here.

To increase thus the power of the city legislature would be by no means to go as far in the way of executive control by the council as was formerly the practice of New York, or as is now the successful practice in England. Just where the limit of the council's functions shall be drawn is a matter of expediency perhaps more than of theory. No sharp line, certainly, can be found laid down by general principles. But that the city council should be the chief, and not a merely subordinate or coördinate, factor in determining the city budget seems to be a proposition defended by reason as well as by precedent. The scarcely fortunate experience of New York city, during the days when the council actually held the purse, cannot be used as a conclusive argument in opposition, for the whole budget system was then in its infancy. The chief objection to giving power of any kind to the council in New York has been its proverbial corruptness. But a large part of the people have at last come to believe that the only hope of improving our city legislators is to increase their power, and to make their office one worth having. With the new civic spirit which has been shown of late years, with the added authority which the consolidation of the great metropolis will give, there would surely be hope that much better citizens might be secured in a municipal assembly of proper dignity and power, than have ever sat in the powerless city council. The charter commission has promised us this change, but it seems likely that they have made an error in not giving any substantial increase of authority to the city legislature. The new powers nominally bestowed upon it are subject to quite as many restrictions in other directions as in the budget. Even with some added grants of authority upon the statute book, the force of custom, if nothing else, will tend, almost inevitably, to keep the council far inferior to the board of estimate and apportionment as a factor in municipal affairs.

§ 48. *The Tilden Commission Plan.*

Although it is perhaps no longer a question of practical politics, the plan of financial control proposed by the Tilden commission on city government, in 1877, has attracted so much attention that it demands mention.[1] It was in brief that general and detailed power over the city revenues and expenditures should be given exclusively to a 'board of finance,' composed of from six to fifteen members according to the size of the city, and elected by citizens paying taxes on a valuation of $500 or paying rent of $250 yearly. This scheme has still many advocates, and strong arguments are adduced in its favor. Quite aside, however, from the practical difficulty of ever securing an amendment to the state constitution restricting the suffrage in this way, there are doubts as to its justice and expediency.[2] It is certainly no wonder that the middle and upper classes revolt against the domination of the corrupt bosses who draw their support largely from the multitudes of ignorant, poor, and largely foreign voters in our great cities. The administration of a board thus constituted might perhaps, for the time being, be an

[1] Assembly Documents, 1877, No. 68.

[2] For a much fuller and more conclusive criticism of this whole plan, see Professor H. C. Adams' *Public Debts*, chapter on Municipal Debts. It is indeed true that at present in many of our smaller cities and villages there are provisions for elections, at which only taxpayers may vote, on the question of raising taxes beyond the ordinary limit, or of borrowing money. But even here the authorities who submit the question and who oversee the spending of the money are elected by general vote, and the matter is quite different from putting the entire control of city expenditures in the hands of a body representing only property owners.

improvement, but there would be a constant danger of disregarding the interests of the small taxpayers and the non-taxpayers. And whatever may be said, these classes really contribute a very large share to support the city, and are thereby entitled to a voice in controlling disbursements. Not merely is a material proportion of taxes shifted directly upon the poor by increasing their rents;[1] indirectly also more still is laid upon them by reduction of wages and increase of prices. Even if this were not the case, the argument that the city is in every way analogous to a business corporation and should be governed by those who pay is far from sound. A city is a place of residence, in which countless numbers of citizens who, under present social conditions, cannot acquire taxable property to any considerable extent, are practically compelled to live. Without them the industries which make up the city would not exist at all. Non-taxpayers are part of the great municipal family, every detail of the municipal housekeeping affects them most vitally. They ought surely to have some voice in its management, and under the plan proposed by the Tilden commission they would have practically none. If taxpayers wish to own the city and to manage it in their sole interest, they might try excluding all others from its limits.

While admitting its injustice from an abstract standpoint, some have advocated the restricted

[1] See Seligman, *Shifting and Incidence of Taxation.*

suffrage on grounds of practical expediency, for the good of the excluded as well as that of the other citizens. Any argument in behalf of this position based on the experience of the early days, when such a system prevailed in the city, loses most if not all its weight on account of the wide difference in conditions. The same may be said regarding arguments from the experience of foreign municipalities with limited suffrage. In Great Britain the qualification required — payment of an annual rental of £10 — is very much lower than was proposed in New York ($250). It has already been forcibly pointed out by the Pennsylvania commission which studied this same question, that so high a requirement as was suggested by the Tilden commission would probably shut out many really intelligent and worthy citizens. In Germany every citizen has some voice in the election of the municipal council (which controls the finances), although the wealthier classes choose more representatives proportionally than do the poorer. It may fairly be questioned whether the excellence of city governments in these two countries may be attributed so much to the restricted suffrage as to the general traditions and character of the people, who have a reverence for government quite unknown to Americans. In Germany, at least, the preference of property has not been without evil results; the poor have often received less benefit than they should from city expenditures and have been made to bear more than a just share of city taxes. Moreover, even if our municipal administration should be temporarily improved by a property qualification for voting, might not the policy be injurious, in the long run, to the welfare of society, by checking growth in civic knowledge and devotion on the part of the non-voters? The ultimate hope for good government must be in uplifting the mass of citizens, the poor as well as the rich, and though its effects at times seem slow, the ballot is a great educator.

§ 49. *Analysis of City Expenditures.*

The net total of actual annual outlay is not given in the comptrollers' reports. The gross expenditures on the regular budget account only, amounting to $45,621,094 in 1896, are the figures usually cited; but, as was explained in § 33, by no means all city income and outlay is covered by the budget. In seeking this net total it is perhaps best to disregard certain minor recurrent expenditures, under the head of 'special and trust accounts,' such as those for teachers' pensions and the like, where the city practically acts only as an agent for collecting and disbursing moneys. We may, however, properly include with the city's expenditures the amount paid on street enterprises destined to be repaid by special assessments, since such assessments are in a sense only a form of taxation; the amount thus spent in 1896, after deducting a transfer of $250,000 from the budget, was $4,261,649. We must also add the amount appropriated, from the receipts of excise licenses, to charitable institutions and to the police and firemen's pension funds,[1] $1,262,853. The small sum paid from the interest fund directly for interest on bonds held by the public, $123,500, is a current expenditure; while the amount transferred from this fund to the redemption fund, together with the amount of net revenue received by the latter fund from sources aside from the appropriation account, are also to be counted as so much outlay, since practically the city debt is reduced by the sums thus added to the sinking fund, and the revenues so pledged are withdrawn from use to meet other expenditures. This net addition to the redemption fund in 1896 was $7,552,876. Adding together all these classes of outlay, we obtain as the total expenditure for really current purposes in 1896 $58,821,973, about a million more than the revenue. The expenditures of Greater New York will be probably not less than eighty millions yearly.[2]

In classifying these annual expenditures, the broadest lines may be drawn, as already suggested, between the expenditure for state taxes — not properly belonging with the city budget at all — and for unavoidable debt payments on the one hand, and those for more contingent purposes on

---

[1] Part of this apparently reimbursed by assessments on firemen.
[2] Corresponding to income; see *ante*, p. 178.

the other. Of the total outlay for 1896, $6,402,009 was for state taxes, $16,232,875 for the debt service, and $36,187,088 (or nearly two-thirds) for other or contingent purposes. $7,676,376 of the debt payments and $5,524,502 of the contingent payments did not enter into the budget proper; all the remaining amounts were included in it.

Confining ourselves now to the budget outlay proper, in accordance with ordinary custom, it will be more satisfactory to use the figures for the original appropriations rather than those for the actual payments from the treasury, since the former are less apt to fluctuate from exceptional causes. The appropriations for 1896 may be grouped, following in part the classification proposed by Professor Clow, as shown on the following page.

From these figures it will be seen that, excluding state taxes, the largest single item in the annual budget is that for maintaining the great police force, while the items for schools and for interest on the city debt (practically all of which appears in the appropriations) are both nearly as great. Each of these three heads amounts to about an eighth of the total budget. Should the expenditures not entering the regular budget be added, the largest form of outlay would be that for debt redemption, more than ten millions in 1896, and the next largest that for public works, more than eight millions, if outlay on special assessment ac-

APPROPRIATIONS, 1896[1]

State taxes		$6,402,009
General administration:		
Mayor	$26,000	
Council	88,800	
Finance department	316,400	
Department of taxes and assessments	162,520	
Commissioners of accounts	65,000	
Civil service commission	27,500	
Law department	205,050	
Bureau of elections	515,294	
Printing, stationery, etc.	277,200	
Judgments	125,000	
Miscellaneous	600,409	2,409,173
City debt:		
Interest	5,566,597	
Principal	2,989,901	8,556,498
Public safety and health:		
Police	5,925,410	
Fire protection	2,345,355	
Health department	519,508	
Street cleaning	3,020,700	
Building inspection	265,000	12,075,974
Public convenience and welfare:		
Public works (streets, water, buildings, etc.)	4,133,530	
Parks and parkways	1,219,255	
Public charities	1,543,417	
Donations to private institutions	1,543,301	8,459,504
Public justice:		
Courts	1,765,929	
Department of correction	475,999	
Sheriff, coroner, and register	308,682	2,550,611
Public education:		
Schools	5,679,302	
College of City of New York	150,000	
Normal college	150,000	
Libraries	63,500	6,042,802
Total appropriations		$46,496,571

[1] Original appropriations, *City Record*, January 14, 1896. Some changes were made during year, but the total remained the same.

counts be included. The largest group of strictly budget expenditures is that for securing 'public safety and health,' including in one sense the most fundamental municipal tasks; but by counting in the outlay for assessment enterprises, the group classed as 'public convenience and welfare' would be made fully as great.[1]

§ 50. *Growth of Expenditures since* 1871.

For the purpose of studying the progress of the yearly expenditures since 1871, we may best simplify matters by confining ourselves to the budget proper, disregarding special assessment enterprises partly because subject to excessive fluctuations, and also debt expenditures on the sinking fund accounts, because of the wide changes in policy from time to time. The classification of the annual appropriations into those for absolutely fixed purposes — state taxes and debt charges — and those for more contingent objects, is especially important for comparing different years. The movements of these two great classes since 1874 (they are not distinguishable earlier) are shown by lines A and B in Diagram C of the Appendix. Their rapid divergence from the practical equality of 1874 is very striking. While contingent appropriations,

[1] Comparison of the relative expenditures for different purposes by other American cities is practically impossible with the present methods of accounting used. The census figures of 1890, though very uncertain, show in general a considerable degree of equality in the relative distribution of expenditures by different cities. See vol. on *Wealth*, p. 556. See also, *ante*, p. 179.

after a slight fall in 1875–8, rapidly rose, fixed appropriations were reduced by 1892 to barely one-half of their amount in 1874. There was a specially remarkable decrease at the very outset in state taxes,[1] which had been swollen by a deficiency in the state sinking fund; while since 1875 these taxes have constituted one of the most fluctuating items in the budget. The annual interest charge has also been reduced greatly since 1877, when it was no less than nine and a half millions, and constituted more than a third of the appropriations on city account. The reduction has been partly due to the actual decrease of the city debt during part of the time, but more to a gradual fall in the average rate of interest, owing to the payment or refunding of the bonds of the war and Ring periods with their high rates. The sudden decrease in interest payments in 1889 was due to a change in the law regarding the sinking fund, as were the great reductions in the appropriations for debt redemption in 1878 and again in 1889.[2] The rapid rise in all three classes of fixed appropriations in 1896 was responsible for two-thirds of the great increase of the gross budget as compared with the preceding year.

Had it not been for the steady decrease in fixed appropriations, the increase in contingent appro-

[1] See Diagram D. All these figures are compiled from comptroller's reports.
[2] See §§ 53, 54.

priations since 1874 could scarcely have been so rapid. Owing to that decrease the total budget was kept for fully fifteen years below the figure reached in 1874 (except in 1876), although the contingent appropriations rose, meantime, nearly 40 per cent. The only breaks in the upward movement of these appropriations were in 1882 and 1886, in the economical, not to say, perhaps, parsimonious, administrations of Mayor Grace, and specially rapid increases in expenditure followed immediately after these years. The unusual rise in 1885 was chiefly due to the payment of a large judgment for water meters put in during the Ring period. On the other hand the steady increase of the budget since 1890 has been due to increases in almost every department.

Without studying in detail the fluctuations in the items of expenditure, a general glance at Diagram D will show that in most departments the growth during the past quarter century has been fairly gradual, corresponding to the increase of population, although for the most part at a more rapid pace. Sudden variations, due to exceptional causes, of course, sometimes appear. The progress of the various appropriations may be more roughly but more easily compared by means of percentages or index numbers, showing the relative amount of the chief heads at decennial periods, 1876, 1886, and 1896. The former year, which is taken as a basis and called 100, marks the lowest point of the expenditures since 1871, the latter their highest point. The figures following may be more clearly appreciated by aid of Diagram E of the Appendix.

INDEX NUMBERS SHOWING GROWTH OF APPROPRIATIONS

	1876	1886	1896
Population [1]	100	133.6	179.7
Assessed valuation	100	128	181
Total appropriations	100	97	133
State taxes, interest, and redemption	100	66	79
State taxes	100	58	89
Interest	100	77	58
Redemption	100	42	145
Contingent appropriations	*100*	*131.7*	*195.2*
Police	100	118	176
Education	100	107	155
Public works	100	193	228
Fire protection and building inspection	100	149	198
Street cleaning	100	152	416
Charities and correction	100	133	173
Public parks [2]	100	205	374
Courts	100	111	145
Donations to asylums, etc.	100	137	175
All other	100	138	203

While the gross budget has thus grown much less rapidly than population or assessed valuation, the contingent appropriations have increased con-

[1] As estimated by Board of Health.

[2] Including certain street expenses. The separation of the department of improvements in the 23d and 24th wards is so recent that it is disregarded.

siderably faster than either—95 per cent in twenty years. This rapid growth is not, indeed, in itself a ground for complaint. It is the common experience of cities, for they are continually undertaking new tasks, and doing more proportionately for their citizens. It is perfectly conceivable that, without going too far into 'socialistic' enterprises, New York might still, with true economy, expend a considerably larger proportion of the people's income in collective undertakings. The real problem is to secure a proper return for money spent, not merely to cut down outlay. Probably no unbiassed critic, however, would maintain that the expenditures of the metropolis during the past two decades had shown marks of striking economy in any sense whatever.

These index numbers show, further, that the forms of contingent expenditure which have increased less rapidly, during the period since the Ring, than population, are those for education, courts, charities and correction, and donations to institutions. The appropriations for schools, indeed, hardly increased at all for many years; but this was accompanied by most unfortunate curtailment of facilities, and especially by failure to provide sufficient room. The rapid growth of appropriations for this purpose, under the administration of Mayor Strong, cannot fail to be generally approved. The most remarkable increase in expenditure has been for street cleaning, till recently the least satisfactorily performed of all municipal functions. Though, following the advice of a special committee of citizens, larger appropriations began to be made about 1891, little improvement was accomplished till the last administration, by still greater outlay judiciously employed, worked a revolution. The apparently rapid increase in park expenditures is partly misleading, being due to added outlay for street improvements in the upper part of the city, under charge (till very recently) of this department. The department of public works is the only one where the rate of increase in expenditure has been materially less since 1886 than before, but this is partly due to the inclusion of so much street work under the park department.

CHAPTER XI

THE CITY DEBT

THE net debt of New York city, at the close of 1896, was more than double that of Brooklyn, which, in turn, was considerably greater than that of any other American city. The consolidated city will, at the outset, have an indebtedness equal to five times that of Boston — the next most heavily indebted American municipality, — to one-fourth that of all our American cities combined, and to more than three-fourths of the united debts of all the American state governments. It is no wonder that the people of the metropolis are so profoundly interested in their city debt, which will amount to about $60 *per capita* in the greater city. The immense burden is the more subject to unfavorable comment because no small part of it represents the result of corruption and fraud; not only is the legacy of the Tweed Ring yet largely unpaid, but considerable mismanagement has attended many of the debt issues since that time.

The study of the city debt involves a consideration of the constitutional limitations upon the issue of bonds, the control of the legislature over such issues, — which has caused so much complaint in the past, and which the Greater New York charter promises to do away almost entirely,— the powers of local authorities as to the creation of debt, the complicated provisions for meeting the principal and interest of bonds, and finally a brief survey of the actual progress of the debt and of the chief bond issues since the Ring period.

§ 51. *Constitutional Limitation of Debt.*

In most of our American states general restrictions of some sort upon the borrowing of local bodies have been established, either by constitutional or legislative act, during the past thirty or forty years. These limitations have arisen as the result of experience of the thoughtlessness with which our 'booming' municipalities are apt to rush into premature public works or to incur burdens for posterity to meet. It is for the interest of the state as a whole, and of every subdivision that is likely to wish to borrow, that the credit of every public financial unit within its borders should be sound.

The first constitutional limitation of local debt in New York, adopted in 1875,[1] followed the example of numerous other states by prohibiting the loaning of public credit to private individuals or corporations, or the purchase of stock in corporations by municipalities — a restriction intended to prevent a very common abuse, especially in granting bonuses to railways. A far more important

[1] Constitution of 1846, Art. 8, § 11.

provision was inserted in the constitution in 1884, an almost unanimous popular vote showing how much its desirability was felt. This amendment, which at first applied only to cities over 100,000, but was extended by the revised constitution of 1894 [1] to all counties and cities, restricts the indebtedness of any city to 10 per cent of the assessed valuation of its real estate. This limit applies to assessment bonds, but not to revenue bonds issued in anticipation of taxes, nor to stocks issued after the adoption of the amendment for supplying water, but such stocks must be payable within twenty years, and a sinking fund for them must be created by raising annually by taxation the necessary proportion. Such water debt is also to be counted in estimating the total that determines whether more money can be borrowed. This 10 per cent limit is higher than that established in almost any other state, but usually elsewhere the percentage restriction applies to the entire assessed valuation, not merely to that of real estate.

This amendment of 1884 created considerable commotion in New York city finances. The real estate valuation of the city was then $1,119,761,597, the gross bonded debt as defined in the constitution, $126,871,138; [2] and the city would be unable for many years to borrow money except for water purposes, unless the constitution could be so interpreted that the large sinking fund accumulations,

[1] Art. 8, § 10.   [2] Comp. Rep. 1894, pp. 142, 158.

then $34,823,735, could be subtracted in estimating the debt. Mayor Edson held with the corporation counsel that this deduction could not be made, but it is charged that he took this position out of personal or political opposition to the scheme of extensive new parks beyond the Harlem, whose opening would require large bond issues. It was further declared at first that Mayor Grace took the same stand on his accession, and for the same reason, but, however that may be, only a few months later the commissioners of the sinking fund, of which he was a member, decided to construe the limitation as applying only to the net debt, and advertised for the sale of $2,000,000 of dock bonds. Large bondholders at once secured an injunction to prevent their issue, and this remained in force throughout 1885, so that none but water bonds were issued. In 1886 the matter was carried to the court of appeals, which unanimously reversed the lower court.[1] The opinion, which was by Justice Danforth, dwelt especially upon the purpose and nature of the sinking fund in the minds of its founders and of the legislature. The words of the ordinance of 1813: "Whereas it is highly useful to establish a fund out of which purchases of the New York city stock may from time to time be made . . . whereby . . . the redemption of the same will be regularly progressing," and other connected phrases, were held to

[1] Bank for Savings v. Grace, 102 N. Y., p. 313.

show that the council considered such purchases as equivalent to redemption; while the fact that the legislature of 1873 had authorized the cancellation of such stocks held by the fund as were redeemable therefrom was also cited. Only city bonds being held by the sinking fund, it was maintained by the court that they were virtually redeemed, and that the "constitutional prohibition . . . is aimed at an actual, not a theoretical indebtedness."

Under this decision the 10 per cent limit did not for a decade hamper at all the finances of the city. The net debt at the close of 1896 was only $6\frac{3}{4}$ per cent of the assessed valuation of real estate. The court decision of that year, however, refusing to approve certain plans for the great rapid transit system, on the ground that its cost would force the debt beyond the legal bound, shows that the limitation may yet have some direct effect in restricting loans. The annexation of Brooklyn, whose net debt already stands nearly at the limit, will narrow the margin of the greater city. Perhaps wiser forms of debt restriction might be either, as has been done in a number of states, to set one limit, subject to extension, — within a second limit, if desired, — whenever a popular vote, perhaps by a two-thirds majority, should favor it; or, if such a department could be kept free from partisan influences, to establish a state board of trained officials to have supervisory control over the management of municipal debts, in some such way as is done by the Local Government Board in England. A combination of the two methods might work satisfactorily. Certainly a city of such enormous resources and such future prospects as Greater New York, has little to fear from the accumulation of a debt considerably larger than the present one, if it be economically applied for wise public improvements, and especially for such as are likely themselves to prove a source of income. Paris has a city debt nearly four times as great as that of New York, but she has magnificent public works to show for it, her people seem not to be appalled by its magnitude, and the city credit is high.[1]

§ 52. *Legislative and Local Authorization of Debt.*

Besides the general constitutional regulation, the New York state legislature retained, up to the enactment of the charter of 1897, full control of the purposes, and often of the details of loans by the metropolis. General grants of borrowing power were, indeed, made for a few regularly recurrent purposes; for example, the city could issue, without special laws, revenue and assessment bonds; dock bonds, not over $3,000,000 yearly; bonds for acquiring new lands and building dams, etc., at the Croton watershed, and for a few less

[1] Shaw, *Municipal Government in Continental Europe*, pp. 134 ff.

important objects.[1] For most loans, however, special legislative acts were required; these differed widely in the extent of their regulation over details. In many cases an absolute limit, usually in round numbers, has been placed on the amount of bonds; in others, as with the new aqueduct begun in 1884,[2] an indefinite sum sufficient to accomplish the enterprise has been authorized. As a restrictive agency these legislative limits have usually been of little or no significance. Bond acts really desired by the city were passed with little hesitation, and if the bounds fixed were too narrow, extensions could be readily secured. On the other hand the legislature has often, with quite as little thought, or perhaps with partisan motives, enacted laws requiring the creation of debt, at the instance of a limited number of citizens or officials, and against the opposition of the most representative authorities in the city. Its interference in this regard has indeed been the subject of most constant and bitter complaint; nor is it easy to exaggerate the lack of consideration, the ignorance or the partisanship with which our legislators have exercised their power over the city's debt.

The comparatively limited degree of discretionary power left to the city authorities regarding debt issues has been considerably divided among different boards and officers. The city council

---

[1] Consolidation Act, §§ 132–162.   [2] Laws, 1884, Chap. 490.

long since lost every shade of control over indebtedness; but the board of estimate and apportionment, with its growing supremacy concerning other features of the finances, has extended its power in this direction also. Loans authorized by statute almost always require the order of some local body or officer before the comptroller can actually issue bonds, while certain details as to the term, interest, and form of bonds are usually left for city authorities to determine. At the outset the board of estimate[1] was given all authority over these matters, except such as was specifically conferred on other officers; but these exceptions were formerly rather important, both in the charter and in the special bond acts themselves. Thus during the Ring period the commissioner of public works had obtained the right to authorize several classes of bonds without other consent; and this right was retained unchanged till 1882, as regards bonds for improvements at the source of water supply, where it led, according to the charges of the Union League Club, to serious evils.[2] In the latter year,[3] however, the board of estimate secured the power to approve or disapprove the requisitions of the commissioner. Again, the commission which constructed the new aqueduct during the last decade was empowered to demand the issue of bonds by

---

[1] Consolidation Act. § 204.
[2] Alleged Frauds in the City Government, 1884, p. 9.
[3] Consolidation Act. § 141.

the comptroller; but here, too, the board of estimate was given at least nominal supervision over the enterprise by the requirement that contracts and various other acts of the aqueduct board should be submitted to its approval.[1] In certain other cases departments have been given the initiative in debt creation, but subject to the approval of the board of estimate and apportionment.[2] The most important subtraction from the control of this board has been that made by the authority given to the sinking fund commission, only two of whose five members belong to the board of estimate. The commissioners of the sinking fund still possess sole power to authorize the issue of dock bonds, and have occasionally been given charge of some other specific enterprise, — such as the erection of the criminal court house in 1887–93.[3] To them belong, naturally, certain other general duties of debt management; they approve bids for the sale of bonds, make proper provisions for payments, arrange the investments of the sinking fund, etc. It has been their prerogative also to declare that any given class of stock shall be free from city taxation, which has been the usual but not invariable practice since it was rendered possible by a law of 1880[4] and by a general ordinance of the council.

---

[1] Laws, 1883, Chap. 490.

[2] *E.g.* board of education, Laws, 1884, Chap. 458; 1888, Chap. 136.

[3] Laws, 1887, Chap. 371.   [4] *Ibid.*, 1880, Chap. 552.

While some of the details of debt management have been left unaltered by the Greater New York charter, the general provisions as to the authorization of bonds have been completely reorganized, the changes made being considered by the charter commission as one of the most salient features of their work. In widest contrast with the present necessity of constant appeal to the legislature for authorization of bond issues, the corporation is hereafter to have independent power, subject to the constitutional limit and to certain requirements of the charter itself as to sinking funds, to borrow money for any public enterprise. Of course no provision made by one legislature can bind its successors, and nothing short of a constitutional amendment prohibiting special legislation of this sort can prevent the state government from hereafter enacting laws interfering with the exercise of this power by the city, either generally or as to special bond issues; indeed, acts compelling the city to borrow against its will may perhaps continue to be passed in the future, as so often before. Nevertheless, this provision of the new charter cannot fail to have a powerful moral influence, and it will doubtless lead ultimately to a large measure of local autonomy. The charter commission has certainly taken a long step in advance.

The commissioners, however, felt, perhaps too strongly, that the great power thus granted the city might lead to abuse, and they have accordingly required the consent of several local bodies to authorize loans. It is expected that the initiative in enterprises involving bonds will ordinarily be taken by the board of public improvements — that important new body consisting of a president and ten *ex-officio* members, including, besides other officers, all the heads of departments concerned with public works. This board will be familiar with the technical details, and can intelligently advise concerning such enterprises. After approval by the board of improvements, the board of estimate and apportionment must give its assent before bonds can be issued, and if over $100,000 is involved, the municipal assembly must likewise approve. In case any measure providing for a public work is first proposed in the municipal assembly, it must, before final action, be submitted to the board of improvements for a report estimating the cost, etc. In default of a favorable recommendation from this board, a five-sixths vote of the assembly will be necessary to pass the ordinance. Four bodies, — including the two houses of the assembly, — each in its general powers and dignity nominally of very high standing, will thus have a mutually restraining control over the creation of indebtedness. There seems much justice in the criticism that this piecemealing of authority will lead to deadlock, or will prevent proper location of responsibility. Unless, however, some great revolution in the general character of the

x

aldermen and councilmen takes place, they are scarcely likely in practice to have as much weight in debt management as the board of estimate and apportionment, which will have the advantage of precedent for its action in this direction.

§ 53. *Debt Redemption — Act of* 1878.

If the legal regulations as to the creation of city debt, both under the former charter and under that of 1897, are somewhat complex and inconsistent, those regarding its redemption are yet more so. The plan of setting aside for the service of the debt certain specific kinds of revenues, and especially their division into funds for interest and for redemption, has been a source of constant financial entanglement. The ever recurring difficulty has been that one or both of the sinking funds have proved more than sufficient for the purposes to which they were limited; while only by legislative act could any diversion of the revenues be made, and then at the risk of charges of violated faith. Simpler methods of debt service have been introduced as to some later bond issues, but the old anomalies have been at the same time perpetuated and further complicated.

At the opening of the financial period now under consideration, after the fall of the Ring, the debt system was already extremely inconsistent and unwise.[1] Only a small amount of interest on the old water bonds was legally pay-

[1] See *ante*, pp. 98, 149.

able from the interest fund, which turned a surplus of one to two millions yearly into the general fund. The redemption of a somewhat larger amount of bonds — chiefly for water and parks — had been charged upon the redemption fund, but its revenues had so increased that the accumulations were going on at evidently double or treble the necessary rate. Notwithstanding the superfluity of the two funds, all the great war debt, and nearly all of the immense issues of the period succeeding the war and of the Ring *régime*, had been made payable principal and interest from taxation. So far as the interest fund was concerned, this arrangement did no harm further than to complicate the accounts, since the surplus of the fund went to the same fund from which general appropriations, including those for interest, were paid. But a real hardship was inflicted on the taxpayers by the provision as to the redemption fund, since they were being compelled to pay from annual taxes the bonds which were now constantly falling due, at the very moment when revenues which should be available for the purpose were being uselessly heaped up.

No change in this unfortunate system was made till 1878, and meantime all the large bond issues of the post-Ring period, like those just before, were made a charge on general appropriation account and not on the sinking funds. By the latter year the redemption fund had risen to more than 60 per cent in excess of all the bonds redeemable from it, and was still increasing nearly three millions a year.[1] Worse yet, there would fall due in the next year or two far larger amounts of bonds to be met by taxes than ever before, and, as no gradual accumulation had been made to meet these, an exceedingly heavy burden threatened to fall on the overtaxed people. The immense floating assessment debt, moreover, required some adjustment, or yet more severe hardships would be incurred.

Comptroller John Kelly appears to have been the author of the first elaborate scheme for solving these financial difficulties. He proposed[2] to make the redemption fund applicable to all bonds then outstanding, except revenue bonds; to authorize the raising by taxation of not over $1,000,000 in any year, to meet stocks falling due in that year for which the fund was not sufficient; and to allow the city to refund any obligations in excess of these limits. The legislative bill containing these provisions, in its original form, was vetoed by Governor Robinson,[3] who charged that practically no greater security was given to the stocks to which the sinking fund had been originally pledged than to assessment and other bonds falling due long

---

[1] Debt December 31, 1877, payable from fund, $18,762,043; amount of fund, $31,080,007. *City Record*, 1878, p. 913.

[2] Assembly Bill, No. 166, 1878.

[3] Public Papers of Governor Robinson, 1878, p. 41.

before these. He likewise objected to further postponement of maturing debt, and accordingly urged that $1,000,000 would be a more proper minimum than maximum limit to be levied yearly for redemption. The bill was amended somewhat in accordance with his suggestions and became a law.[1]

It is strange that the old idea that by pledging particular revenues, aside from taxes, to debt redemption, the credit of the city would be improved,[2] should have persisted when it was generally (although indeed wrongly) supposed to be evident that such revenues would no longer be sufficient even to meet the existing debt, much less to meet future additions, and that for the remainder taxa-

---

[1] Laws, 1878, Chap. 383.

[2] It is possible, though hardly probable, that when the sinking fund was first established, one of the reasons for its character may have been the belief that the payment of the specific revenues set aside could be enforced by *mandamus*, giving thus added security to creditors. But as the sinking fund ordinance was passed *after* the issue of the bonds, it is difficult to see that it constituted a contract, or that a *mandamus* as to these revenues would have any more force than a general one ordering payment. At any rate such an argument could have had no proper weight in 1878, for at that time the custom of setting aside specific revenues was at least uncommon in other municipalities, while the courts had held repeatedly that holders of city bonds could obtain *mandamus* to compel the levy of a tax to pay their claims, even if the law authorizing the bonds had not specifically ordered such tax, and much more so if the law had prescribed that taxes must be levied. It is simply inconceivable that New York should fail to pay its bonds under a system providing for taxes to pay them. See Dillon, *Municipal Corporations*, ed. 4, § 849 ff.

tion must be the only security. The opportunity lay ready to hand in 1878 of adopting a simple and rational plan of debt redemption. All that was necessary was henceforth to turn all the city's miscellaneous revenues into the general or appropriation account; and taking as a basis those accumulations of the sinking fund not required for the bonds already guaranteed by it, to add thereto annually from the appropriation account precisely such sum as would be needed to amortize the rest of the debt. No holder of bonds to which the sinking fund had been originally pledged could possibly suffer by such a change.

The merit of the plan of systematic and proportional debt redemption was indeed felt by the framers of the act of 1878, and it was provided that for all bonds thereafter to be issued a sinking fund must be accumulated by raising a fixed annual proportion out of taxes. As to the debt already outstanding, however, the old system was continued with new and complicated adjustments. Owing doubtless less to a fixed policy than to the anticipation that the miscellaneous revenues would be insufficient to meet both principal and interest of the existing debt, no attempt was made to increase the scope of the interest fund, which was still to be applied only to the interest on old water bonds. With characteristic complication, however, the revenues then pledged to the interest fund were left under that name, while the annual surplus of the fund, which soon would be fully nine-tenths of its amount, was to be transferred to the redemption fund, to augment the revenues already devoted to it. The redemption fund thus strengthened was made available for redeeming any bonds, except revenue bonds, outstanding at the date of the law; but, in accordance with the suggestion of Governor Robinson, an emphatic provision was inserted that no such payment should impair the security of the bonds originally chargeable to the fund, which were declared a preferred lien. As the sinking fund was thus enabled to pay assessment bonds, unpaid assessments on the proceedings for which these bonds were issued were pledged to it. The section regarding taxation to cover deficiencies in the fund, as amended after the governor's veto, required that, whenever the commissioners of the sinking fund should certify that it would be insufficient to pay stocks due in the next calendar year, the city should levy the sum required; "provided, however, that the amount so to be raised by tax and paid into the sinking fund . . . shall not in any one year be less than the sum of one million dollars, nor more than two million dollars."

It would appear a very free interpretation to treat these words as meaning that only in such years as the sinking fund was insufficient to pay the then actually maturing bonds should any tax be levied. It seems rather to mean, and such was clearly the purpose of the governor, that at least $1,000,000 should be raised *every* year toward the principal of the debt outstanding in 1878; yet, doubtless because it soon became evident that the reconstituted sinking fund would be more than able to meet its obligations, unaided, this provision for levying taxes to supplement it was disregarded, or otherwise interpreted. In 1879, indeed, precisely one million was inserted in the budget for redeeming the old debt, but since that year practically no taxes have been levied to pay debt outstanding at the time this law was passed, the sums that have actually been raised representing the proportion required annually on stocks issued after that date, together with sundry minor payments on revenue bonds, etc.

The provision for issuing consolidated stock to postpone maturing debt, which, in spite of Governor Robinson's objections, was still retained in the law as adopted, has been actually made use of but twice, although in each case to large extent. The most immediate purpose of this provision was to enable the funding of the large amount of assessment bonds that fell due in 1878 and 1880; no less than $9,700,000 of fifty-year bonds were issued for this purpose. Again, in 1896, it was felt that the sinking fund would be unduly depleted if compelled to redeem the large amount of Ring debt then maturing, and $8,377,000 of refunding bonds were accordingly issued. These refunding stocks constitute a lien on the sinking fund prior to all others except that of bonds originally secured by it.

The important features of this law of 1878 were, then, the practical consolidation of the interest fund with the redemption fund, the application of the latter to the payment of all funded debt *then outstanding*, and the requirement of gradual amortization out of taxes for future bonds. Awkward as was the arrangement, it lightened the burdens of taxpayers. With all the allowances which are necessary, probably this act made the annual tax levy for the following decade approximately two millions a year less than it would have been had the old debt system remained in force.

For some time, both before and after the passage of the act just described, considerable opposition was shown against the whole sinking fund system, and especially against permitting the few men controlling it to retain in their possession uncancelled such vast amounts of city bonds. The movement went so far that Mr. Theodore Roosevelt even introduced at Albany a bill [1] requiring the destruction of all stocks held or acquired for the sinking fund, but providing that precisely the same sum should annually be paid to the commissioners of the fund as the interest on its accumulations would have amounted to. If this provision were faithfully carried out, the security of creditors

[1] Assembly Bill, No. 89, 1882.

would be exactly the same as before, and they could not justly complain of ill-faith. Able students of finance have approved such a plan. On the other hand, as was explained by the comptroller,[1] no serious danger was really to be feared from the non-cancellation of bonds, while, from lack of clear comprehension of the change of policy, the city's credit might have been temporarily impaired, had the proposed law been actually passed.

The opposition[2] which the comptroller and sinking fund commissioners had shown to Mr. Roosevelt's bill seems hardly consistent, for in the same year, 1882, a large number of bonds were actually cancelled by them. The circumstances of this action were these: As far back as 1873[3] the destruction of such bonds held by the sinking fund as were by law redeemable therefrom had been authorized by the legislature; but, as there was no provision for continuing interest payments to the fund in corresponding amount, the local financiers felt that to act under this authority would be to break faith with bondholders. But after the law of 1878, which required the transfer of the entire surplus of the interest fund to the redemption fund, it was evident that precisely the same sum would be turned over to the latter fund if a certain amount

[1] Comp. Rep., August, 1881. p. 13.
[2] Letter to Assembly Committee on Cities. *City Record*, 1882, p. 619.
[3] Laws, 1873, Chap. 335, § 102.

of interest now being paid, from the interest fund, upon bonds held by it were simply stopped. Accordingly $6,030,972 of bonds held by the redemption fund, upon which the other fund was paying interest, were cancelled by the city authorities in 1882.[1] A general cancellation of sinking fund bonds was again proposed in 1885, under stress of the constitutional limit on debt; but, as the courts soon allowed the accumulations of the fund to be deducted in estimating the limit, the measure was not pushed.

§ 54. *Debt Redemption under Present Laws.*

Barely a decade was the act of 1878 in operation before new legislative 'tinkering' of the sinking fund became necessary. The objection was raised,[2] with some reason, that no change could be made without violating the contract which that law had declared to exist between the city and its creditors; but as it was now evident that the fund would soon more than equal all the bonds charged to it, no attempt was made to urge the point in court. As usual the city financiers had underestimated the geometrical increase in the sinking fund revenues, and needless accumulations were piling up, while heavy and rapidly growing sums were being added to annual taxes, as required by law, to raise the proper yearly proportion of bonds issued after 1878. Already in

---

[1] Comp. Rep., August, 1882, pp. 10–12; December, 1882, p. 11.
[2] *E.g.* by Mr. Coleman, *New York Times*, November 1, 1890.

1888 the tax required toward the debt created for the new aqueduct — subject to the special provision of the constitutional amendment of 1884 — amounted to over $800,000, while that levied to amortize other bonds was nearly $700,000.[1] Meanwhile, during the ten years since 1878, the ordinary revenues of the sinking fund, not counting the sums contributed by taxation, had been able, without reducing the capital of the fund, to pay off about 40 per cent of the bonds outstanding in 1878, to which alone they were applicable; and with the progressive increase in the revenues, it was likely that accumulations sufficient to cover the entire amount of these bonds would be made within ten or twelve years, while a considerable portion of them could not be retired till well into the next century.

The main features of the law passed in 1889[2] to relieve this situation were (1) the application of the sinking fund miscellaneous revenues to the redemption of the entire city debt, present and future (except the water debt, where the constitutional amendment of 1884 required taxation for the sinking fund), instead of merely to bonds outstanding in 1878; and (2) the stopping of interest on the accumulations of the redemption fund. The sums which up to this time had been raised from annual taxes for amortizing bonds issued since 1878, and for interest on bonds held by the sink-

[1] Comp. Rep., 1888, p. 57.   [2] Laws, 1889, Chap. 178.

ing fund, were hereafter to be removed from the budget. A provision was indeed retained requiring taxation to supplement any deficiency in the fund, but this has never proved necessary. Moreover the second change was not made in the bald way in which it has just been stated, but the fiction of a large separate interest fund, which had been kept up under the law of 1878, was called into play, and it was provided that the entire amount of interest on stocks held by the redemption fund should be paid from the interest fund instead of from taxation. In other words the same revenues of the interest fund, which under the law of 1878 had gone to the redemption fund as 'surplus,' were now to go to it as interest, and a corresponding annual addition to the fund from regular appropriations was to be discontinued.

This law, as an immediate effect, reduced the appropriation of 1889 for debt redemption from $2,269,842 to $1,294,073 (the latter being the amount required for the water debt under the constitution), and that for interest from $7,129,048 to $5,728,772;[1] and similar large reductions in the burden of annual taxation have resulted each year from its operation. A necessary consequence of the measure of 1889 was the separation from the sinking fund accumulations in general of those made to pay the water stock under the constitutional amendment of 1884, the latter stock being

[1] Comp. Rep., 1889, p. 84.

now on an entirely different basis of redemption from all the rest of the city debt. There became, accordingly, two redemption funds, the larger being designated as No. 1, and the one for water bonds as No. 2.

The sinking fund provisions of the new charter of 1897 unfortunately fail to simplify the finances, — indeed, by the consolidation with other municipalities some new complications will arise. All existing sinking funds of each municipality are continued, and the greater city, except in one or two cases, is to carry out the requirements now made concerning them, whether by raising annual taxes or setting aside specific revenues. In case, however, all the water bonds of the various subdivisions issued since 1884 have been properly provided for according to the constitutional amendment of that date, the existing sinking funds for these may be consolidated, and water bonds hereafter issued may be charged to the same fund. For all other debt hereafter created by the metropolis there is to be established a new fund, to be supplied primarily from annual appropriations raised by tax. When, however, the bonds charged to any of the present sinking funds are wholly 'discharged, liquidated, or cancelled,' the specific revenues devoted to them are to be paid to the newly established fund. This provision is somewhat vague, and it is to be hoped that it will not be interpreted, in connection with another prohibiting cancellation of sinking fund bonds before maturity, so as to require heaping up of accumulations after the funds have fully equalled the bonds payable from them, but before such bonds are due. The old sinking fund for interest is continued also, its surplus going to the old redemption fund as at present.

The sinking fund of Brooklyn, which will now be transferred to the greater city, is relatively of very small amount, and is increased solely by annual taxes levied under the constitutional amendment of 1884 and under certain special acts, and by interest on its accumulations. The interest on the Brooklyn water debt is provided for entirely by the income from the water system, which indeed furnishes a small surplus to the general fund.[1]

§ 55. *General Progress of the Debt since* 1871.

In considering the general movements of the city debt since the fall of the Tweed Ring, three main periods may be distinguished: from 1872 to 1874, from 1875 to 1884, and from 1885 onward. The fluctuations in the debt may best be studied by means of Diagram B.[2] The funded indebted-

---

[1] See Brooklyn Comp. Rep., 1895, pp. 103 ff., 236 ff.

[2] The diagram (see Appendix) shows only the resultant of issues and redemptions. The following table giving the amounts of annual funded loans and redemptions will aid in interpreting the diagram. Figures before 1875 are not available; others are compiled from the reports of the commissioners of accounts in the *City*

ness of the city — by which phrase is designated that represented by long-time bonds, excluding revenue and assessment bonds — increased very rapidly during the three years of the first period, almost solely on account of the funding of revenue

Record, and from comptroller's reports, from year to year. Both figures for 1896 include $8,377,000 of bonds refunded.

Year	Bonds Issued	Bonds Redeemed
1875	$4,144,346	$3,329,000
1876	5,244,734	4,802,425
1877	3,523,624	1,582,704
1878	8,379,182	3,690,499
1879	1,832,673	4,816,155
1880	4,406,251	4,374,665
1881	2,996,500	1,449,012
1882	2,791,961	7,699,126
1883	2,654,783	1,764,549
1884	5,193,081	4,581,235
1885	4,950,000	3,826,080
1886	3,875,845	3,668,349
1887	11,912,154	10,062,171
1888	7,857,215	4,010,839
1889	14,819,132	5,150,200
1890	8,878,294	4,696,300
1891	6,957,346	3,654,500
1892	8,070,116	4,226,815
1893	9,853,927	147,200
1894	10,486,041	4,143,900
1895	13,669,828	2,829,700
1896	24,378,827	14,422,752
Total 22 years	$166,875,866	$98,928,181

bonds and other floating obligations bequeathed by the Ring. In the decade constituting the second period there was a relative economy of bond issues; redemptions nearly kept pace with them, while the sinking fund grew largely, notwithstanding these payments, thus reducing the net debt. Large borrowing was indeed almost impossible, for not only were the people thoroughly alarmed and indignant at the immense burden so recently thrown upon them, but the city credit was such that loans could be placed only at high interest. On two-thirds of the immense loans from 1872 to 1874, 7 per cent had to be paid. As late as 1878 the city could secure no better rate than 5 per cent on the funding bonds. The people were therefore little inclined to borrow further, and of the forty-one millions of new loans contracted during the decade from 1875 to 1884 a considerable part were unavoidable refundings of old obligations. By the latter year, however, the situation had much improved: the net debt, which had stood at fully 10 per cent of the assessed valuation during the '70's, was reduced to less than 8 per cent; while loans could now be floated at 3 per cent interest. Accordingly the city began to borrow largely for the new aqueduct and other long postponed public improvements. Since 1884, in fact, the bond issues, $125,708,730, have been more than double the redemptions, and have averaged over twice as much yearly as during the preceding ten years. Nevertheless, the sinking fund has increased so rapidly, and the rate of interest has been reduced so greatly, that the amount paid from the budget for interest was only about $5,500,000 in 1896 as against $9,500,000 in 1876. The average rate of interest on the city debt (weighted according to the amount at each rate) fell from 6.1 per cent in 1880 to about 3.9 per cent in 1895.[1] This remarkable change is partly due to reduction in the general market rate, but shows also a great improvement in city credit. It is a matter of just congratulation to New York's financiers that, by exempting their bonds from local taxation, they have been able to sell at par large blocks bearing only $2\frac{1}{2}$ per cent interest; and though $3\frac{1}{2}$ was the rate on the large issues of 1896, the increase was due solely to the general political and financial disturbance, and, moreover, large premiums were received.

[1] The following table shows the amount at the respective rates:—

Year	2½%	3%	3½%	4%
1880	....	....	....	2,800,000
1895	14,274,237	93,132,620	5,612,974	9,319,494

Year.	5%	6%	7%
1880	28,504,944	56,620,078	45,609,996
1895	15,855,027	31,542,943	15,820,600

The broad fluctuations of the amount of temporary bonds (lines B and C, Diagram B) may be noted as contributing to the movement of the net debt, in which they are reckoned. The unprecedented extent of assessment enterprises during and after the Ring period increased the assessment bonds outstanding to over twenty-two millions in 1876, but they were greatly reduced by the funding of 1878, and by the redemption of bonds from the sinking fund, in 1884, by virtue of the debt act of 1878. Since then there has been a slow but steady increase in this class of indebtedness. The great reduction of revenue bonds in 1874 was due to the funding of the floating debt left from the era of misrule. Thereafter the annual amount left outstanding of these bonds, issued during the year in anticipation of taxes, varied little till toward the close of the '80's, when more prompt collection of taxes reduced them greatly, and in 1896 would have brought the amount unpaid at the end of the year to zero, had it not been for the 'special' revenue bonds not redeemable till 1897.

The movements of the sinking fund (line D) are subject to the opposite influences of accumulations from revenue and depletions by redemption of bonds. The growth of the fund was approximately steady from 1872 to 1890, since when, partly because of smaller payments, the increase has been much more rapid. The net debt (line E) which represents the sum of the funded debt, assessment, and revenue bonds, less the sinking fund, rose for a few years after the downfall of the Ring, but then declined rapidly from 1876 to 1886; since that time there has been an almost equally fast increase till the net indebtedness in 1896 reached within one or two millions of the figures twenty years ago. It will be observed that during the Ring *régime*, and again in 1878, the net debt, owing to the vast amount of temporary bonds outstanding, exceeded the funded debt by a small amount.

If, now, by means of index figures, we compare the progress of the city debt for 1876, 1886, and 1896, with that of the annual appropriations already pointed out, we find a very different picture. Taking 1876, when the net debt was at its maximum as the result of the Ring period, for a basis, we have:—

PROGRESS OF CITY DEBT

	1876	1886	1896
Population	100	133.6	179.7
Assessed valuation	100	128	181
Total appropriations	100	97	133
Variable or contingent appropriations	100	131.6	195.2
Funded debt	100	102.5	154.9
Total bonded debt, including assessment and revenue bonds	100	88.8	133.9
Sinking fund	100	145.8	274.3
Net indebtedness	100	75.4	98.8

These figures show that, during these twenty years, the funded debt and the total debt have increased considerably less rapidly than have population, assessed valuation, or contingent appropriations; that the funded debt has grown considerably faster, but the total debt at almost the same pace as the gross budget; while in net indebtedness there has been an absolute decrease as against very large increases in the figures for population, valuation, and appropriations.

§ 56. *Chief Bond Issues since* 1871.

In tracing now the chief purposes for which loans have been made since 1871, we may, for convenience, group together the first two periods above distinguished, since several bond issues were distributed partly over both. A large part of the debt contracted from 1872 to 1884 may be attributed, directly or indirectly, to the Ring's misrule. The more than sixteen millions [1] of consolidated stock issued to fund revenue bonds and other floating debt; the $9,700,000 required to refund assessment bonds; the $3,899,494 for meeting the state sinking fund deficiency; the nearly equal sum for completing the change of the aqueduct between 93d and 113th streets; the $4,196,000, chiefly borrowed early after the Ring period, for water mains under a Tweed law; and, finally, the $5,707,734

---

[1] Figures following obtained chiefly by comparing debt tables in Comp. Rep., 1884, p. 78, with those of Joint Investigating Committee of 1871, pp. 122–124.

of 'city improvement stock' for street openings — all these may be considered as, to no small extent, a legacy from the era of misgovernment. The most important of the remaining loans during these years were for improving Central Park and for extending the sources of water supply, each of which required more than five millions; for the New York and Brooklyn bridge ($4,638,500); and for constructing docks, about a million yearly being borrowed for the latter purpose from 1872 to 1884.

The main objects for which bonds have been issued during the great borrowing period since 1884 have been (1) water supply, (2) new parks, (3) dock improvements, (4) bridges over the Harlem, (5) new schoolhouses, and (6) repaving of streets.

By far the most expensive enterprise ever undertaken by the city has been the new Croton aqueduct begun under a law of 1883. The need for this work had been for years a crying one. The conduct of the task has been interesting, because of the political motives and of the frauds and litigation connected with it.[1] The evil of state interference found here its most extreme expression. Under the original law the construction of the aqueduct was directed by a commission composed of the mayor, comptroller, commissioner of public works, and four other members, not connected

---

[1] See Report of Special Committee, Senate Documents, 1889, No. 57. The minority agreed in most of the charges.

with the city government, named in the law. The constitution of this body marked a sufficient usurpation by the state of properly municipal power to justify complaint, but it did not satisfy the politicians. Contracts for more than half of the work had been let by this board to the firm of O'Brien & Clark, Mr. O'Brien being chairman of the Democratic state central committee. It is charged that it was the desire of Mr. O'Brien to escape too careful scrutiny of his estimates and bills by the comptroller and mayor in the interests of the city, that led him to make a 'deal' for a reorganization of the aqueduct commission with certain Republicans in the legislature, who, as had been suggested by the speaker of the assembly, thought it "wise to increase the Republican end of that commission in order that the men should not be voted solidly for the Democratic party."[1]

In 1886, accordingly, a bill was run through in a somewhat surreptitious manner, removing the mayor and comptroller from the aqueduct board and putting in their place three persons appointed by the governor. The commission, as thus reconstituted, was composed almost solely of mere politicians, and its work proved far from satisfactory. Mayor Hewitt declared in a letter to the governor: "It is an abomination in the eyes of the citizens of New York, and its history has been one con-

[1] See Report of Special Committee, Senate Documents, 1889, No. 57, p. 699, testimony of Mr. Hamilton Fish.

tinued scandal."[1] Some of the abuses of the aqueduct management were made public in 1888 by a senate investigating committee; and, finally, at a special session of the legislature called in July, on the recommendation of Governor Hill, who acknowledged the injustice of the law of 1886 which he had approved, the board was reconstituted to consist of the mayor, comptroller, commissioner of public works, and four members named by the mayor. Without studying in detail the character and extent of the frauds which were discovered in the aqueduct contracts, suffice it to say that by the substitution of material of poorer grade, by the construction of unnecessary retaining walls in the tunnel, and by excavation in excess of specifications, large sums were added to the cost of the work, while heavy claims for similar charges were rejected. There have been numerous lawsuits over these claims, in which the contractors have for the most part been worsted, and scarcely a year has passed without an effort being made in the legislature to enforce their payment by special act.

The total amount of bonds issued for this great work up to the close of 1896 was no less than $33,695,000.[2] This sum includes the cost not

---

[1] See Report of Special Committee, Senate Documents, 1889, No. 57, p. 42.

[2] Following figures from Comp. Rep., 1894–1896, statements B and D.

merely of the immense tunnel-aqueduct, which was completed several years before the water was actually conveyed by it, but also of new dams and improvements of various sorts, mostly at the source of supply, for which large outlay is still being made. Considerable amounts of bonds of another class are also being issued yearly for acquiring new lands at the Croton watershed.

The agitation for larger park space, like that for more water, dated back many years, and the addition to the city in 1874 of the extensive tracts beyond the Harlem suggested the devotion of part of this territory to the purpose. Opposition to this plan was manifested on the part of certain officers, but there seems no doubt that the general public sentiment was largely in its favor. The territory, selected by commissioners appointed by the mayor under a law of 1883, was so extensive that several years were required to carry through the condemnation proceedings; and meanwhile, as often happens in such cases, much speculation took place in the lands affected, so that the city paid a round price for them. The bonds for paying awards, mostly issued in 1889, have amounted to $9,822,000. While these large parks have been established, the city has also, during the past two or three years, entered quite extensively on the policy of opening small parks in the heart of the town itself. Corlear's Hook, Mulberry Bend, St. John's, Washington Bridge, and other smaller parks and squares have been established at a cost of several millions. Work in improving and adorning these, as well as the large parks in Westchester county, has little more than begun, and doubtless much will ultimately have to be spent upon them. The public speedway, recently commenced, a project somewhat similar in purpose to the parks, has cost the city a considerable amount, while if the 'Grand Concourse' in the annexed district is actually carried out it will involve very large outlay. That New York is not entirely behind in the modern movement for more space and more means of recreation for city dwellers, is evident from the fact that in the twelve years from 1885 to 1896 she expended more than twenty millions on her parks and boulevards; while with this might properly enough be included more than three millions spent on the Museums of Art and Natural History.

For the new Harlem River bridges and improvements, together with half a million for the New East River bridge, there have been issued since 1884 bonds to the amount of $6,745,464; for new schoolhouses and sanitary improvements, more than twelve millions; and for repaving streets, nearly seven and a half millions, besides minor issues for special streets. Some of the first schoolhouse bonds ran for a ten-year term only and are already falling due; the later ones are for twenty years. It will be remembered that according to the assessment laws it is impossible to charge the cost of renewals and repairs of pavements upon the abutting property unless the owners petition, and an immense amount of repaving has had accordingly to be done at general expense. Only unusual circumstances can justify the creation of debt for such purposes as building schoolhouses and paving streets, since in a large and rapidly growing city the probabilities are ordinarily that approximately an equal amount of such improvements will be necessary every year; they are properly current rather than extraordinary expenses. But in New York, during the Ring misrule and the succeeding years of unavoidable restriction in both taxation and borrowing, the condition of the schoolhouses and of the streets became exceptionally bad, and thereafter to have placed the cost of immediately necessary work on the taxpayers would doubtless have been unjust. Further large bond issues for all the purposes just mentioned are still being made.

Without dwelling specifically upon the rather numerous minor issues of bonds, the following table may be given as summarizing all the loans since the fall of the Ring.[1] The dates of issue are roughly indicated in the case of the more important stocks.

[1] Figures chiefly obtained by comparing tables in Report of Joint Investigating Committee, pp. 122-124, with statements B and D in Comp. Rep. of 1884 and 1896.

THE CITY DEBT

Bonds Issued September 16, 1871, to December 31, 1896

Water supply:		
New aqueduct, 1884–1896	$33,695,000	
Water mains, 1871–1875, 1896	4,683,500	
Other purposes	12,959,772	$51,338,272
Parks:		
Improvement of Central Park, 1871–1880	5,661,000	
Purchase of new lands, 1889–1896	14,161,304	
Miscellaneous improvements	4,458,500	24,280,803
Public buildings and sites:		
School-houses, chiefly 1884–1896	14,011,851	
Armories, 1884–1895	3,544,998	
Museums of Art and Nat. Hist.	4,054,103	
Court-houses and miscel. buildings	5,332,444	
Lands and sites for buildings	1,144,478	28,087,875
Street improvements; boulevards:		
City impr. stocks (openings), 1871–1883, 1895	6,486,506	
Boulevards, 1871–1883, 1894–1896	3,855,350	
Repaving, general, 1889–1896	7,393,500	
Miscellaneous	1,555,194	19,290,550
Bridges:		
New York and Brooklyn	5,672,566	
Other, chiefly over Harlem	7,069,434	12,742,000
Docks		28,553,000
Refunding old debt[1]		
Consolidated stock, Ring debt	16,695,249	
Funding assessment bonds, 1878–1880	9,700,000	
Refunding consol. stock of Ring period, 1896	8,377,000	
State sinking fund deficiency	3,899,494	38,671,743
Debt of annexed territory, 1881, 1896		1,642,943
Miscellaneous		660,361
Total issues		205,267,553
Debt September 16, 1871		81,351,158
		286,618,711
Bonds redeemed, 1871–1896		100,429,469
Debt December 31, 1896		186,189,242

[1] The bonds for the liquidation of claims and judgments, issued during the '70's, are omitted, as they ran for only a few years and were mostly funded by consolidated stock, so that to include them would have been duplication.

§ 57. *Present State of Debt. Effect of Consolidation.*

Various subdivisions of the debt are made in the comptrollers' reports according to the respective relations to the sinking fund, — the bonds originally charged thereto under the ordinance of 1844, the second lien bonds under the act of 1878, etc., being separated from one another. Since, however, under the present law all the funded bonds of the city now outstanding, except those for water supply issued under the constitutional amendment of 1884, may be, and almost beyond question will be, redeemed from sinking fund No. 1 (that now supported solely by the miscellaneous revenues), these technical distinctions may be disregarded here. We need only to retain the broad division between bonds respectively redeemable from sinking fund No. 1 and from sinking fund No. 2. It is of interest, however, to notice that only $2,500,600 of the old water and park bonds, to which the sinking fund was originally pledged, remain outstanding; and as it is only on these that the 'sinking fund for interest' pays interest (aside from the nominal payment on the bonds held by the redemption fund), the amount subtracted from the interest fund, before the transfer of its surplus to the redemption fund, is very small, and will become zero before many years. The following is a statement of the situation of the debt December 31, 1896: —

City Debt, December 31, 1896[1]

Funded debt:	
Payable from sinking fund No. 1	$147,419,242
Water debt payable from fund No. 2	38,770,000
Total	186,189,242
Temporary debt:	
Assessment bonds	9,718,448
Revenue bonds	2,433,326
Total bonded debt	198,341,017
Amount of both sinking funds	77,630,491
Net debt of all classes	120,710,526
Net debt, less revenue bonds	118,277,200

The amount of sinking fund No. 1 was $65,904,946, so that the net funded debt to which it will be applicable was $81,514,296. Sinking fund No. 2 amounted to $11,725,544, and the net water debt under the constitutional amendment of 1884 was thus $27,044,456. Comment has already been made on the interest of these various bonds, which now is at a weighted average of somewhat less than 4 per cent. The term of the various bonds varies considerably, and very unequal amounts mature in different years. An exceptionally large sum fell due in 1896, and again in 1901, 1904, 1907, 1908, and 1915–1916, the amounts maturing will be large; but under the sinking fund system this inequality is comparatively unimportant as regards particular years, provided, as is actually the case, there is a fairly even distribution as between longer periods. A majority of the

[1] Statements B and E. Comp. Rep., 1896.

bonds recently issued have been made due and payable in twenty years from date, but many thirty-year bonds are also issued. More than $25,000,000 of stocks, largely created in 1878 and 1889, have been made payable at option after twenty or thirty years, but are not due for twenty years longer.

The net funded city debt, in the sense used by the state constitution, at the close of the last fiscal year ($118,277,200), was equal to 5.6 per cent of the assessed valuation of real and personal property, and represented $59.32 of indebtedness *per capita*. Comparison with other American cities may be made by means of the United States census of 1890. The relative *per capita* indebtedness is of most importance, the proportion borne by debt to assessed valuation being of little significance because of the widely varying methods of valuing property. Material changes in the following table would be necessary if figures for 1896 were available: —

PER CAPITA DEBT OF AMERICAN CITIES, 1890[1]

Jersey City	$106.56	Pittsburgh	$42.02
Cincinnati	83.32	Minneapolis	38.98
Baltimore	73.22	Philadelphia	28.29
New Orleans	69.81	Cleveland	23.51
Boston	62.82	Milwaukee	14.26
New York (1896)	59.32	Chicago	11.98
St. Paul	54.55	Detroit	10.76
St. Louis	47.87	San Francisco	2.50
Brooklyn	42.96	All cities over 4000	31.39
Buffalo	42.51		

[1] U. S. Census, compiled from report on Wealth, Debt, and Taxation, Vol. I.

It will be seen that five large cities had, in 1890, heavier debt burdens than that now borne by New York. Since that year, moreover, Brooklyn has borrowed so largely as to nearly equal New York in *per capita* indebtedness, while the proportion borne to the assessed value of property is considerably greater than in New York. In fact, since the consolidated city assumes also the payment of Kings county bonds, the annexation of the sister city places the debt in a much more unfavorable condition than before as regards the constitutional limit of 10 per cent of the real estate valuation. The gross debt of Brooklyn in 1895 was $57,728,521, leaving the net debt, deducting the small sinking fund, $52,037,000 or 9.6 per cent of the real estate valuation. Kings county, with practically the same territory as the city, owed nearly thirteen millions in 1895, and two or three millions of bonds have been issued by the other bodies united by the law of 1897. The net debt of Greater New York at the date of consolidation, January 1, 1898, will be about 185 or 190 millions, approximately 8 per cent of the assessed valuation of real property.

§ 58. *The Sinking Fund and Future Debt Issues.*

The large additions to the city debt thus to be made by consolidation will not, according to the new charter, be chargeable upon the present sinking funds of New York city; but the metropolis will be compelled to carry out all existing provisions of law for sinking the bonds of the former separate bodies — chiefly by raising taxes. Nor, as we have seen, will the present funds be charged directly with stocks hereafter created, for which primarily taxation is to be the means of redemption. A study of the present capacities of the sinking fund No. 1 will show, however, that, if the law can be so interpreted as to allow the transfer of its surplus as soon as accumulations reach the present amount of bonds, and before they mature, it will soon be able to aid largely in redeeming bonds hereafter issued, and, indeed, will perhaps be more than sufficient to meet them. Redemption fund No. 2 may be disregarded here, since its accumulation must be at a perfectly definite rate, and from taxation.

There have been few changes since 1844 in the classes of ordinary revenues from city property, franchises, etc. (aside from taxes and assessments) set apart to the interest and redemption funds. The most important has been the removal from the redemption fund of excise licenses, which now constitute a distinct feature in the finances. Some additions to the annual revenues of the funds have been made by devoting to them the surplus earnings of the New York and Brooklyn bridge, receipts from railway franchises, and other minor sources; but the great cause of the rapid increase which has taken place is the growth of the income from docks and from Croton water rents, which contribute nearly nine-tenths of the net revenues of redemption fund No. 1 and of the interest fund.[1] Under the present law practically all of the revenues originally pledged to these two funds go ultimately to the redemption fund, which receives almost no other real income. The receipts of the interest fund for 1896 were $4,796,775, but all save about $120,000 of this was transferred to the redemption fund as interest on bonds held by it and as surplus. The net revenue of the redemption fund, excluding the small amount received from assessments and excluding the transfers just mentioned, was $2,879,601. Now in order to estimate the future growth of the redemption fund, we may take as a basis the total net revenues of the redemption and the interest funds combined, since soon the interest payments from the interest fund on bonds outside the other fund will cease entirely, as will the income of the redemption fund from assessments. The rate of increase in these revenues for the future may be roughly estimated from that shown in the past twenty years, which is indicated by the following figures, the years 1875-95 being chosen as more typical than 1876-96:

	1875	1880	1885	1890	1895
Net revenues . . .	$3,160,552	$3,296,300	$4,818,681	$5,892,962	$7,731,119
Index numbers . .	100	104	152	186	244

[1] See table, p. 183.

Thus the annual revenues, hereafter practically all available for the redemption fund, have multiplied two and one-half times within twenty years, while the rate of increase has been constantly becoming more rapid. It will certainly be an exceedingly conservative assumption to suppose that these same revenues twenty years hence will, unless some change of policy in fixing charges is made, be double what they are now. On this hypothesis the income of the sinking fund for 1916 would be $15,352,752 (double $7,676,376 for 1896); and, if the increase be assumed as in arithmetical progression, the average annual income from 1897 to 1916 inclusive would be $11,514,564, and the total additions to the redemption fund No. 1 would be $230,291,280. On January 1, 1897, the amount of debt which, under the new charter, is primarily chargeable to this fund, less the amount already accumulated by the fund, was only $81,514,296, and it will probably not be much greater when the charter takes effect. It is more than probable that the sinking fund will within ten years have entirely provided for this indebtedness, the average maturity of which is over fifteen years. If then the ambiguous words of the charter above quoted are held to mean that the revenues of the fund cannot be diverted till the bonds charged to it are actually redeemed, either hardship will arise, as so often before, from unnecessary accumulations, or some change in the

law will be required. In fact it is by no means
unlikely that the revenues at present pledged to
the sinking fund would be more than able, un-
aided by taxation, to provide for all bonds hereafter issued by the greater city, except water
bonds, for which taxes are constitutionally required,
— but it is of course impossible even to guess at
the amount of money that will be borrowed in
the future.

Many New York citizens are very proud of the
manner in which the redemption fund has grown,
and have a vague belief that it enables the city to
borrow without burdening its taxpayers. As a
matter of fact, the sinking fund system is extremely crude. We have seen how it has pro-
duced hardships in the past, which only awkward
devices of transfers of revenues and changes in
the applicability of the redemption fund, requiring
special legislative act, have in part removed. The
system under the new charter is even more complex than before, and while possibly no hardships will again result, it is difficult to see why
the framers of the charter should have perpetuated the old conditions, at least longer than
was necessary to fulfil present obligations. It
would have been quite as safe for bondholders,
much simpler, and probably would have distributed the burden of debt payment more evenly
than is likely to prove the case, had the plan of
raising annual taxes for bonds hereafter created,

as required by the charter, been adopted without the further provision for turning over to the new sinking fund the surplus of the old sinking fund. The system of appropriating special classes of revenue, instead of fixed annual sums, to the debt, cannot give that perfectly proportional and certain reduction which is so desirable in managing local indebtedness.[1] It is never advisable except when credit is so low that only by having their fingers directly on the means of repayment will moneylenders offer loans. The system to which the metropolis has clung so closely is, in fact, as Professor Ross[2] declares, "characteristic of new countries in the earlier stages of financiering, or of nations threatened with disaster to public credit. . . . It is a survival of the time when general national credit was unknown, and loans were raised by pledging specific funds to pay interest and principal." Surely New York is not so far behind the great majority of our American municipalities that she needs to adopt this antiquated system while they incur loans on the security of sinking funds raised by annual taxes. The specific revenue system in New York has already caused so many difficulties and required so many patches by act of the legislature that any prejudice in its

---

[1] It is often very undesirable in national financiering to continue sinking fund accumulations while the country is actually borrowing largely, but in municipalities the conditions are entirely different.

[2] Sinking Funds, p. 95.

favor should have long since been dispelled. The plan of pledging specific revenue from certain income-creating works to the service of the debt created for their construction does indeed aid in clear comprehension of the working of municipal investments, but even here the object may be accomplished by merely keeping an additional set of accounts. At any rate this advantage has never even been sought by New York financiers.

A further strong objection to the present sinking fund system is that it confuses the people as to the real cost of government. The payments for the interest and redemption of the debt in New York, as everywhere else, should and do constitute just as real and immediate a burden on the taxpayers as any other form of public outlay, unless of course bonds have been issued for income-earning investments. Yet owing to the fact that a large part of the expenditures on the debt do not appear in the regular budget account, many citizens fail to appreciate this burden. By the complicated practice of keeping the accounts of the three sinking funds, which will be yet further involved under the new charter, the actual outlay for the debt service is made still more difficult to ascertain.[1] Under the simple plan of

---

[1] This lack of clearness is only partly remedied in one of the tables of the comptroller's reports (Statement G), which, immediately under the expenditures on appropriation account, gives those from the sinking funds. It is evident that the real annual

gradual amortization from taxation, the entire expenditures for interest and redemption would have their place in the regular appropriation account, and the people would realize clearly that the debt payments constitute a real and direct burden upon them. All the miscellaneous revenues would then be merged in the general fund; a change which would produce the further incidental advantages that, without the complications of the present scattering of these revenues among the general fund, the redemption fund, and the interest fund, it could be seen clearly and at once just how much they contributed to the city finances; and, more important still, that without difficulty the management of every source of municipal income could be brought under the single supervision of the body possessing the general control of the budget.

This objection as to the obscurity resulting from the present sinking fund system is not a mere theoretical one. There can be no doubt that many citizens of New York quite misunderstand the nature of the sinking fund. The newspapers not infrequently explain with *sang froid* that the 'sinking fund will take care of' money borrowed, with no burden to taxpayers, and even city officials who have charge of the creation of debt are

---

contribution toward the debt is not represented by the amounts paid to redeem maturing bonds, which fluctuate widely, but by the additions made to the sinking fund for redemption itself.

said sometimes to fall into this fallacy. There is a manifest tendency to look upon the fund as a sort of self-sufficient entity, a widow's cruse that by some legerdemain will allow the people to spend money without taking it from their pockets.

CHAPTER XII

AUDIT, ACCOUNT, AND FINANCIAL RESPONSIBILITY

§ 59. *Auditing and Accounting System.*[1]

The methods of accounting and auditing are often omitted in financial studies as comparatively unimportant, but from the bearing that they have on the general honesty and efficiency of the administration, the main outlines of practice in New York deserve mention.

The two chief financial officers are the comptroller and the chamberlain. The former, who is elected by the people every three years (every four years under the new charter), has the more important and discretionary functions, and is denominated the head of the finance department. The chamberlain merely heads a bureau in the department, although he is appointed directly by the mayor, and his duties are almost purely ministerial. All moneys of the city, from whatever source, pass ultimately through the hands of the chamberlain, but not all receipts come through the comptroller's office, nor are all disbursements

---

[1] For general outline see Consolidation Act, §§ 123-126, 163-165; Comp. Rep., 1892, pp. 58-66.

ordered by him. The collection of various forms of revenue is in the control of departments to which they specially relate — water rents being paid to the department of public works, dock rents to the dock department, etc.; while the sinking fund commissioners directly draw warrants on the sinking funds. All moneys received are turned over to the chamberlain daily and at once deposited in bank. The city depositories, which are designated by majority vote of the mayor, comptroller, and chamberlain, must agree to pay interest on the daily balances at a rate fixed for each quarter by those officers. No bank may hold more of the city's money than amounts to half its capital and surplus.

A general outline of the system of accounts has already been given in § 33. Besides a record of cash receipts and payments, separate accounts are kept by both comptroller and chamberlain of the sums appropriated under each head, which are treated as credits, and of the expenditures charged to them. The comptroller is required to furnish each department weekly a statement of the unexpended balances of its various appropriations; while the chamberlain is forbidden to pay any warrant drawn against an exhausted appropriation.

Before any claim upon the city can be paid it must go through a rather long process. For the most part each separate bill of each individual must be paid by a distinct warrant of the comptroller; there are no gross payments to departments — except to the police department — to be by them disbursed in detail. The first audit of bills, however, is naturally by the department concerned. In departments governed by several commissioners, a formal vote of the board, duly recorded, is required to approve bills, such action being, of course, based on reports by inspectors and auditing officers connected with the department. The effect of approving a claim is to draw a requisition on the comptroller, which must be accompanied by a voucher containing the necessary statements concerning its validity, usually verified by oath, the receipt, signed in advance, etc. But this departmental audit is by no means final; the bill must pass the scrutiny of the auditing bureau of the finance department, which is headed by two auditors. There expert accountants examine the vouchers to see if all the numerous technical requirements have been complied with; and, more important than this formal procedure, the bureau does a vast amount of actual inspection of work and supplies, especially in the case of contracts, to ascertain whether fair value has been received. Although only ten or a dozen inspectors and engineers are employed by the bureau, they discover many defects and omissions that have been passed over by the more numerous departmental inspectors. During 1892 they made about 19,000 inspections and examinations, and reported adversely in nearly 3000 cases; while in 1894, out of 38,010 vouchers and pay-rolls examined by the auditing bureau, 1847 were returned for correction to the departments.[1]

If a claim is found correct, the auditors duly certify to that effect and prepare in blank a warrant addressed to the chamberlain, which states on its face the precise purpose of the payment and the appropriation or account to which it is charged.[2] All warrants must be signed by the comptroller in person, and until recently had to be countersigned by the mayor himself; but this proving too great a burden, the duty is now performed by his chief clerk. A check on one of the city depositories is inseparably attached to each warrant, and this must be signed by the chamberlain personally, before the claimant can receive his money.

There are two exceptions to this method of paying bills. The first is with regard to the police department, which has a separate treasury, and receives monthly from the comptroller warrants for one-twelfth of the amount of each main head of the police appropriation. So far as the pay of the force is concerned, this arrangement is not spe-

---

[1] Comp. Rep., 1892, p. 58; 1894, p. 17. The number of inspections and of adverse reports does not determine definitely the number of vouchers sent back for correction.

[2] Warrants on the appropriation account are designated as 'A,' those on special and trust accounts as 'B' warrants.

cially anomalous,—it merely constitutes a second paymaster's bureau,—but when it is extended to payments for miscellaneous purposes it seems to make the department too independent of the auditing supervision of the comptroller. This disadvantage is partly overcome, however, by a provision that the comptroller may require duplicate vouchers to be filed in his office. The other exception to the general auditing system is the very natural one of pay-rolls. Warrants covering the collective salaries and wages in each division of each department are drawn to the city paymaster. He pays day laborers in cash, while salaried officers receive checks signed by the paymaster, but, like ordinary warrants, prepared in blank under the supervision of the auditing bureau.

Practically the only change in the auditing system under the Greater New York charter is that additional auditors will be appointed, part of whom are to act on claims arising in the separate boroughs.

§ 60. *Financial Records and Reports.*

If, in the early days of the city and again during the Ring period, there was great lack of publicity regarding financial details, the evils that arose from this lack have caused the enactment of laws requiring frequent publication of the most minute transactions. Records of every branch of the administration are kept in great detail, and abstracts giving the essentials are published weekly in the

City Record.[1] The *Record* is a daily journal devoted solely to city business, and its contents have so increased that they now fill from five to six thousand finely printed pages yearly. Especially every action of a department relating in any way to expenditure must be reported, — the main features of contracts entered into during the week, the bills audited, the amount of requisitions drawn on the comptroller, etc. The chamberlain and the comptroller publish separate weekly statements; the latter giving, not merely receipts and payments according to the main heads of account, but the bonds issued, the amount of the city debt, a list of contracts made by all departments, the openings of bids for contracts attended by the comptroller, and other details. Quarterly reports also are required of every department;[2] the finance department makes two, one giving general financial transactions, the other, that of the auditing bureau, containing a list of all separate warrants drawn, with the payee, the purpose, etc., in detail.

Most departments make also annual reports. The legal provisions regarding those of the finance department are very unsatisfactory. The fiscal and budget year corresponds with that of the calendar, yet a report covering the year ending December 31 is not required by law, while two reports are required for periods of twelve months ending at other dates. The first of these

---

[1] Consolidation Act, § 51.   [2] *Ibid.*, § 49.

is the official 'annual statement of the receipts and expenditures' by the comptroller, which must be published two months before the annual election, for the year ending on the first of the month when it is made. This practice dates from the old days when the city election was held in April, so that the report actually covered the calendar year preceding. When the election was changed to November, this section of the charter was retained unaltered,[1] and the report now covers the year ending July 31. The budgets of two years are thus involved, and the report becomes not only superfluous, but confusing. Another act[2] requires the accounts of the chamberlain to be closed on the last day of November; the commissioners of accounts must then examine them, together with all the vouchers, and publish a summary of the accounts for the preceding twelve months, with a detailed statement of the city debt. If the finance department did no more than the law thus requires, it would be very difficult to follow the financial transactions of the city, and this was indeed the case from 1870 till, in 1879, the department began the practice of making its last quarterly report a summary of the year. In 1883 the summary was made a document distinct from the quarterly report; and since then this annual statement, which is what is ordinarily understood by the 'comptroller's report,' has been enlarged and improved,

---

[1] Consolidation Act, § 126. [2] *Ibid.*, § 164.

and various tables and comparisons with previous years have been added till, at last, it has come to present a very satisfactory view of the city finances.

The charter of Greater New York provides that the report of the finance department, now published annually in August, shall be made only once in two years. While making no definite provision for continuing the present series of reports covering the calendar year, it establishes a bureau of general municipal statistics, which is to publish an annual volume containing financial and other statistical tables. It is to be hoped that ultimately the financial statements of the metropolis will be made much more easy of comprehension and more logical than they now are.

§ 61. *Inspection of Accounts and Official Responsibility.*

So numerous and complex are the reports of the various departments that it is practically impossible for citizens, or for officers whose duties are not specially connected with the accounts, to understand them and detect errors or frauds. This difficulty the charter of 1873 sought to remedy by establishing two 'commissioners of accounts,'[1] appointed by the mayor and specially subject to his direction, whose sole duty it is to examine printed reports, and more particularly original papers and accounts. Besides their annual report

[1] Consolidation Act, § 110.

on the finances for the year ending November 30, these commissioners make quarterly examinations of the accounts of the comptroller and the chamberlain, and not merely report as to their correctness, but publish detailed statements that are little more than duplicates of those of the finance department itself. Besides these regular tasks, they undertake from time to time, at the bidding of the mayor, special investigations of the business methods and accounts of particular departments; for this purpose they are empowered to summon witnesses and compel testimony. It is probably true, as has been sometimes charged, that the action of the commissioners of accounts has usually been to considerable degree perfunctory, giving little additional security against mismanagement.[1] The investigations into the city government, now and then made by special committees of the state legislature, awaken much more popular attention and produce more direct results in the way of modifications of law and practice than do those of the commissioners of accounts. Unfortunately, partisan motives enter to such an extent into these legislative investigations that they, too, are usually of comparatively little value.

[1] Testimony before the Fassett Investigating Committee showed that the commissioners then in office were decidedly incompetent and did very little personal work on the accounts, and that committee was of the opinion that the commissioners had never accomplished anything of value. Senate Documents, 1891, No. 80, pp. 2567 ff.; part 5, p. 119.

Various other detailed provisions of law,[1] for securing responsibility of public officers, have grown out of the abuses against which the charters of 1853, 1857, and 1873 were aimed. All official records and accounts must be open to the inspection of any taxpayer. On the affidavit of the mayor, comptroller, a commissioner of accounts, or of any five aldermen or taxpayers, an order may be issued by a judge of the supreme court, directing any officer to be summarily examined touching his use of public moneys, and other witnesses may also be summoned. Severe penalties for fraud and bribery in all their forms are prescribed. Aldermen and officials are forbidden direct or indirect interest in contracts or expenditures. A provision of no small importance in this general direction is that all fees and perquisites of every officer, except the sheriff, who still retains one-half his fees,[2] must be turned over to the city treasury, fixed salaries being paid in place of such remuneration.

By means of all these provisions for full accounts, frequent reports, and liability to investigation, — provisions scarcely modified in the charter of 1897, — New York has secured a fair degree of official responsibility and honesty, so far as purely financial matters are concerned. A few instances of peculation and fraud have been discovered since 1873, and doubtless not a few more have never

---

[1] Consolidation Act, §§ 50-64.   [2] Laws, 1890, Chap. 523.

seen the light; but anything like the extensive mismanagement that prevailed even before the Tweed period hardly exists now. Serious evils indeed have existed in the city government during the past twenty-five years; inefficiency, neglect, misuse of official power, have been flagrant enough, but open and direct stealing of city money has not often occurred.

In indirect ways, however, hardly within reach of law, the city treasury often suffers. Among these may be mentioned an occasional abuse of the contract system. The law provides that, in case the value of the work or material for any particular purpose exceeds $1,000, it must be performed or furnished by contract, unless by three-fourths vote the council orders otherwise. Contracts are let, after due advertisement for bids, by the heads of the departments concerned, but the comptroller is always represented at the opening of proposals. The contract must be awarded to the lowest bidder, unless all bids are rejected. Bidders must deposit a security for good faith, and the accepted contractor must give bonds. The comptroller is required to certify that there remains unexpended and unpledged, to the credit of the appropriation or account concerned, a sufficient sum to cover the estimated amount of the contract, and this amount must be treated thereafter as pledged to the purpose.[1] Of the almost inevi-

---
[1] Consolidation Act, § 123.

table abuses that have connected themselves with this contract system, the most common is that resulting from 'unbalanced bids.' These are most frequent and striking in the case of street grading, and the term may be most readily understood by an illustration from a job of this kind. Street grading usually involves two classes of work, — rock excavation and earth excavation. The city engineers estimate the respective quantities that will be required, and the bids are at so much per cubic yard for the number of yards estimated of each kind. Not infrequently these rates are utterly disproportionate to the true value, the one being excessively high, the other excessively low; that is, the bid is unbalanced. To cite an actual case,[1] the successful bid for one job in 1883 was for 20,000 yards of rock excavation at 2 cents per yard; 10,000 yards of earth at $1.62½ per yard, the actual values of such work being perhaps $1.20 per yard for the former and 30 cents for the latter. The product ($16,650) of these widely unbalanced bids — at the estimated amount of excavation of each sort — was lower than the bid of any other contractor. Now, as often happens, the relative quantities of the two classes of work turned out very differently from the estimates; there proved to be only 9241 yards of rock and 20,576 of earth; so that at the rates named, which always hold regardless of the actual amount of work done, the

[1] *New York Tribune*, December 9, 1883, pp. 1, 2.

contractor ultimately received $33,620. The rationality of making unbalanced bids is simply that the contractors, by their familiarity with the peculiar conformation of rock and earth in different parts of Manhattan Island, are often able to judge more accurately than are the city engineers as to the true amount of excavation of each class. Unbalanced bids are sometimes also made on jobs of other kinds.

This practice was the cause of considerable agitation during 1883 and 1884, and a legislative committee took up the matter.[1] Several flagrant instances of overcharge were brought forward, and it was even alleged that there was collusion on the part of city officers in making intentionally incorrect estimates. Probably some truth lay in all this, but it was hardly proved conclusively. The department of public works declared that, while in a considerable proportion of its contracts bids were unbalanced, yet in the long run the estimates of the city engineers averaged so nearly correct that practically no loss was suffered; and further maintained that it was impossible to overcome the practice under the existing law requiring the award to the lowest bidder. The movement made to enact laws requiring bids to be in gross sums for the entire work, or otherwise to do away with the system of unbalanced bids, finally subsided with-

[1] Senate Documents, 1884, No. 57, pp. 31 ff. See also *New York Tribune* for December, 1883.

out action being taken, and such bids still continue to be quite frequent. In the case of street grading, however, danger of loss has been largely removed by taking greater pains in estimates, borings being made for each job with no little care.

At the time when these charges just described were made, it was also alleged that in a great many instances the provision requiring works valued at over $1000 to be done by contract was evaded, in violation of the express terms of law, by breaking up jobs into parts whose aggregate far exceeded that amount.[1] Several instances were cited in which this had doubtless been done, but no way of remedying the difficulty has appeared save by greater strictness in the enforcement of existing laws.

[1] Senate Document cited, pp. 35 ff. *Tribune*, dates cited.

CONCLUSION

§ 62. *Concluding Remarks.*

A summary of the history and the present form of the financial system of New York has already been given in the introductory chapters, and it is necessary here merely to call attention to a few general aspects of the subject. Our study has shown us that the outer form and the practical working of the financial system have been intimately dependent upon the condition of the general municipal administration and of state and national politics. The control of the purse is indeed naturally of prime importance in municipal affairs, and both the form and the spirit of the city government will be reflected very perfectly in the financial management, while on the other hand any change in the form of the financial system tends strongly to affect the character of the general administration. Unfortunately, the two influences which have acted most powerfully in determining the charter history and financial history of the metropolis have been the desire to gain political advantages and the desire to check existing abuses; and the natural result has been that most changes in the form of government have been mere patches, mere expedients to accomplish an immediate end, rather than carefully studied, systematic changes. The new cloth and the old have not always gone well together; indeed, the new has often rent greater gaps in the old. In 1830 and again in 1849, to be sure, somewhat more systematic attempts were made to reorganize the city government, but the former largely failed to change the real nature of the administration, and the political conditions soon after the charter of 1849 became such that the government was distorted out of all semblance of reasonableness. The innovations of the Tweed charter had no logical basis; it was merely a device to increase the power of the Ring; yet so great was the strength of precedent, so little the independence of the framers of the charter of 1873, that the anomalies of the previous law were largely perpetuated. Even the charter of Greater New York has attempted to combine warring elements, simply because precedent exists for them individually.

If the history of the general frame of government has been thus one of inconsistency, that of the separate features of the finances has been no less so. The budget system, considered as a system, has passed from bad to worse. The sinking fund has never been managed in a scientific manner; temporary makeshifts have modified the system only when its hardships became unendurable. The management of special assessments likewise has been often readjusted in this unsystematic fashion, under the stress of immediate needs, and remains still complex and inconsistent. Above all is the power to authorize debt issues unduly complicated. In all these respects the charter of Greater New York does little to effect improvement.

It is, to be sure, true that in some ways this method of patchwork legislation has its advantages. Revolutionary changes, even though logically defensible, are often practically dangerous, not to say impossible. Especially where customs, rather than laws, are adjusted gradually in accordance with new conditions, the result is apt to be more satisfactory than if a sudden transition were made. But unfortunately New York's charter and financial history shows little of this natural growth, this evolution. Such quite extraordinary circumstances as the extreme strength of party feeling during the war, as the unparalleled corruption of the Ring period, have worked changes in the municipal organization which, perpetuated in written law, have remained unmodified under widely different conditions. Both the officers of the city and the state legislators, who have had most to do with framing the statutes which govern the city, have for the most part been ignorant of general principles and, indeed, far from familiar with the actual conditions which they sought to remedy;

while partisan motives likewise have largely determined their action. The result is that the city has not had a frame of government which worked smoothly, either because it was logical or because it was a natural outgrowth; the government has been both theoretically and practically one of discord and confusion.

Fortunately civic spirit in the city is rapidly growing. Reform movements, indeed, have been often mere flurries, subsiding as soon as the city elections are over. We must not hope for any sudden and complete change in the people or in the form of the administration. But there is growing a deeper movement, one which aims at thorough understanding of needs and of methods, and from this ultimately will come better things. So complex are many of the financial details in the city government that it can scarcely be expected that the body of the citizens will soon thoroughly comprehend them and demand improvement. There is more hope for reform in the finances by a reorganization of the general administration, and above all by the election, and the reëlection, of able and disinterested public officials. Nevertheless, the anomalous nature of the present budget system, even as modified by the Greater New York charter, the undue complication of authorities in enterprises involving special assessments or bond issues, the unscientific management of public works and franchises in the past—these at least are financial matters which every citizen should and can understand, and in which he should insist upon reform. It would seem, moreover, that popular interest might be sufficient to demand that the new bureau of municipal statistics, which is to be established, shall publish in its reports, and in newspapers of general circulation, brief and clear statements concerning the city finances, avoiding the technical complications which now exist in the accounts, and explaining in simple terms the significance of the figures presented. Such comprehensible financial statements would surely prove of great practical value.

APPENDIX

TABLE OF WORKS CITED

NOTE. — Many of the authorities consulted consist of long series of annual publications, and minor changes in title from year to year often occur. The present form of title, in the case of series continued up to this time, is employed in the citations. The deviations in the earlier names are not sufficient to cause the reader any difficulty in discovering the works referred to. Not a few of the documents and series cited separately, and which are bound as separate volumes, appear likewise in the sets of collected documents published from year to year by the city of New York and by the state of New York. In addition to the works below, a large number of unofficial pamphlets, circulars, speeches, etc., have been consulted for impressions as to the general political situation and state of public opinion.

PUBLICATIONS OF THE STATE OF NEW YORK

(Except where stated, published at Albany)

Constitutions of the state of New York, adopted 1821, 1846, 1894. With amendments.

Proceedings and debates of the constitutional convention of the state of New York held in 1867 and 1868. Albany, 1868.

Records of New Netherland. English manuscript translation.

Laws of the province of New York passed from 1691 to 1775. Editions: 1691-1773. Peter Van Schaack. 2 vols. New York, 1774.

1691–1762, Livingston & Smith. 2 vols. New York, 1752, 1762.

1773, 1774, 1775, original folios, no title-page.

Laws of the state of New York passed at the 1st to 120th sessions of the legislature, 1777–1897.

Editions: 1777–1801, reprinted by state. Albany, 1886.

1778–1792, Greenleaf. 3 vols. New York, 1798.

1802–1804, Webster. Albany, 1804.

1805–1897, original official editions.

Some of the specific laws — the charters, etc. — are so important that they might be mentioned here as separate documents, but their location may be found by consulting index and footnotes of this book. The present law governing New York city is: "An act to consolidate into one act and to declare the special and local laws affecting public interests in the city of New York." Laws of 1882, Chap. 410. The Greater New York charter will be found in separate form as well as in the laws of 1897, Chap. 378.

Journal of the senate, 1st to 120th sessions, 1777–1897.

Journal of the assembly, 1st to 120th sessions, 1777–1897.

Documents of the senate, 53d to 120th sessions, 1830–1897.

Before 1830, bound with senate journal.

Documents of the assembly, 53d to 120th sessions, 1830–1897.

Before 1830, bound with assembly journal.

These collective sets of documents contain all the publications of the state except those specifically named in this table. Those most noteworthy are: —

Tilden Commission. Report of the commission appointed to devise a plan for the government of cities in the state of New York. Assembly documents, 1877, No. 68.

Fassett Committee. Testimony taken before the senate committee on cities. 5 vols. Part V contains the conclusions of the committee. Senate documents, 1891, No. 80.

Bills of the senate, 1830–1897.

Bills of the assembly, 1830–1897.

Reports of cases decided in the court of appeals (New York Reports), vols. 1-153, 1847-1897. Albany or New York.

Reports of cases in the supreme court of the state of New York (Hun's Reports), vols. 1-99, 1874-1897.

Public papers of the governors, 1777-1896.

PUBLICATIONS OF THE CITY OF NEW YORK

(All published at New York)

The *City Record:* official journal. Daily, June 24, 1873-date. This is devoted solely to city reports, advertisements, etc. It contains all the proceedings and reports of the city council and departments, except the comptroller's report for the year ending December 31. Many of these reports, especially annual ones, are also printed in separate form, but for convenience the *City Record* is usually cited in the text.

Charters of the city of New York: Dongan charter, 1686; Montgomerie charter, 1730, granted by royal governors. Published in all compilations of city laws, and in the corporation manuals from 1850-1870. Charters granted by the state legislature in 1830, 1849, 1857, 1870, 1873, 1882 (consolidation act), 1897. See Laws of New York for those years.

Laws and ordinances ordained and established by the mayor, aldermen, and commonalty. The compiler of the ordinances in 1838-1839 knew of the following previous editions: 1763, 1786, 1793, 1797, 1799, 1801, 1803, 1808, 1812, 1817, 1821, 1823, 1827, 1834. Also editions in 1845, 1859, 1866, 1880.

Records of the burgomasters and schepens of New Amsterdam. English manuscript translation.

Minutes of the city council. Manuscript, 1665-1830.

Proceedings of the board of aldermen, vols. 1-224, 1830-1897.

Proceedings of the board of assistant aldermen (or councilmen), vols. 1-136, 1830-1875.

Proceedings of the council approved by the mayor, vols. 1-64, 1831-1896.
Documents of the board of aldermen, 1830-1878.
Documents of the board of assistant aldermen, 1830-1875.

These two sets of documents contain often, though not always, the annual comptroller's reports, and various other series which also appear separately bound. The most important document cited, aside from series, is: "Report of the special committee appointed to investigate the Ring frauds, together with the testimony." Documents of 1877, No 8.

Proceedings of the board of supervisors of the county of New York, 1809-1874. 1809-1850 first printed, New York, 1865.

Documents of the board of supervisors of the county of New York, 1857-1874. Bound with proceedings till 1864. These contain the comptroller's county reports, estimates, etc.

Annual report of the comptroller of the city for the year ending December 31, 1830-1870, 1880-1896. Also for 1879 in *City Record*.

Annual report of the comptroller of the city for the year ending August 1, 1852-1858, 1873-1897. For 1873-1879, 1883-1896 only in *City Record*. Several of these reports are for the year ending June 30, and titles vary. See as to legal requirements concerning comptrollers' reports, *ante*, p. 351.

Reports of the commissioners of accounts, quarterly, semi-annual, and annual. In *City Record*, 1873-1897. Somewhat irregular as to date of issuance and period covered. At present the annual report shows the state of the treasury November 30.

Annual report of the comptroller exhibiting the receipts and expenditures of the county of New York for the years 1859-1870.

Proceedings of the joint investigating committee of supervisors, aldermen, and associated citizens appointed to examine the public accounts. New York, 1872.

Minutes of the board of estimate and apportionment, 1871–1897. Also in *City Record* after 1873.

Annual messages of the mayors for the years 1830–1897.

Annual report of the board of commissioners of the Central Park. Nos. 1–13, 1857–1870.

Report of the comptroller on the establishment of a sinking fund for the redemption of the city stock. New York, 1813. 8 pages.

Journal of the city convention of 1829. In Kent's edition of the city charter, 1834.

Journal of the convention in relation to the charter of the city of New York, 1846.

Manual of the corporation of the city of New York for the years 1841–1866, 1868–1870. Edited by D. T. Valentine from 1842–1866.

MISCELLANEOUS

Adams, Henry C. Public debts: an essay in the science of finance. New York, 1887.

Black, George Ashton. The history of municipal ownership of land on Manhattan Island. New York, 1891 Columbia College studies in history, economics, and public law, vol. 1, No. 3.

Brooklyn, Comptroller's report, 1895.

Citizens' association of New York. Annual reports and numerous pamphlets published from 1864–1874. Collected by the association in one volume, no title-page.

Committee of seventy. An act to reorganize the local government of the city of New York. New York, 1872. Also Assembly bill 118, 1872.

Durand, E. Dana. The city chest of New Amsterdam. In Half Moon series. New York, 1897.

Green, Andrew H. Municipal debt of the city of New York. New York, 1874. 24 pages.

Green, Mrs. J. R. Town life in the fifteenth century. New York, 1894.

Hoffman, Murray. A treatise upon the estate and rights of the city of New York as proprietors. New York, 1853.

O'Callaghan, E. B. History of New Netherland. New York, 1846.

New York Tribune, 1842-1897.

New York Times, 1851-1897.

New York Commercial Gazette, 1829.

Parton, James. The government of the city of New York. *North American Review,* vol. 103, 1866.

Paulding, J. Affairs and men of New Amsterdam in the time of Governor Peter Stuyvesant. New York, 1843.

Rosewater, Victor. Special assessments: a study in municipal finance. New York, 1893. In Columbia College studies in history, economics, and public law, vol. 2, No. 3.

Ross, Edward A. Sinking Funds. Baltimore, 1892. In Publications of American Economic Association, vol. 7, Nos. 3-4.

Schwab, J. C. History of the New York property tax. Baltimore, 1890. In Publications of American Economic Association, vol. 5, No. 5.

Seligman, Edwin R. A. The shifting and incidence of taxation. Baltimore, 1892. In Publications of American Economic Association, vol. 7, Nos. 1-2.

—— Essays in taxation. New York, 1895.

Shaw, Albert. Municipal government in Great Britain New York, 1895.

—— Municipal government in continental Europe. New York, 1895.

Statistisches Jahrbuch der deutschen Städte, 1891-1896. Breslau.

Tilden, Samuel J. The New York city ring . . . reply to the *New York Times.* New York, 1873.

Valentine D. T. Political history of New York. In Corporation Manual for 1854.
—— Financial history of the city of New York. In Corporation Manual for 1859.
Union League Club. Alleged frauds in the city government of New York. New York, 1884.
United States Census, 1890. Wealth, Debt, and Taxation.
Wingate, Charles F. An episode in municipal government. *North American Review*, vols. 119, 120, 121, 123.

FINANCIAL TABLES

The following tables are compiled for the most part directly from the comptroller's annual reports. In some cases summary tables have been followed: in others it has been necessary to consult the *City Manual*, the proceedings of the Council, the report of the Fassett Committee, and other sources. Individual references cannot be conveniently cited. For 1871 to 1873 some figures are entirely wanting, no reports, or only partial ones, being published. The explanations in the text should be used in connection with the tables.

TABLE I
Budget, Taxes, and Special Assessments

Year	Appropriations (from Taxes)	Appropriations less State Tax	Assessed Valuation	Tax Rate	Expenditures on Assessments
	$	$	$	cents	$
1830	509,178	....	125,288,518	.42	202,301
1831	572,104	....	137,560,259	.41	229,937
1832	665,385	....	144,902,328	.46	212,900
1833	971,854	....	166,491,542	.59	268,384
1834	835,605	....	186,548,511	.45	389,184
1835	965,602	....	218,723,703	.46	353,381
1836	1,085,130	....	309,500,020	.36	805,455
1837	1,244,972	....	263,747,350	.47	1,113,838
1838	1,486,993	....	264,152,941	.56	746,873
1839	1,352,826	....	270,869,019	.51	506,553
1840	1,354,835	....	252,233,515	.53	670,927
1841	1,394,836	....	251,194,920	.58	213,619
1842	2,031,382	....	237,805,651	.80	144,663
1843	1,747,516	....	229,229,079	.79	99,186
1844	1,988,118	1,832,462	236,727,143	.86	57,683
1845	2,096,191	1,952,194	239,995,517	.88	137,767
1846	2,526,146	2,379,208	244,952,004	1.05	259,495
1847	2,581,726	2,458,200	247,153,299	1.05	408,685
1848	2,715,510	2,588,414	254,163,523	1.08	570,888
1849	3,005,762	2,851,437	256,197,143	1.18	432,565
1850	3,230,180	3,100,749	286,061,816	1.14	619,458
1851	2,924,384	2,764,325	320,110,857	.92	943,615
1852	3,378,335	3,016,325	351,768,426	.97	1,074,137
1853	5,069,650	4,836,269	413,631,382	1.23	1,190,485
1854	4,841,255	4,456,288	462,021,734	1.05	1,408,938
1855	5,843,822	5,372,204	486,998,278	1.20	2,378,817
1856	7,075,425	6,340,482	511,740,491	1.38	926,032
1857	8,066,566	7,171,482	521,175,252	1.56	429,550
1858	8,621,091	7,210,383	531,194,290	1.64	101,941

TABLE I (*Continued*)

Year	Total Appropriations	Appropriations less State Tax	Assessed Valuation	Tax Rate	Expenditures on Assessments
	$	$	$	cents	$
1859	10,225,399	8,897,393	551,923,122	1.80	2,059,701
1860	10,121,358	8,789,100	577,230,656	1.69	1,879,470
1861	11,551,016	9,442,381	581,579,971	1.60	942,454
1862	11,103,746	8,890,816	571,967,345	1.73	1,318,356
1863	12,945,212	10,404,655	594,196,813	2.03	642,504
1864	14,875,702	12,138,622	634,615,890	2.16	1,661,767
1865	19,147,919	16,123,919	608,784,355	2.99	1,178,765
1866	18,890,398	15,987,549	736,988,058	2.30	1,736,196
1867	23,653,324	19,762,780	831,669,813	2.67	1,829,644
1868	25,928,758	20,364,332	907,815,529	2.66	3,090,040
1869	26,485,847	21,998,927	964,257,164	2.27	9,071,406
1870	30,906,263	26,001,762	1,047,427,049	2.25	9,772,509

Year	Total Appropriations	Appropriations less State Tax	Contingent Appropriations[1]	Assessed Valuation	Tax Rate	Expenditures on Ass'ts.
	$	$	$	$	cents	$
1871	31,478,148	?	?	1,076,253,633	2.17	?
1872	34,058,680	28,313,681	?	1,104,098,087	2.90	?
1873	30,154,187	24,036,822	16,356,059	1,129,240,573	2.50	?
1874	34,872,391	27,098,910	17,583,147	1,154,029,176	2.80	6,099,130
1875	36,171,472	28,159,086	17,404,322	1,100,943,699	2.94	5,639,479
1876	34,934,801	27,701,611	16,163,704	1,111,054,343	2.80	5,004,145
1877	31,005,805	26,842,921	16,099,415	1,101,092,093	2.65	1,559,433
1878	30,104,077	26,192,751	15,848,069	1,098,387,775	2.55	1,175,099
1879	30,247,750	26,496,688	16,542,087	1,094,069,335	2.58	577,369
1880	29,668,771	26,097,439	17,445,653	1,143,765,727	2.53	729,265
1881	31,759,205	27,488,445	18,583,102	1,185,948,098	2.62	1,014,951
1882	29,434,031	26,606,744	18,140,113	1,233,476,398	2.25	2,446,903
1883	30,676,785	27,457,815	18,874,373	1,276,677,164	2.29	1,848,098
1884	34,067,585	29,815,007	21,146,521	1,338,298,343	2.25	1,438,243
1885	34,078,405	30,494,964	23,046,393	1,371,117,003	2.40	1,358,107
1886	33,802,320	29,602,714	21,289,312	1,420,968,286	2.29	922,140
1887	34,343,022	30,084,495	21,716,900	1,507,640,663	2.16	1,967,301
1888	37,051,053	32,986,864	24,096,859	1,553,422,431	2.22	2,174,858
1889	34,983,385	32,950,231	24,137,356	1,603,839,113	1.95	1,854,520
1890	35,148,097	30,628,445	24,242,019	1,696,978,390	1.97	1,994,233
1891	35,992,891	32,342,361	25,883,368	1,785,857,338	1.90	2,522,776
1892	35,881,205	32,482,701	27,140,501	1,828,264,275	1.85	2,733,909
1893	37,444,154	33,889,696	27,264,663	1,933,518,529	1.82	4,724,339
1894	38,664,257	34,551,981	27,540,791	2,003,332,037	1.79	3,623,130
1895	40,076,960	36,522,640	29,461,355	2,016,947,663	1.72	4,454,567
1896	46,496,571	40,094,561	31,538,061	2,106,484,905	2.14	4,261,649
1897	49,486,297	44,035,187	34,208,259	....	....	....

[1] *I.e.*, total appropriations, less state taxes, interest, and redemption payments.

TABLE II
City Debt — 1830–1896

Year	Funded	Assessment	Revenue	Sinking Fund	Net Bonded Debt
	$	$	$	$	$
1830	570,300	....	432,000	227,744	774,556
1831	500,000	....	498,000	257,087	741,913
1832	500,000	....	793,400	398,590	894,810
1833	500,000	....	542,500	206,155	836,344
1834	500,000	....	499,500	254,465	745,034
1835	1,500,000	....	139,978	261,050	1,378,928
1836	2,939,487	....	200,000	339,655	2,799,832
1837	3,398,687	....	600,000	382,093	3,016,594
1838	5,034,740	....	800,000	363,103	5,471,637
1839	7,716,105	....	414,230	618,368	7,511,967
1840	10,442,369	400,000	310,000	699,133	10,453,236
1841	12,481,661	200,000	347,947	831,095	12,198,513
1842	14,096,701	....	587,433	1,018,975	13,665,159
1843	14,333,637	....	260,000	1,266,693	13,326,944
1844	14,476,986	....	600,700	1,499,856	13,577,830
1845	14,657,088	....	1,170,250	2,065,530	13,761,808
1846	14,830,194	....	1,393,173	2,284,607	13,935,760
1847	14,851,783	....	1,508,092	2,485,949	13,873,826
1848	15,016,783	....	1,956,253	2,994,472	13,978,564
1849	15,241,783	....	2,273,453	3,690,866	13,774,370
1850	15,037,383	....	766,050	3,583,206	12,220,227
1851	15,288,908	....	869,340	4,052,069	12,106,179
1852	14,890,856	55,000	1,434,125	3,896,266	12,483,715
1853	14,910,856	284,925	1,945,561	4,631,167	12,510,175
1854	15,114,856	100,000	3,569,009	5,171,308	13,612,557
1855	15,204,856	800,000	3,600,600	5,594,719	14,010,737
1856	15,384,156	649,900[1]	4,489,365	4,936,378	15,587,053
1857	17,593,168	1,150,000	3,490,900	5,093,880	17,140,188
1858	17,224,898	1,095,700	4,368,700	5,277,555	17,411,743
1859	17,801,489	1,098,200	4,976,250	6,364,394	17,511,555
1860	20,305,344	1,898,200	1,230,100	5,107,703	18,325,941
1861	22,343,344	1,925,600	1,080,900	6,262,542	19,087,302

[1] In addition to these $1,600,000 of assessment bonds for Central Park assessments were outstanding from 1856 to 1860.

TABLE II (*Continued*)

Year	Funded	Assessment	Revenue	Sinking Fund	Net Bonded Debt
	$	$	$	$	$
1862	25,738,042	2,330,000	855,300	7,233,421	21,689,921
1863	32,157,342	2,013,000	....	7,985,151	26,185,191
1864	40,188,824	1,692,000	700,800	8,767,393	33,814,231
1865	41,347,424	2,019,200	2,276,100	9,669,127	35,973,597
1866	42,154,176	2,042,600	991,000	11,229,231	33,958,545
1867	43,584,776	2,904,072	417,325	13,984,313	32,721,861
1868	44,586,858	4,395,872	3,222,700	16,501,109	35,704,321
1869	56,018,879	7,608,572	2,412,600	18,321,313	47,717,738
1870	68,998,146	10,525,100	11,966,200	18,115,894	73,373,522
1871	87,238,608	14,944,000	6,369,100	20,182,321	88,369,386
1872	93,773,659	16,927,372	8,114,197	23,348,074	95,467,154
1873	99,492,219	21,927,372	10,449,979	24,841,100	107,028,471
1874	118,241,557	20,851,000	2,711,200	26,823,788	114,979,969
1875	119,056,903	21,322,200	4,142,927	27,748,307	116,773,724
1876	119,631,313	22,371,400	6,104,844	28,296,247	119,811,310
1877	121,440,133	21,329,500	6,051,424	31,120,315	117,700,742
1878	126,128,815	13,481,500	5,951,875	32,143,787	113,418,403
1879	123,145,333	13,262,100	6,039,966	33,021,985	109,425,414
1880	123,176,919	10,358,100	5,524,244	32,993,024	106,066,240
1881	124,724,407	9,676,100	4,328,095	36,110,300	102,618,301
1882	119,817,241	10,657,095	4,246,534	34,332,388	100,388,432
1883	120,707,475	9,973,095	2,983,883	38,134,544	95,529,909
1884	121,319,320	5,551,817	2,358,825	34,823,735	94,406,229
1885	122,443,239	3,032,000	3,670,525	36,113,813	93,031,951
1886	122,650,735	3,332,000	5,618,367	41,205,470	90,395,633
1887	124,500,719	3,768,000	4,554,346	39,521,884	93,301,181
1888	128,347,095	4,098,000	3,302,730	44,324,690	91,423,135
1889	138,016,028	3,823,000	2,462,187	45,638,142	98,663,072
1890	142,198,022	4,173,000	207,188	48,513,792	98,064,418
1891	145,500,869	4,798,000	34,600	52,783,433	97,550,036
1892	149,344,171	5,817,802	366,083	56,532,406	98,995,651
1893	159,050,898	7,419,951	666,073	65,708,442	101,428,481
1894	165,393,039	8,598,042	1,699,033	69,912,260	105,777,854
1895	176,233,167	9,355,429	2,564,510	75,703,087	112,450,020
1896	186,189,242	9,718,448	2,433,326	77,630,491	120,710,526

TABLE III
BUDGET EXPENDITURES BY DECENNIAL PERIODS [1]
1830–1890

	1830	1840	1850	1860	1869	1880	1890
Population	197,112	312,710	515,547	805,658	942,292	1,206,299	1,515,301
Assessed valuation	$125,288,518	$252,233,515	$286,061,816	$577,230,956	$964,257,164	$1,143,765,727	$1,696,978,390
Gross budget expenditures	676,618	1,605,742	3,368,163	9,785,056	26,532,761	29,754,553	34,985,680
Budg. exp. less state tax	676,618	1,605,742	3,238,732	8,473,657	22,045,841	26,183,221	30,465,928
Budget exp. less state tax and debt payments	641,618	1,455,411	2,818,323	7,564,399	18,164,331	17,539,328	24,265,690
Per capita expenditure	$3.43	$5.13	$6.53	$12.14	$28.14	$24.66	$23.09
Percentage of expenditure to valuation	0.54%	0.63%	1.18%	1.70%	2.75%	2.60%	2.06%
State taxes	....	....	$129,431	$1,311,399	$4,486,920	$3,571,322	$4,519,641
Interest (budget)	$52,118	$150,631	330,409	837,601	2,725,878	8,422,293	5,119,722
Redemption (budget)	....	....	90,000	71,657	1,155,632	221,610	1,080,617
Common Council	2,500	8,861	27,248	75,895	295,304	122,712	81,023
Mayoralty	4,017	4,750	6,416	28,198	56,751	39,701	26,797
Law department	....	4,801	17,600	45,574	110,655	160,186	188,816

FINANCIAL TABLES

	1830	1840	1850	1860	1870	1880	1890
Finance department	$4,500	$8,149	$13,637	$105,779	$254,440	$262,127	$287,666
Department of taxes	5,359	11,423	9,820	51,515	55,643	107,784	112,562
Lighting	49,381	120,675	185,408	431,355	1,188,484	510,612	765,767
Water supply (except debt)	37,978	6,046	162,478	154,128	418,410	645,790	728,361
Streets, sewers, and public works	50,378	160,840	287,188	914,784	1,333,210	1,005,129	1,656,458
Parks				104,728	250,000	551,101	1,122,404
Charities and correction	131,021	254,000	400,000	746,199	953,000	1,318,793	2,124,750
Health	1,252	4,677	7,229	161,060	194,936	256,425	390,434
Police	99,521	271,709	487,541	1,395,122	2,901,133	3,277,069	4,587,599
Cleaning streets	25,976	149,930	158,637	325,371	570,570	809,703	1,315,912
Fire department	23,462	76,788	44,969	167,573	907,940	1,387,991	2,123,367
Board of education	25,995	94,411	374,553	1,278,781	3,150,000	3,422,307	4,149,563
Judiciary	38,417	55,040	76,535	323,185	754,869	1,263,351	1,456,971
Printing and advertising	3,486	23,800	51,615	153,473	443,768	166,352	241,740
Asylums, etc.	4,000	6,921	9,863	109,661	939,219	930,399	1,154,644
Elections	1,881	7,704	7,269	148,914	84,809	177,469	499,685
Docks and wharves	34,038	80,886	149,829	186,928	563,483	......	......

[1] Compiled from comptroller's reports of respective dates. The classification of purposes is nearly the same as that of recent comptroller's tables. There was no grouping of items before the '70's, and I have had to exercise a judgment not always quite certain as to some items. Because of the impossibility of entire accuracy, I have made no attempt to balance the separate items with the total, but have omitted "miscellaneous" expenditures, which amount usually to two or three per cent of the total. The figures include only expenditures on the regular budget account, not those on assessment enterprises, through the sinking funds, etc.

TABLE IV — THE BUDGET[1]

ANNUAL MODIFICATIONS IN THE ESTIMATES

1874-1897

YEAR	DEPARTMENTAL	PROVISIONAL	RECTIFIED BY ALDERMEN	FINAL ESTIMATES [2]
1874	39,491,051	38,530,299	41,662,090	39,138,945
1875	38,693,052	36,657,062	36,864,572	36,171,472
1876	37,893,682	35,423,231	35,547,691	34,904,269
1877	33,987,530	32,089,970	33,186,696	30,984,269
1878	31,848,282	30,082,385	30,346,085	30,079,077
1879	30,976,072	29,284,470	29,962,821	30,007,097
1880	30,698,728	29,297,072	29,328,872	29,642,991
1881	32,066,645	31,524,744	31,621,456	31,354,322
1882	31,398,030	29,212,623	29,710,596	29,412,831
1883	31,999,558	30,327,864	30,711,762	30,593,535
1884	35,253,376	33,373,157	33,856,947	34,046,165
1885	34,888,217	33,472,740	33,977,902	33,881,905
1886	43,306,569	36,054,325	37,019,856	35,736,320
1887	36,600,435	34,101,619	34,759,844	34,157,273
1888	38,868,242	36,689,186	37,091,186	37,051,053
1889	40,455,009	37,029,604	37,227,638	37,637,069
1890	39,683,638	36,264,249	36,295,449	35,148,097
1891	38,223,822	34,600,336	34,745,336	35,960,891
1892	38,264,395	35,905,212	36,115,212	35,881,205
1893	39,062,517	36,521,008	36,652,008	37,444,154
1894	43,286,791	38,296,633	38,413,133	38,664,257
1895	43,432,713	38,699,593	38,799,593	39,976,960
1896	50,505,675	45,154,701	45,154,701	46,496,571
1897	47,439,009	45,372,186	45,373,386	49,486,297

[1] Compiled from *City Record*.
[2] Note that these are not always the same as the ultimate appropriations as given in Table I.

TABLE V

Summary of Bond Issues, etc., for the Four Periods since 1812

	1812-1849	1850-1868	1869-1871 (Sept. 16)	1871-1896	Total
Funded bonds issued:					
Water supply	13,236,695	5,420,800	2,536,000	51,338,272	72,531,767
Parks	....	10,048,571	1,041,000	24,280,804	35,370,975
Public buildings and sites	2,035,000	4,555,437	1,881,000	28,087,875	36,559,312
Streets and boulevards	....	851,700	5,653,139	19,290,550	25,795,389
Bridges	....	....	450,000	12,742,000	13,192,000
Docks	....	500,000	500,000	28,553,000	29,553,000
War purposes	....	13,593,600 [1]	90,000	....	13,683,600
Funding and refunding	900,000	4,112,800 [1]	28,650,932	38,671,743	72,335,475
Miscellaneous	1,446,330	229,000	921,952	2,303,304	4,900,586
Total issued	17,618,025	39,311,908	41,724,624	205,267,553	303,922,110
Debt at beginning of period	....	15,241,783	44,586,858	81,351,158	
Redeemed during period	17,618,025	54,553,691	86,311,482	286,618,711	
	2,376,242	9,966,833	4,960,324	100,429,469	117,732,868
Funded debt at close	15,241,783	44,586,858	81,351,158	186,189,242	186,189,242
Assessment bonds at close	....	4,395,872	12,592,500	9,718,448	
Revenue bonds at close	2,223,453	3,222,700	22,766,200	2,433,326	
Total bonded debt at close	17,465,236	53,205,430	116,709,858	198,341,017	
Sinking fund at close	3,690,866	16,501,109	19,422,333	77,630,491	
Net bonded debt at close	14,774,370	35,704,321	97,287,525	120,710,526	

[1] War debt, December 31, 1868; bonds for repayment of taxes, December 31, 1868, $1,364,800. Refundings, etc., disregarded.

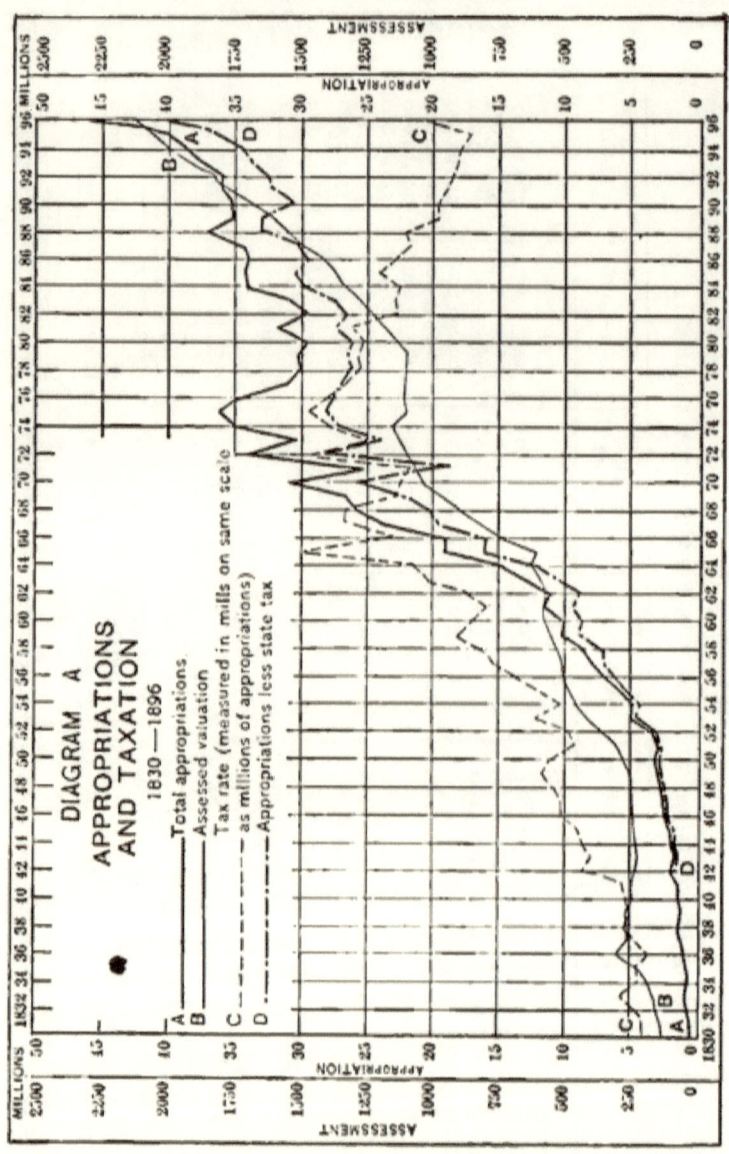

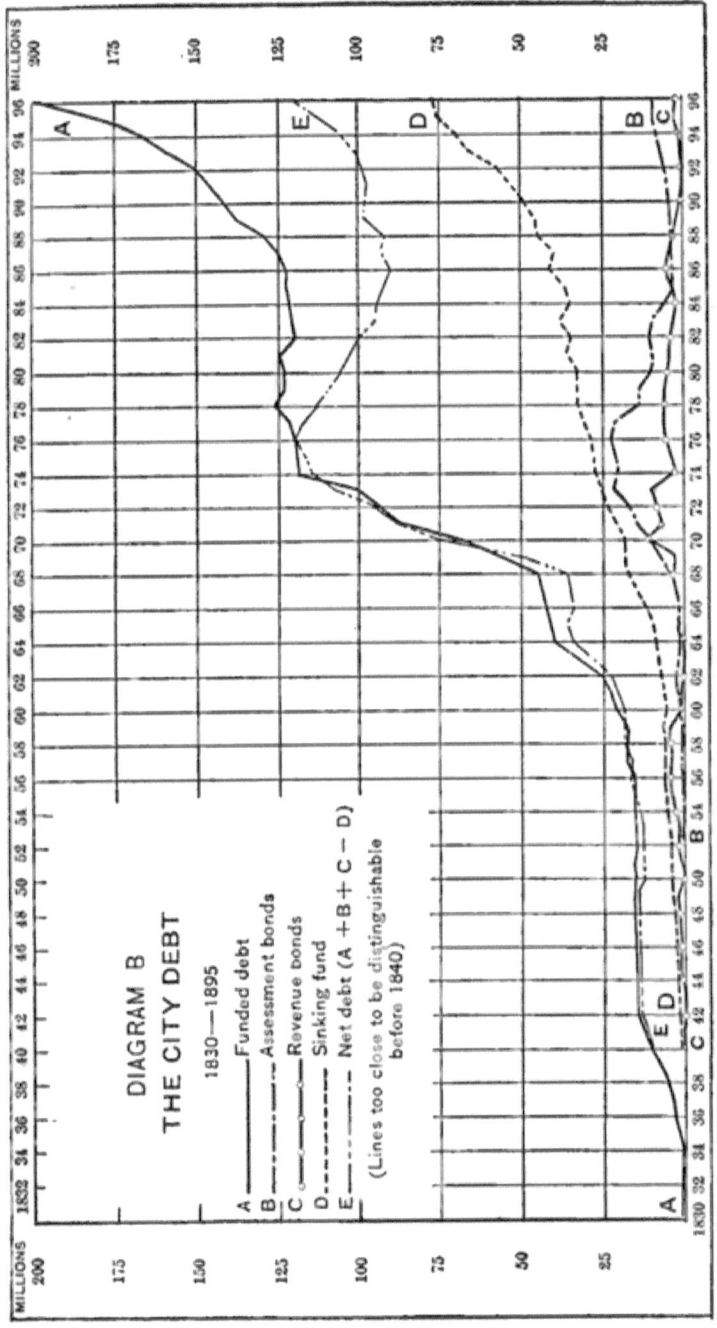

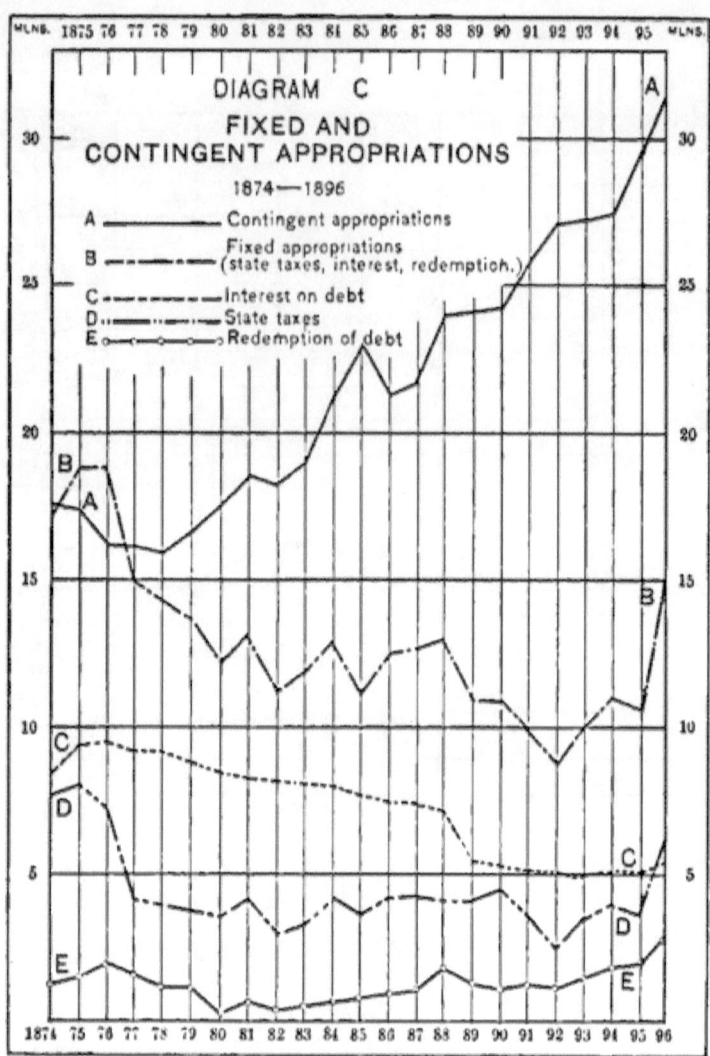

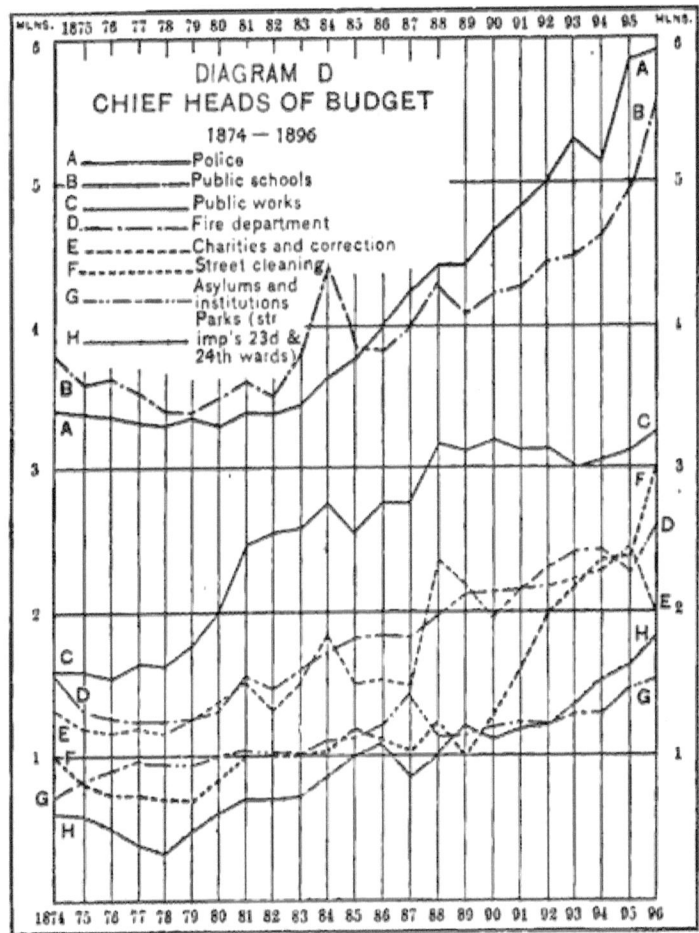

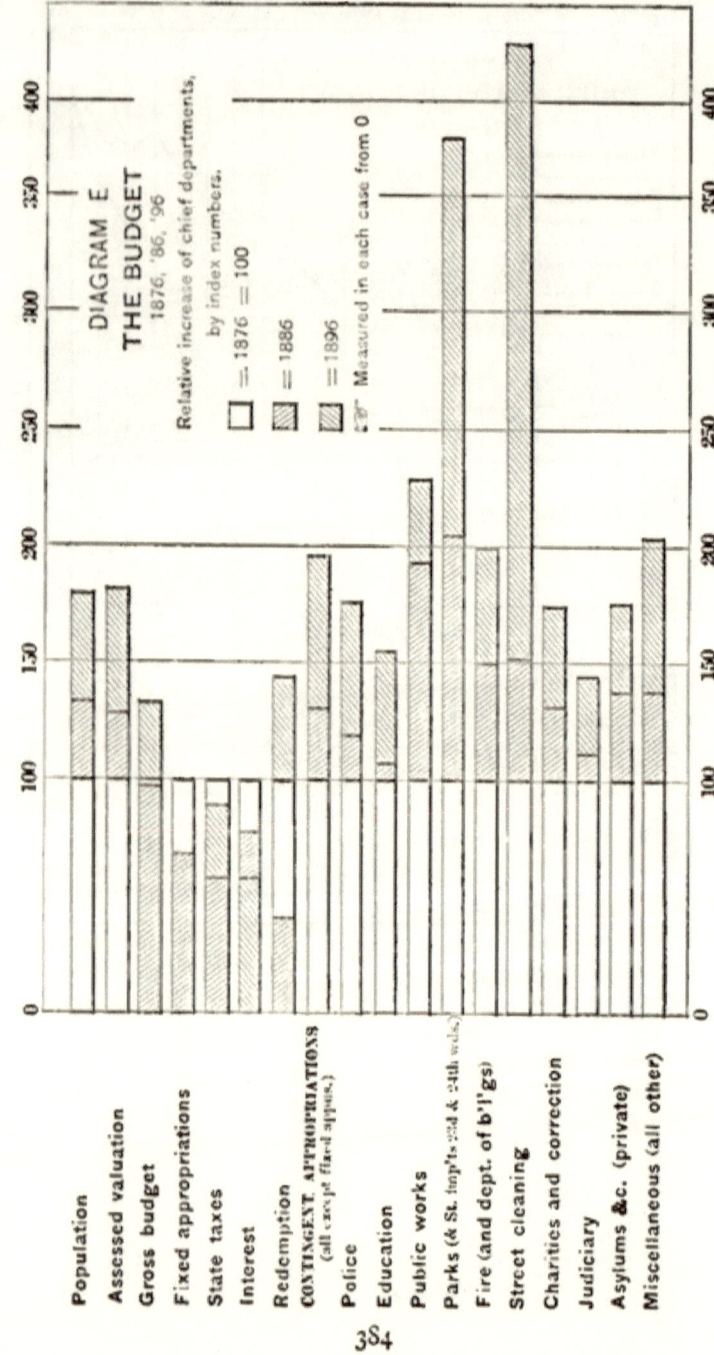

INDEX

Accounts, commissioners of, established, 162; duties, 351-353.

Accounts, imperfection of early system, 50; reorganization, 1859, 111; confusion of sinking fund, 342; description of system, 345-349; reports, 349-352; inspection, 352-354.

Accumulated debt bonds, 124.

Advertising, printing, etc., transfers of appropriations for, 90; judgments for, 91; Ring expenditures, 114, 139.

Aldermen, president of, member of board of estimate, 162, 253; his influence, 274; *see* Council.

Almshouse department, expenditures, 1798, 30; 1830, 31; financial independence, 82; expenditures, 1850-1869, 83; changed to charities and corrections, 80.

Appointment of officers, exclusive power of council, 37, 42; abuses by council, 62, of police, 62, 74; restored to mayor, 77; under Ring charter, 126; proposed system of Committee of Seventy, 157; council to confirm, 160; power of confirmation removed, 165, 172.

Appropriations, city, absence of system to 1830, 29; system introduced, 44; imperfect working, 46-50; evil of additional, 48; further slight regulations, 1853, 70; great additional, 1852, 72; rapid increase, 75; power of independent departments, 81-87; of county government, 85, 86; legislative control, 88-97; additional, 1850-1856, 89; abuse of transfers, 90; three-fourths vote required, 97; submitted to mayor and comptroller, 94, 97, 127; by board of estimate and apportionment, 131; juggling by Tweed Ring, 132-134; increase, 1869-1871, 138; special revisions authorized, 1872-1875, 152, 153; proposed system of Committee of Seventy, 157; outline of present system, 253-257; in Greater New York, 257, 277-281; weakness of council, 258-261; fixed charges and legal restrictions, 261-263, 274; actual procedure and motives, 264-275; underestimate to influence elections, 276; criticism of system, 277-281; Tilden commission plan, 281-284; analysis of budget, 285-289; progress since 1871, 289-294; accounts of, 346; tables of, 372, 374, 376-378; diagrams, 380-385; *see also* Estimate and apportionment.

Appropriation account, 178.

Armories, fraudulent Ring expenditures, 114, 140; bonds for, 332.

Art, Museum of, expenditures, 330.

Assessment bonds, introduced, 1852, 108; rapid increase under Ring, 145; funding, 1878, 209;

386 *INDEX*

payment from sinking fund, 209; constitutional limit applies, 211, 297; description of, 216; no special law for issue, 300; recent reduction of amount, 323.

Assessment of taxes, increase of valuation, 1800–1830, 31; method of, 187, 188; evasion of personal property, 190–195; on real estate, 195–197; for state taxes, 196; table of valuations, 372; diagram, 380.

Assessments, board of revision of, established, 109; powers, 217.

Assessments for local improvements, 201–220; *see* Special assessments.

Assessors, board of, 217, 218; deputy, 187, 192.

Assistant aldermen, no power in tax levy, 28; name changed to councilmen, 73.

Asten, Thomas B., tax commissioner, 268.

Audit of accounts, fraudulent 'special,' 1868, 122; by *ad interim* board, 1870, 128; general process, 346–349; bureau of, 347.

Auditors, in finance department, 347.

Barker, E. P., tax commissioner, 272.

Baths, proposed appropriation for, 260.

Berlin, street railways in, 248; gas plant, 249.

Boards, *see* Departments, Assessors, Council, Estimate and apportionment, etc.

Bonds, *see* Debt.

Boston, expenditures of, 186; debt of, 295.

Boulevards, 'the,' established, 104, 110; recent expenditures, 330.

Bounties, bonds for, in Civil War, 102–104.

Bribery, penalties, 74, 354; to secure Ring charter, 125, 126.

Bridges, bonds issued for, 147, 326, 330, 332; revenues from Brooklyn, 230, 337.

Broadway, widening 'job,' 1870, 144.

Broadway railway, franchise 'job,' 1884, 236; percentage paid by, 239.

Brooklyn, treatment of finances, vii; consolidation with New York, 166–168; receipts of, 179; personal taxes in, 195; sinking fund, 319; heavy debt, 336.

Brooklyn bridge, bonds for, 147, 326, 330; revenues from, 230, 337.

Brouwer Straate, assessment for paving, 12.

Budget; *see* Appropriations.

Burgomasters of New Amsterdam, appointment, 8; financial management by, 9–11.

Cabinet government, contrasted with city council, 278, 279.

Central Park, control by state commission, 78; appropriations for, 84; established, bonds, 99, 100; improvement under Ring, 147; power of commission as to streets, 202; bonds for, 1871–1884, 326.

Chamberlain, office established, 15; duties prescribed, 1788, 26; appointment and duties, 345, 346, 348; inspection of his accounts, 351, 353.

Charitable institutions, private, rapid increase of donations, 1850–1869, 114; excise revenues go to, 256; required donations to, 261; restrictions on appropriations to, 263; increase of appropriations to, 293.

Charities and correction, department of, established, 80; expenditures, 1860-1869, 82; expenditures, 1871-1896, 293; *see also* Almshouse.

Charter of New York city, general history, 1-6; first Dutch, 8; English royal, 13, 14; convention of 1829, 42; of 1830, 42-45; convention of 1846, 67; reorganization, 1849, 67-70; amendments, 1853, 70-75; reorganization, 1857, 76, 77; other changes, 78-80; failure of proposed convention, 80; complex character, 1850-1869, 114-118; reorganization by Tweed Ring, 125-127; proposed by Committee of Seventy, 155-158; reorganization, 1873, 159-161; general character of present, 161-163; amendments since 1873, 163-166; of Greater New York, 168-172; influence on finances, 359; unsystematic development and character, 360-362; *see also* Greater New York charter.

Chicago, receipts and expenditures, 179, 181, 186.

Cities (generally), early independence of European, 7, 15; receipts of American, 179; expenditures of American, 186, 289; franchises and property, 224, 247; proper function of council, 279-281; Tilden commission plan, 281-285; limited suffrage, 282-285; debts of American, 295; constitutional limitations on debt, 296, 300; state board to control debt, 300; comparative *per capita* debts, 335.

Citizens' Association of New York, influence on appropriations, 95; favors legislative commissions, 117; supports Ring charter, 126.

City council, *see* Council.

City hall, erection, 33.

City improvement stock, for street openings, 110, 206, 326.

Civil War, bonds for bounties and riots, 102-104.

Clow, F. R., classification of expenditures, 287.

Coleman, Michael, tax commissioner, 192, 194, 266, 271.

Commissioners, *see* Accounts, commissioners of, Sinking fund, Legislative commissions, etc.

Committee of Seventy, fight against Tweed Ring, 136; propose charter, 155-158; influence on charter of 1873, 159, 160.

Common council, *see* Council.

Comptroller, office established, 28; to prepare estimates, 46; term four years, 77; appoints charities commissioners, 80; added power in appropriations, 94, 97, 127; special audits by, 1868, 122; power of appointment by, 127; member board of estimate, 131; office made elective, 165; control of contracts, 216, 355; influence in board of estimate, 264, 271; election and functions, 345; must sign warrants, 348; reports of, vi, 351, 352; *see also* Accounts, Finance department, Reports.

Connolly, Comptroller Richard B., becomes Ring member, 122; share in spoils, 129; deposed, 136.

Consolidated Gas Company, 247.

Consolidated stock, 130, 312, 325.

Consolidation, *see* Greater New York.

Constitution of New York, convention of 1867, 79; grants local veto of bills, 165; limits railway franchises, 235; limits city debt, 296-300.

Contracts for city work, council not to be interested, 70; restric-

tions established, 74, 77; weekly reports of, 350; officers forbidden interest, 354; how let, 216, 355; unbalanced bids for, 355-357.
Convention on city charter, 1829, 42; 1846, 67; 1862, 80.
Cooper, Peter, as reformer, 72, 95.
Corporations, loan of city credit to, prohibited, 296.
Council, common, election, etc., colonial, 15; controls entire administration, 29, 37; character of administration, 38; separation of two boards, 42; attempt to remove executive power from, 43, 60; executive power removed, 69; early corruption, 61, 71; reorganization, 'councilmen' established, 1853, 73; rearrangement of districts, 77; opposes legislative interference, 86, 87; proposed restoration of power, 156; minority representation, 161; failure and abandonment of same, 163, 164; composed of one board, 161; growing weakness, 164; reorganization as 'municipal assembly,' 1897, 168; remission of taxes by, 188; power in special assessments, 202, 203, 205, 216; street railway 'jobs,' 236; appropriations submitted to, 255, 256; appropriating power under charter of 1897, 257, 278; present lack of power or interest, 258-261; proper sphere in government, 279-281; property qualification in Germany, 288; has now no control of debt, 301; debt power under new charter, 305; prohibited interest in contracts, 354.
Councilmen, board of, name established, 73.
Counsel to the corporation, made member of board of estimate, 254.

'County liabilities,' fraudulent payments, 128, 135.
County of New York, government separated from city, 78; growth of expenditures, 85, 86; court house, 102, 141, 142, 147; war bonds of, 103; consolidated with city, 126, 153.
County supervisors, taxes levied by aldermen as, 28; separate board, 78, 85; Ring formed by, 120; abolished, 126.
Court house, county, commenced, 102; Ring frauds in, 141, 142, 147; criminal, 303.
Courts, expenditures for, 31, 114, 293; control of street openings, 214, 215; decision as to transfer of appropriations, 268; as to debt limit, 298; mandamus to compel debt payment, 309.
Croton aqueduct, construction, 52-54; management and revenues, 224-226; construction of new, 326-328; *see also* Water supply.

Debt of New York city, for fortifications, 1653, 9; for docks, 1676, 20; floating, eighteenth century, 24; first permanent, 1812, 33; history to 1830, 33-37; 1830-1850, 51-57; for aqueduct, 52-54; funding floating, 56; proposal to require vote, 68; 1850-1868, 97-106; for Central Park, 99, 101; for war purposes, 102-104; funding floating, 1860, 102; assessment bonds introduced, 108; increase in annual charges for, 113, 114; for 'adjusted claims,' etc., under Ring, 122, 124, 130; progress under Ring, 145-149; manner of calculating charges, 186; purpose of revenue bonds, 189, 267; provisions as to assessment bonds, 209, 211,

216; fixed charges in budget, 261, 263; reduction in budget charges, 267; payments for interest and sinking, 287, 290; constitutional limitations, 296-300; effect of consolidation, 299; legislative control of creation, 300, 301; control by local authorities, 302, 303; exemption from taxation, 303; control under Greater New York charter, 304, 305; recent changes in sinking fund system, 306-318; general progress since 1871, 319-325; interest rate, 322; temporary debt, 323; chief bond issues since 1871, 325-332; present state, 333-336; comparison with other cities, 335; tables of, 374, 375, 379; diagram, 381.

Deficiencies, taxes for, 50; funding of, 30, 56, 102; percentage to cover, 110, 189, 200.

Democratic party, first gains power, 39; in Croton aqueduct board, 53; abuses by, 1850-1860, 76; opposes legislative control, 86; secures majority in legislature, 125; division in party, 125, 126; two wings of, 271; control of board of estimate, 271.

Departments, executive, appointment by council, 37; attempt to establish independent, 43, 60; established by law, 69; appointed by mayor, 77; certain, governed by state commissions, 78, 79; term four years, 80; power of independent, 81-87; lobbying as to tax laws, 95; under Tweed charter, 127; proposed minority representation in, 157; council to confirm appointments, 160; appointment and removal by mayor alone, 165, 168, 172; bipartisan boards, 165; estimates of appropriations, 254, 265; distinction of functions from legislative, 279; audit of bills by, 347; reports of, 350; investigations into, 353.

Depositories of city moneys, 346.

Docks and wharves, established by Dutch, 11; grant of lands for, 19; revenue from, 55, 75; bonds issued for, 98; reorganization of department, 1870, 128; present management and revenue, 227-229; issue of bonds for all expenditures, 257, 300; bonds since 1871, 326, 332.

Donations to private institutions, 114, 256, 261, 263, 293.

Dongan, Governor Thomas, charter and grants, 13.

Draft riots, 1863, bonds for, 103.

Dutch, finances under rule of, 7-13.

Edson, Mayor Franklin, opinion as to debt limit, 298.

Education, *see* Schools.

Elections, early partisanship in, 39, 62; proposed requirement for bond issues, 68; Ring frauds, 123; on consolidation question, 166; reduction of estimates to influence, 276.

Elevated railways, franchises and profits, 244-246.

England, early city charters in, 7, 15; early special assessments, 23; sinking fund fallacy, 35; water supply in cities, 224; municipal gas plants, 247, 248; success of city councils, 280; limited municipal suffrage, 284; state control of local debt, 300.

Equitable Gaslight Company, 246.

Estimate and apportionment, board of, established, 131; first action, 132-134; reconstituted, 152; composition and duties, 253-256;

under Greater New York charter, 257; disregard of council's action, 258; complaint of fixed appropriations, 261-263; practical procedure, 264-267; transfer appropriations, 267-269; character, partisan motives, etc., 269-277; meagre reports of meetings, 274; anomaly of system, 278; control of debt issues, 302, 305.

European cities, *see* England, Germany, Paris.

Ewen, Comptroller John, on additional appropriations, 49.

Excise licenses for liquor traffic, management by Dutch, 9, 10; grant by English governor, 18; receipts from, 182, 184; appropriation of moneys from, 256, 286.

Executive, *see* Mayor, Departments.

Expenditures, compared with state and United States, vi; character, colonial period, 22, 23, 25; increase of to 1869, 30, 64, 82-86, 112-114; effect of inflated currency, 113; juggling by Tweed Ring, 138-140; present, how calculated, 186; compared with other cities, 186; analysis for 1896, 285-289; fixed and contingent, 287; increase since 1871, 289-292; *see also* Appropriations.

Fees, importance under Dutch, 10; present receipts, 182; paid into city treasury, 354.

Ferries, privilege secured, 18; increased revenue, 75; present management and revenue, 230-232.

Final estimate, requires unanimous vote, 254; how fixed, 255; changes from provisional estimate, 258-261, 265, 266; legislative changes after adoption, 267; *see also* Appropriations.

Finance, board of, proposed by Tilden commission, 282.

Finance department, organization and duties, 345-349; records and reports, 349-352; *see also* Accounts, Comptroller, Reports.

Finances of New York city, importance of, v; outline of history, 1-6; outline of system, 172-177; unsystematic development, 360; need of reforms, 362.

Fines, receipts from, 182.

Fire department, Dutch taxes for, 11; expenditures, 1830, 31; paid department, under state commission, 79; expenditures to 1869, 85; pension fund, 256; growth of expenditures, 288, 292.

Fire of 1835, bonds for aid, 56.

Flagg, Comptroller A. C., advocates reforms, 71.

Floating debt, in colonial days, 9, 24; funding of, 30, 56, 102, 124, 130, 209, 325; *see also* Assessment bonds, Revenue bonds.

Fortifications, construction, 1653, 9.

Fourth Avenue, railway depressed, 153.

Franchises, municipal, abuses, 1850-1852, 71; regulations on grant, 73, 74; summary of revenue from, 183, 185; importance of revenue, 222-224; general management, etc., 230-252; for ferries, 230-232; street railways, 232-246; lighting works, etc., 246, 247; in foreign cities, 248; recent movement for reform, 249-252.

Fraud, penalties for, 354; now limited in extent, 355.

Freemen, limitation of rights to, 16.

Garvey, A. J., payments to, 141.

Gas plants, franchises, profits, municipal plants, etc., 246-249.

INDEX

General fund, established, transfers to, 101; revenues, 181; how receipts estimated, 256.
Germany, municipal waterworks in, 224; municipal gas plants, 249; property suffrage, 284.
Governor, state, appointment of mayor by, 15; of police commissioners, 79; approval of removals, 162.
Grace, Mayor W. R., vetoes franchises, 236, 240; appropriations under, 261, 275; opinion as to debt limit, 298.
Grant, Mayor H. J., board of estimate under, 271.
Greater New York,' effect of consolidation on finances, vii; history of consolidation, 166-168; charter of, 168-172; estimated receipts, 179; estimated debt, 336.
'Greater New York' charter, history and character, 166-172; assessment enterprises under, 203-205; budget system, 257, 277-281; control of debt issues, 304, 305; sinking fund provisions, 318; audit system, 349; financial reports, 352; unsystematic charter, 360, 361.
Green, Comptroller A. H., installation, 1871, 136; reforms by, 150, 151; member Greater New York commission, 166.
Greenwich Street Elevated Railway, 244.

Hall, Mayor A. O., lobbying as to tax law, 95; election, 123; probable share in frauds, 129; message of 1871, 131.
Harlem River, expenditure for bridges, 330.
Havemeyer, Mayor W. F., on party influences, 63; proposes charter reforms, 159.

Haws, Comptroller Robert T., reforms by, 90, 111.
Health department, under state commission, 79, 84.
Heere Gracht, assessment for paving, 12.
Hewitt, Mayor A. S., appropriations under, 275; condemns aqueduct board, 327.
Hoffman, Governor John T., election, 123; vetoes charter of Seventy, 158.
'Home rule' for cities, 165, 169.

Ingersoll, J. A., payments to, 142.
Inflation of currency, 1862-1869, 113.
Interest, on city debt, rapid increase, 1850-1869, 113; high rates, 104, 149; fixed charge in budget, 261, 263; amount of expenditures, 287, 290; reduction in rate since 1871, 321, 322.
Interest on taxes and assessments, 181, 200; on city deposits, 346.
Interest, 'sinking fund' for, established, 55; transfer of surplus, 101; surplus goes to redemption fund, 310; pays interest on redemption fund bonds, 317; receipts, 1896, 338.

Judgments, abuse of, 91, 92.
Judiciary, expenditures for, 114, 292.

Kelly, Comptroller John, proposes sinking fund law, 308.
Keyser & Co., payments to, 142.
Kings county, debt of, 336.

Lands, grants by royal governors, 18, 19; income from, 34, 55, 226.
Leases, regulations for granting, 73, 226.
Legislative commissions, established for certain city departments, 78-80; control of expen-

ditures by, 83-85; criticism of, 115-118; abolished, 126.
Legislature of New York, early control of taxation, 20, 27; partisan interference in city charter, 77, 78, 80; commissions for city affairs, 78-80, 115-118, 126; direct interference in appropriations, 88-97; becomes tool of Tweed, 119; local disapproval of bills, 165; franchises granted by, 234, 245; present influence on appropriations, 261-263; detailed control of debt, 300, 301; loses control of debt under new charter, 304; investigations of city departments, 353.
Licenses, general, receipts from, 182; theatrical, 256; see also Excise licenses.
Lighting, public, first taxes for, 1761, 25; expenditures, 1798, 30; 1830, 31; franchises for, 246.
Long Island city, consolidated with New York, 167.
Lotteries, public, as source of revenue, 24.
Low, Seth, member of charter commission, 168.

Manhattan Elevated Railway Company, 245.
Markets, granted to city, 18; revenues from, 36, 37, 227.
Mayor, appointed by governor, 15; by council, 38; elected by people, 42; given veto, 42, 73; to appoint officers, 77; added power as to appropriations, 94, 97, 127; limited power under Tweed charter, 127; member of board of estimate, 131; power of appointment and removal, 156, 161, 165, 168, 172; disapproval of legislative acts, 165; veto on appropriations, 257; influence in board of estimate, 270, 273; vote as to city depositories, 346; countersignature of warrants, 348; controls commissioners of accounts, 352, 353; may investigate officers, 354.
Mercein, Comptroller Thomas R., proposes sinking fund, 34.
Metropolitan board of health, 79, 84.
Metropolitan fire department, 79, 85.
Metropolitan police district, 79, 83, 84.
Metropolitan Street Railway Company, 237, 241-243.
Ministers, public support, 10, 21, 25.
Minority representation, in county supervisors, 78; proposed by Seventy, 157, 158; introduced for council, 161; abandoned, 163, 164.
Montgomerie charter, 14.
Morris, Mayor Robert H., charges against council, 48, 60.
Museums, expenditures for, 330.

Natural History, Museum of, 330.
New Amsterdam, finances of, 7-13.
New York city, outline of history, 1-6; consolidation, 166-168; see also Charter, Greater New York charter.
New York county, see County of New York.
New York Printing Company, 140.
New York state, see Governor, Legislature, State.
New York Times, exposes Ring frauds, 135.
New York Transcript, Ring payments to, 139.
Newspapers, favor Tweed Ring, 123; unsatisfactory study of finances, 276, 343.
Nicolls, Colonel Richard, charter and grants by, 13, 18.

O'Brien, James, heads Young Democracy, 125; exposes Ring frauds, 135.
O'Brien & Clark, aqueduct contracts let to, 327.
Officers, city, investigations of, 354; prohibited interest in contracts, etc., 354; *see also* Appointments, Departments.
Opening streets, *see* Street openings.

Paris, great city debt, 300.
Parks, Central, established, 99, 100; control of Central, 78, 84; improvement under Ring, 147; power of department as to streets, 202; assessments for, 206, 213; apparent rapid increase in expenditure, 294; recently established, bonds, 298, 330, 332.
Parliamentary government, study of appropriations in, 264, 265; contrasted with New York council, 278.
Party politics, influence in city, 1800-1850, 39, 62; in Croton aqueduct, 53; during war time, 76-80; present influence in budget, 270-276; in debt control, 301; in new Croton aqueduct, 326; in charter history generally, 359.
Pavements, assessments for, 216; *see also* Streets.
Paymaster, city, duties, 349.
Personal property, evasion of taxes, 190-195.
Philadelphia, expenditures, 186.
Police department, early 'watch,' 11, 21, 23, 30, 31; appointed by council, 62; by ex officio board, 74; rapid increase of expenditure, 64; control by state commission, 79, 83, 84; grounds for state control, 117; bi-partisan board, 165; pension fund, 256; number and pay fixed, 261; appropriations for, 287, 292; monthly payments to, 348.
Poor relief, early taxes for, 21; *see also* Charities and correction.
President of the aldermen, elective office, 165; member of board of estimate, 162, 253; influence of, 274.
Printing and advertising, abuse of transfers for, 91; judgments for, 91; Ring expenditures, 114, 139.
Provisional estimates, procedure, 254, 257, 260; great changes in final estimates, 258, 265, 266; reduced to influence elections, 276, 277.
Public buildings, loans for, 56, 57, 98, 332.
Public drives, bonds for, 104, 110, 330.
Public improvements, *see* Public works, Streets.
Public improvements, board of, established by charter of 1897, 170; power in assessment enterprises, 294; in debt control, 305.
Public works, autonomy of Greater New York, 169.
Public works department, commissioner member board of estimate, 131, 152; power as to assessments, 203, 207, 216; transfers of appropriations for, 268, 269; expenditures of, 287, 294; power to authorize bonds, 302; collects water rents, 346; unbalanced bids for contracts, 357.

Railways, street, early franchises and abuses, 71, 74; summary of franchises and revenues, 232-243; taxes on, 243; elevated, 244, 245; in Europe, 248; proposed underground, 249.

394   *INDEX*

Rapid transit, act of 1875, 244; proposed underground system, 249.
Real estate, early grants to city, 18, 19; early rents and sales, 34, 36, 55; taxation of, 187, 190, 195–197; present revenue from, 226.
Receipts, summary of, 177–185; *see also* Revenues.
Receiver of taxes, 189.
Repaving streets, not at expense of owner, 216; bonds for, 330.
Reports, financial, use in citations, vii; reorganization of system, 1859, 111; confusion of, 342; requirements and character, 349–352; need of simplifying, 363.
Republican party, interferes in city, 76, 78; adopts charter, 1873, 155, 159; deal as to aqueduct board, 327.
Revenue bonds, increase and funding, 56, 57, 102; for 'adjusted claims' under Ring, 122, 124, 130; funding, 124, 130, 325; purpose of, 189, 267; not included in debt limit, 297; issued under general law, 300; recent reduction in amount, 323.
Revenues (generally), Dutch preference of indirect, 9, 10; English grants of indirect, 18; importance, 19; indirect, 1798–1830, 30, 31; summary and classification of present, 177–185; from property and franchises, 221–252; lack of unified management, 255; rapid increase of indirect, 338.
Riots, caused by war draft, 103.
Robinson, Governor L., vetoes sinking fund bill, 308.

Salaries, many fixed by law, 261; instead of fees, 354.
Schoeyinge, construction, 1655, 11.
Schoolhouses, bonds for, 330, 331.
Schools, public, expenditures, 1798,
30; 1830, 31; rapid increase, 64; independence of department, 81; expenditures, 82; moneys received from state, 256; appropriations to sectarian, prohibited, 263; increase of appropriations since 1871, 287, 293; bonds for buildings, 330, 331.
Seventy, Committee of, fight against Tweed Ring, 136; propose charter, 155–158; influence charter of 1873, 159, 160.
Sewers, assessments for, 216.
Sharp, Jacob, Broadway railway franchise, 71.
Sidewalks, assessments for, 216.
Sinking fund, established, 1813, 33–36; amount, 1830, 37; separation of interest and redemption funds, etc., 1844, 55; transfer of surplus of interest fund, 100, 101; rapid increase to 1870, 106; slow increase under Ring, 149; payments to, classed as current expenditures, 286; deducted in fixing debt limit, 298; unnecessary accumulations, 307; extended applicability, 1878, 308–313; transfer of interest to redemption fund, 311; cancellation of bonds in, 313, 314; further extension of applicability, etc., 1889, 316–318; system under new charter, 318, 319; increase since 1871, 323; amount and classes, 1896, 334; rapid increase of revenues, 338; probable future capacity, 339; crudity of system, 340–342; confuses taxpayers, 342–344.
Sinking fund commissioners, established, 34; control of property and franchises, 224, 226, 229; control of docks, 229, 257; general debt control, 313.
Special assessments for local improvements, use by Dutch, 12;

first colonial law, English influence, 23, 24; increased use, 32; for street openings, 32; amount, etc., 1830-1840, 58, 59; amount, 1850-1870, 107; bonds first issued for anticipating, 108; vacations of, 108, 109; board of revision established, 109; Ring frauds in, 142-145; vacations, 144; present system, 201-220; authorization of enterprises, 201-203; authorization under new charter, 204, 205; losses from, and funding of bonds, 206-210; special funds for, 211-213; procedure, street openings, 213-215; street improvements, 216-219; collection, 219; annual amount, etc., 220, 285; tables, 372, 373.

Special and trust accounts, definition, 173.

Speedway, bonds for, 330.

State assessors, action as to city assessments, 196.

State of New York, expenditures, v; bonds for deficiency in sinking funds, 153, 325; *see also* Legislature, Legislative commissions.

State taxes, first levied, 65; levy of, 196, 197; fixed charge in city budget, 261; suits to reduce city apportionment, 266; not proper city expenditure, 286; amount, 1896, 287; amount since 1871, 290.

States, American, expenditures, v; debt, 295.

Steam heating, franchises for, 246.

Street cleaning, expenditures, 1830, 31; transfers of appropriations for, 90; judgments for, 1865, 91, 92; transfers for, 269; increase of appropriations, 293.

Street opening and improvement, board of, 203, 214.

Street openings, assessments first levied for, 32; assessments limited, 110; bonds for city's share, 110, 143, 206, 326; how authorized, 202-204; when cost borne by city, 206; fund for, 212; assessment procedure, 213-215; amount of, 220.

Street railways, first franchises, 71, 74; summary of franchises and revenues, 232-243, 337; overcapitalization, 239-243; Metropolitan company, 241-243; taxes on, 243; elevated, 244, 245; in Europe, 248; underground proposed, 249.

Streets, early assessments for improving, 12, 23, 32; rapid improvement, 1830-1840, 58, 59; 1850-1870, 107-110; Ring frauds in improving, 142-145; authorization of improvements, 202-205; losses on assessments, 207-210; special fund for improvement, 211-213; assessment procedure, 213-219; amount paid for improving, 220; limit of repaving appropriation, 263; bonds for repaving, 330, 331; bonds since 1871, 332; unbalanced bids for grading, 356.

Strong, Mayor W. M., vetoes new charter, 167, 168; increase of appropriations under, 275, 293, 294.

Stuyvesant, Peter, domination by, 8, 9.

Suffrage, municipal, early limitations, 16, 17; advisability of limiting, 282-285.

Supervisors of New York county, aldermen act as, 28; separate board established, 78, 85; Ring formed by, 120; abolished, 126.

Supreme court, control of street openings, 214, 215.

Sweeney, Peter B., becomes Ring member, 121; share of spoils

129; device as to accounts, 129; president of park department, 127.

Tammany hall, reorganization, 121; wins election of 1868, 123; opposition of Young Democracy, 125; secures charter of 1870, 126; representation on board of estimate, 270, 271; false economy, 275; delusive reduction of budget, 277.

Tax laws, required annually, 27; drafted by council, 46; used as means of state interference, 88-96; juggling under Tweed Ring, 128-132; system abandoned, 152, 153.

Taxes, first under Dutch, 10; slight use in early days, 20, 21; date of collection, 26; annual laws required, 27; how levied, 28; rate, 1798, 1830, 31; 1830-1850, 65; penalty for non-payment, 1850, 110; deficiencies in, 111; limited to 2%, 1871, 131; general system, 187-200; levy, 189, 255; assessment, 187-198; evasion of personalty, 190-195; state assessment, 196, 197; collection, 189, 198-200; on street railways, 243, 245; interest on, 256; variability in rate, 275; false arguments from rate, 276; rights of non-taxpayers, 283; city bonds exempt, 303; changes as to debt service, 308-313, 315-317; tables, 372, 373; diagram, 380.

Taxes, receiver of, 189.

Taxes and assessments, department of, 187, 190, 196; president member of board of estimate, 162, 253.

Taxpayers, hearing on appropriations, 255; proposed limitation of suffrage to, 282-285; may investigate accounts, 354.

Telephone lines, franchises for, 246.

Third Avenue Railway, 237, 238.

Tilden commission, plan of finance control, 281-285.

Tilden, Governor Samuel J., fight against Tweed Ring, 136.

Transfers of appropriations, abuse of, 90; prohibited, 91; reëstablished, recent working, 267-269.

Trust accounts, definition, 173.

Tweed Ring, origin and growth, 120-123; secures charter, 125-127; juggling with debt and budget, 128-134; fall, 134-137; summary of frauds, 138-142; special assessments under, 142-145; increase of debt, 145-149.

Tweed, William M., early career, 120; organizes Ring, 122; secures charter, 126; commissioner of public works, 127; auditing frauds, 128; member board of estimate, 131; punishment, 137.

Twenty-third and twenty-fourth wards, street improvements in, 203, 219, 220.

Unbalanced bids for contracts, 356.

Unexpended balances, transfers of, 90, 91, 267-269.

United States constitution, influence on city charter, 42, 45.

Vacation of assessments, law authorizing, 1858, 108; under Tweed Ring, 144; in recent times, 208, 210.

Vanderbilt, William H., taxation of estate, 194.

Vestrymen, taxes collected by, 21, 25.

Vouchers, requirements of, 347.

War, Civil, bond issues caused by, 102-104.

Warrants, how drawn, 348.

Watch, night, Dutch taxes for, 11; expenditures, 1798, 30; 1830, 31.

Water supply, first aqueduct, 52-54; rents from, 55; improvements, 1850-1870, 98; bonds issued by Tweed Ring, 147; present management and revenues, 224-226; limit of appropriation for mains, 263; judgment for meters, 291; effect of debt limit, 297; control of bond issues for, 300, 301, 302; separate sinking fund for, 317, 318; bond issues since 1871, 325, 332; construction of new aqueduct, 326-328.

Watson, James, county auditor, 122; part in Ring frauds, 129.

West India Company, relation to city, 8.

Wharves, built by assessment, 32; *see also* Docks.

Wood, Mayor, disloyal utterances, 117.

Young Democracy, 125, 126.

www.ingramcontent.com/pod-product-compliance
Lightning Source LLC
Chambersburg PA
CBHW022116290426
44112CB00008B/691